PRAISE FOR
THE MAN BETWEEN & MICHAEL HENRY HEIM

"Michael Henry Heim was an unusual person, a scholar of many talents, a dedicated linguist, a gifted translator. With his passing, I have lost a friend. The gap he leaves will not be filled."

—Günter Grass

"This is a wonderful and illuminating account of a wonderful and luminous writer. Heim's impact on American letters was profound and far-reaching. [*The Man Between*] pays handsome tribute to the work of a uniquely adventurous translator, and shows just how much we all owe to him."

—David Bellos

"This delightful collection provides a richly detailed portrait of the life and work of an extraordinary writer, translator, linguist, scholar, educator, benefactor, intellectual—above all, an extraordinary human being. . . . I am proud to have known this brilliant—and yet entirely unassuming and modest—polymath. Readers of *The Man Between* are in for a rare pleasure!"

—Marjorie Perloff

Edited by Esther Allen,
Sean Cotter & Russell Scott Valentino

THE MAN BETWEEN

MICHAEL HENRY HEIM & A LIFE IN TRANSLATION

OPEN LETTER
LITERARY TRANSLATIONS FROM THE UNIVERSITY OF ROCHESTER

Special thanks and gratitude to Priscilla Heim for her help and support in all stages of this project, as well as supplying additional photos from the Heim family's personal archives.

Library of Congress Cataloging-in-Publication Data: Available upon request.
ISBN-13: 978-1-940953-00-7 / ISBN-10: 1-934824-00-6

Printed on acid-free paper in the United States of America.

Text set in Caslon, a family of serif typefaces based on the designs of
William Caslon (1692–1766).

Design by N. J. Furl

Open Letter is the University of Rochester's nonprofit, literary translation press:
Lattimore Hall 411, Box 270082, Rochester, NY 14627

www.openletterbooks.org

CONTENTS

INTRODUCTION

SEAN COTTER

Michael Henry Heim translated, taught translation, and advocated for professional and academic translators. He understood translation deeply and his work encompassed translation broadly, making him a central figure for late twentieth-century literature and translation studies. Any route to understanding the contemporary position of translation in the United States must pass through his life and work. He mastered a mystifyingly large number of languages, from Czech and Russian to Croatian, Dutch, Danish, Spanish, and Hungarian. As the translator of writers such as Milan Kundera, Bohumil Hrabal, Thomas Mann, and Péter Esterházy, Heim created Central European literature in English, giving us not only the texts but also the notion that these books from disparate languages formed a whole. Heim instituted one of the first workshops in literary translation and developed a translator training method that produced not applied linguists, but writers. He advanced translator training at the same time that he improved the working conditions for translators, by arguing for the status of translation as academic scholarship, lobbying publishers to produce translations, and endowing a fund to support translation projects. It is difficult to imagine a translator's life more dedicated or successful. This collection is a biography and

appreciation, a portrait of a man between languages who expanded
the possibilities of a life in translation.

The collection demonstrates this range of possibility in its form.
Rather than a single-author biography, our book is a composite, a
thick description of Heim's career from both his own perspective and
those of the many authors, translators, and publishers whose work
he affected. By placing one version of Heim's influence alongside
another, our approach to biography resembles the way we might
compare a translation to an original, in order to see the translator's
work come to light in the space between. Heim ranged across many
domains and is important to many people. The collection of voices
in this volume, therefore, is modeled on Heim's own definition of
translation. "A good translation," he stated, "will allow a person who
has read the work in the original and a person who has read the
work in translation to have an intelligent conversation about it."[1]
He emphasizes not narrow textual questions but the beginning of a
dialog, the international community of readers a translation creates.
Anyone who met Heim would recognize in this definition his characteristic, expansive generosity, a movement toward inclusion. This
collection is not a Festschrift, but a conversation.[2] This collection
emulates both his translation practice and his generosity, by telling
his story in many voices, which come from the many areas where
Heim made translation important.

Heim's work was dedicated to improving our practice and understanding of translation, and a book dedicated to him allows us to
improve the field of Translation Studies. A focus on the complex
constitution of a translator has been lacking from the wave of interest

1   Interview with Louise Steinman, "Translator Remains Faithful to His 'Un-
faithful' Art," *Los Angeles Times* (30 September 2001), E1.

2   . . . especially since that book already exists: *Between Texts, Languages, and
Cultures: A Festschrift for Michael Henry Heim*; Edited by Craig Cravens, Masako
U. Fidler, and Susan C. Kresin (Slavica Publishing, 2008).

in translation that began in the 1970s and swelled in the past two decades. Heim was a part of this wave, which shifted translation from a domain of language training and linguistics (the field of his graduate work) to comparative literature, cultural studies, and creative writing. The first two fields, in particular, have become allergic to biographical approaches. Works such as *Siting Translation* by Tejaswini Niranjana, *The Practice of Diaspora* by Brent Hayes Edwards, or *The Translator's Invisibility* by Lawrence Venuti have documented the roles translators play in resistance to colonial and patriarchal power structures, networks of cultural exchange, or challenges to the primacy of authorship, while focusing overwhelmingly on the power structure, network, or signature, at the expense of the translator figure. Emblematic of this elision is Paul de Man's 1983 definition: "the relationship of translator to the original is the relationship between language and language."[3] The equation of the translator and language is an indication of Translation Studies' lagging attachment to its roots in structural linguistics. In the same way that Saussure's sign gains meaning only within the context of a larger language system, the translator has been appreciated as an element within these power networks. Only recently have studies addressed "the great scandal of translation" that Gayatri Spivak identifies as "the obliteration of the figure of the translator."[4] A more humanist approach should ask how a life endows a person with the complex set of skills literary translation requires, and in what ways might a person live through translation? Although some new works have come to this human focus—such as the collection *Barbara Wright: Translation as Art*, edited by Debra Kelly and Madeleine Renouard, or Iliya Troyanov's fictional biography of Richard Burton, *The Collector*

---

3   *The Resistance to Theory* (University of Minnesota Press, 1983) 81.

4   Quoted in Esther Allen, ed. *To Be Translated or Not To Be* (Barcelona: Institut Ramon Llull, 2007) 28 – 29.

of Worlds, or even the documentary films *Translating Edwin Honig: A Poet's Alzheimer's* (by Alan Berliner) or Nurith Aviv's *Traduire*, or Vadim Jendreyko's *Woman with the Five Elephants*, about Svetlana Geier, translator of Dostoyevsky into German—translators' lives rarely receive more than a portrait, not a book-length study.

Even this intellectual context, however, has not diminished our interest in the author biography. Translators lag behind our long-standing interest in authors, who seem more creative and more miraculous than a person who, we might naïvely think, simply copies a creative work down in another language. The author's life promises the key to unlock his works. "Ultimately what the biographer seeks to elicit," writes Richard Ellmann in his landmark *Golden Codgers*, "is less the events of a writer's life than the 'mysterious armature,' as Mallarmé called it, which binds the creative work."[5] Yet even Ellmann's translation of Mallarmé in this passage relies on a definition of "armature" as "skeleton," which appears in English only in 1903, five years after the poet's death. Earlier uses of the word refer to defensive "armament," an exoskeleton. What mendicant French sculptor translated this new definition into English, shifting the skeleton from outside to in? It is only thanks to that translator that the armature is hidden from view and becomes mysterious. If creation is mysterious, surely recreation is even more so. The translator's life binds together not one work, but two. The mystery of creation meets the impossible act of translating, a doubly improbable transfer of a text into a foreign system. *The Man Between* enables us better to imagine the translator who lives between works, erecting the armature that binds a creative work to another work in a different language.

•

---

5   *Golden Codgers* (Oxford UP, 1973), x.

Part of the significance of Heim and his work lies in the confluence of two key cultural events of the second half of the twentieth century: the great wave of literature translated from Central European languages and the rise of literary translation within the American academy. Heim is at the center of both of these broad shifts in our collective attention, similar changes in the value we place on "minor" countries and a "secondary" literary practice. This connection is far from accidental, Harish Trivedi has argued, since the transformations of literature wrought by Central European texts were a driving force behind the deeper consideration of translation.[6]

As is still the norm today, Heim studied Czech only as a "second Slavic" language, as part of his doctoral work on Russian linguistics. But on travelling to Czechoslovakia in 1965, he found a culture so lively and attractive that he decided to make it his specialty, and he returned to Prague just three years later, without knowing he would land in the midst of the 1968 Soviet invasion. As Heim recalls in this book, the Soviet soldiers did not know Czech (the Latin alphabet led some to believe they were in Romania), and few Czechs knew Russian. Thanks to the structure of American Slavic studies, the young American scholar was in high demand; he traveled the city, interpreting between the soldiers and Czech people. In the end, he was featured on German television. It is a typical Heim story: an amazing performance in three languages, none of them English.

The United States experienced a rush of interest in Central and East European literature following the Prague Spring, an interest prefigured by the wave of new Czech films and a growing countercultural interest in the United States for works from other countries. Unlike the contemporaneous Latin American Boom, the Central

6 "Translating culture vs. cultural translation," *In Translation – Reflections, Refractions, Transformations,* Paul St-Pierre and Prafulla C. Kar, eds. (Amsterdam: John Benjamins, 2007), 277–287.

European wave featured exceptional diversity in its original languages: a list of mutually unintelligible Slavic languages, as well as several other language families (in the case of Hungarian, German, Romanian, and Albanian). Heim's competence in so many disparate languages is stunning. While there were languages he did not cover (such as Albanian, Polish, Bulgarian, and Slovene), he made do with Czech, French, German, Italian, Hungarian, Slovak, Russian, and what was then called Serbo-Croatian. It is no wonder to read in Michelle Woods's essay that in this moment, when presses were searching for translators of East European literature, Heim appeared to Knopf as "the genius fallen from the sky."

A leader of his generation, Heim brought a library of Central European texts into English. Perhaps best known as the translator of *The Unbearable Lightness of Being*, he also translated, from Czech alone, three other books by Kundera, three by Bohumil Hrabal, and more from Karel Čapek, Jan Neruda, and Josef Hiršal. Then there are the dozens of translations from other languages, including, from the Serbian, two books by Danilo Kiš, Miloš Crnjanski's *Migrations*, and Aleksandar Tišma's *The Book of Blam*; from the Russian, a book of Chekhov's major plays and a selection of Chekhov's correspondence, as well as one novel and one book of prose nonfiction by Vasily Aksyonov; from the German, plays by Bertolt Brecht, a prize-winning retranslation of Thomas Mann's *Death In Venice*, a best-selling book on mathematics by Hans Magnus Enzensberger (whose math he corrected), and Günter Grass's memoir *My Century*, to choose only a few titles from his much longer bibliography. His achievement brings to mind T. S. Eliot's description of Ezra Pound, whom he called "the inventor of Chinese poetry for our time."[7] By bringing works from a host of languages into a single language, English, Heim created a textual Central Europe that otherwise existed

---

7 "Introduction," *Selected Poems* by Ezra Pound (Knopf, 1928), 14.

only in the imaginations of writers separated by their languages. The idea of a cultural zone, drawing on its Austro-Hungarian connection, took shape in English translation. Long before Kundera, in "The Tragedy of Central Europe," lamented the fact that "the West looks at Central Europe and sees only Eastern Europe," Heim had created the body of imaginative works that enabled Kundera's English-language readers to understand his point.[8]

But Heim did more for readers of this region than pave the way for this landmark essay. Heim was on the board of *Cross Currents*, the journal that published critical essays and original work by Kundera and many others, creating yet another version of Central Europe in English, yet another community in translation. *Cross Currents* brought together defining cultural figures—Czesław Miłosz, Vaclav Havel, Adam Michnik, Joseph Brodsky, Susan Sontag—from both sides of the West/East cultural divide. His work for this journal was followed by his tenure on the board of Northwestern University Press, which published many significant works from Central Europe in translation, with an important emphasis on new work after the historic events of 1989. He worked to expand yet another journal, *East European Politics and Societies*, to include the arts and literary culture. He was the founder of the Association for the Translation of Central European Literatures, which paired native speakers of English and Central European languages in a systematic attempt to evaluate the existing works and to initiate needed translations. This list of involvement follows a pattern: Heim worked not only on translations but also on the publishing systems in which translations moved. Far more than books, then, is the translation oeuvre of Michael Heim. He labored to create a translation culture.

Heim taught Slavic languages and literatures and authored an important Czech textbook, but his pedagogical influence extends

---

8 *The New York Review of Books* 31:7 (April 24, 1984), 35.

beyond his work in a specific language. Heim was also a leader in the development of the graduate seminar in literary translation, which was structured to support training in translating any language into English. These workshops were born of the same increased interest in translation that enabled the Latin American Boom and Central European wave. Developed at the same time as, and modeled upon, the creative writing workshop, these courses began in 1964 at the University of Iowa and appeared soon after at the University of Texas (1965) the University of Arkansas (1972), and the University of Texas at Dallas (1978), reaching UCLA in the mid-1980s. As the interviews with Heim and Maureen Freely's contribution in this volume describe in more detail, these workshops marked a fundamental change in approach to translation pedagogy: a new focus on the literary quality of English. Within the American academy, translation before this time had been the purview of either foreign-language departments (modern and classical) or linguistics. This background tended to measure the translation against the standard of the original, and the translations produced are identifiable by the original language's imprint. The workshop setting, while concerned with the adequacy of the translation to the original, measures the language of the translation against the norms of literary English. The resulting translations are marked by this professional competence.

Heim's involvement follows the pattern established in his Central European translations: expansion beyond the confines of his own beginnings, toward a broader community. He moved from the Czech and German to almost all the Central European languages, and from publishing his own translations to the review and advocacy of the vast field of Central European translators. Likewise, Heim extended his concern for translator training beyond his own classroom. In 2004, a group of graduate students and Heim inaugurated a national graduate-student conference on literary translation, which was subsequently held at several schools beyond UCLA. As Esther

Allen's essay demonstrates in more detail, he was a powerful force for the recognition of translation as creative scholarship within the American academy, resulting in that organization's endorsement of translation for consideration for tenure. The most surprising project, however, was his least visible. Heim endowed a fund to defray the cost of translation through grants paid directly to translators. Administered by PEN America, the establishment was anonymous until after Heim's death, and is now awarded annually as the PEN/ Heim Translation Fund. The revelation of this endowment turns out to be absolutely in keeping with Heim's work for the profession of translation. At every turn in his career, we see Heim expanding the range of translation, the status of translation, and the professional possibilities for literary translation, but doing so with quiet competence and humility before the great edifice of literature.

•

The three sections of *The Man Between* follow a similar trajectory to the one we have imagined shaping Heim's professional life, from the person, to personal portraits, to his influence on the culture. The first section, "The Man," begins with extensive selections from a series of interviews Heim gave in 1998, in four languages, to a group of scholars in Timişoara, Romania. Revised in part by Heim, these are the most extensive autobiographical texts he ever produced, telling the story of his childhood, education, and awakening interest in Central Europe, as well as providing comments on translation and translation pedagogy. The interviews are followed by a transcription of his 2011 talk at the Center for the Art of Translation, a systematic overview of recent translation history and a reflection on current translation criticism. His bibliography, compiled by Esther Allen, extends well beyond the modest account Heim gives in the interviews, to document a record of public literary engagement far above the norm.

The pages of "Community" unite portraits of Heim by those who
knew him, worked with him, and simply enjoyed his company. These
include eulogies from his memorial service, attended by hundreds in
2012 in Los Angeles, as well as Andrei Codrescu's remembrance on
National Public Radio. Each essay presents a distinct perspective on
Heim, including the experience of Dubravka Ugrešić, whom Heim
not only translated but befriended, and translated as an expression
of friendship. Michael Flier's account gives details of Heim's own,
groundbreaking tenure case. The essays capture Heim reading while
walking to his university office, collecting recycling, or celebrating
events in his friends' lives. This collection of intimate perspectives
portrays the large circle of personal friends Heim developed, a community of literary souls.

The final section, "Impact," considers the importance of Heim's
work across a range of fields. Russell Valentino describes the rise of
translation within contemporary Slavic studies. Heim's collaborator
on the journal *East European Politics & Societies*, Andrzej Tymowski,
argues for the importance of social science colleagues translating each
other's work across national boundaries. Maureen Freely documents
the pedagogical techniques she learned from Heim while institut-
ing her own literary translation workshop. Against the backdrop of
Heim's publishing career, Michelle Woods examines his nuts-and-
bolts choices in two of his most famous Czech translations, from
Hrabal and Kundera. A translator from Czech who first published
in 1995, Alex Zucker considers the importance of Heim's generation
for contemporary Central European translators. Sean Cotter lists the
vast cultural reverberations and permutations of Heim's most famous
translation choice, the title "The Unbearable Lightness of Being."
The case for translator biographies is made by Breon Mitchell, who
outlines the archival resources he developed at the Lilly Library in
Bloomington, Indiana, including papers from Heim. Esther Allen
articulates the theory in practice that Heim's life exemplified, in the

face of a difficult academic climate, to advance translation as a trans-
formative cultural force.

Work on this book began in 2011, a year before Heim's passing. Completed in 2014, the work is in part a memorial, partaking
in the familiar tropes of loss in translation. But we believe Heim
would be the first to object to a volume centered solely on him. Such
a book could be said to miss the point of a career spent helping
other authors to be read and other translators to come to light. The
broader aim of this book is to collect the voices of the community
created by his translations: not only his friends but also those editors of literature and scholars of politics, those readers of novels and
students of literary English, and those fellow translators who follow
the paths Heim blazed. In doing so we advocate, with Heim, for
the mysteriousness and inherent interest of the lives of translators,
expanded methods for reading translation, and the importance of
translation in our culture.

THE MAN

A HAPPY BABEL

MICHAEL HENRY HEIM

(selected and translated by Sean Cotter with substantial additions in English by the author)

With the support of the Soros Foundation, Pro Helvetia, and the U.S. Information Agency, Michael Heim organized a conference in Timişoara, Romania, in 1999 to promote the mutual translation of literature among the former Eastern Bloc countries. Representatives from all the countries participated. Mircea Mihăieş and Adriana Babeţi, who worked closely with him on the conference, asked if some of their colleagues could interview him during the breaks. He agreed, assuming, as he later wrote, that all that would come of it was a newspaper article. "But three of them and Adriana trailed me incessantly, badgering me with questions, one in French, another in English—French and English were the official languages of the conference—the third in German, and the fourth in Romanian. They told me they were going to translate it all into Romanian (I'm sure my Romanian needed almost as much translation as the other languages), but I didn't really believe them. Then a few weeks after the conference was over, lo and behold they sent me the translation!"

The Romanian volume was published in 1999 as *A Happy Babel* (*Un Babel fericit* [Iaşi: Editura Polirom]). I have selected those parts of the interview that hold special biographical interest or insight into his thoughts on translation. These interviews, the most extensive

3

Heim ever gave, provide rare insight into the formation of a translator, through Heim's background, thoughts on translation, and mode
of expression. The interviews hold more than biographical interest,
however. For online publication in *The Iowa Review*, Heim revised
my initial English versions, making his responses more concise and
the narratives more dramatic. These sections are marked with a line
down the left margin. Something interesting happened during these
revisions, something with the potential to change the way we read
not only Heim's translations, but all translations. As he wrote in an
email, "Returning to the Romanian book more than a decade later,
I took it upon myself to restore my personal diction." Of course, a
personal diction is the last thing a translator is supposed to possess. A
translator should emulate the style of the original, or nobly fall on his
sword. In the interview here, he is restoring his own voice, but this
record allows us to read his translations in a new way, paying close
attention to their textual qualities. If there is a feature that marks
Heim's translations, it is his superb literary skill, through which he is
able to bring the best qualities of the originals to new life in English.

We can appreciate Heim's own storytelling style by comparing
a simple translation from the Romanian interviews to his revision.
Stories like his experience of the Prague Spring gain great pace and
activity. My translation from the Romanian reads as follows:

> In the middle of the night, the phone rang. It was my teacher
> who said that one of her friends had called and said there
> had been an invasion, and she wanted to know if I knew
> anything. I said no, and then I quickly turned on the radio
> to hear what was happening. The Czech radio was off the
> air, and that was a bad sign. Then I found Deutsche Welle,
> where they were talking about a Soviet invasion of Czecho-
> slovakia. After half an hour, I saw the tanks, since I was
> living on Czechoslovak Army Street, and the apartment was

two or three blocks from the Ministry of Defense. In the week that followed, I went back and forth across the city, interpreting between the Czechs and Russians.

Heim revises this narrative into the following:

> At about four in the morning the phone rang. It was my Czech teacher. One of her friends had called to report the invasion was underway. I quickly turned on Czech radio. It had gone off the air, a bad sign. Then I switched to the German station Deutsche Welle, and suddenly things were clear. A half hour later I saw the tanks. The street where I happened to be living was Czechoslovak Army Street, and the apartment was only a few blocks from the Ministry of Defense. In the week that followed, I constantly crisscrossed the city interpreting between Czechs and the soldiers.

Details that might be understood from context are cut: we don't need to explain that the caller "wanted to know if I knew anything" or that he turned the radio on "to hear what was happening." The facts are obvious. These changes come at points that often appear in rough translations from Romanian: the extra "that"s in "who said that" and "that was a bad sign." Indeed, "that" is a bad sign, and its appearance marks places to shorten sentences and thereby add drama—the point of the anecdote, after all.

No one could ever associate Heim's work with that of idiosyncratic translators such as Ben Bellitt, Roy Campbell, or Stephen Mitchell, translators whose renderings are more predictable and easily recognizable. Yet if we read the interviews attentively, we may notice that aspects of his personal diction show up in his translations, a word here and there. For example, Heim tells about getting a haircut in Prague the day before a linguistics conference. This is his revised version:

The barber had read about the conference in the papers, and since barbers like to chew the fat as they work, I regaled him with human interest stories about the star of the conference, the structuralist Roman Jakobson, a world-renowned linguist whose biography I knew well because I had studied with him. He had fled his native Russia after the Revolution ("and a good thing too," the barber interjected) and come to Prague ("and a good thing too"), where he helped to found the famous Prague Linguistics Circle ("didn't know we had one"), and after Hitler's invasion he fled to America, where he still lived ("smart guy!").

The story stands out to me because he uses the same phrase in this passage from Hrabal's *Dancing Lessons for the Advanced in Age*, where the speaker tells the story of an automatic pistol:

> . . . my brother took it apart and we couldn't put it back together, we were so desperate we wanted to shoot ourselves, but we couldn't because we couldn't put it back together, a good thing too or I wouldn't have been able to go to church to see the ladies . . .[1]

The overlap of "a good thing too" is too small to be called an intrusion of the translator's English diction into the text. (In fact, both uses of the expression are translations from Czech, appearing in stories from different authors.) Rather, this moment directs our attention to the translation as a text, with its own English rhetoric. We notice not tics of diction, but the fact that the text is meticulously, skillfully shaped. Heim once wrote that a translation must "exploit

---

1   Heim's translation of Bohumil Hrabal, *Dancing Lessons for the Advanced in Age* (New York Review Books, 2011) 7.

all the resources of the target language." How rarely do we allow a translator that much freedom. How often do we train ourselves to ignore, in particular when reading prose, the meaning created by textual characteristics of the translation.

When I read a passage, for example the opening of *The Encyclopedia of the Dead* by Danilo Kiš, I am drawn toward those features of the translation that emphasize their Englishness. The first story of this collection presents "Simon Magus," a rival miracle worker in the time of Jesus, whose story has two endings: he dies either by first flying and then plummeting back to earth, or by being voluntarily buried alive. These two narrative paths begin with a description of travelers' paths:

> Seventeen years after the death and miraculous resurrection of Jesus the Nazarene, a man named Simon appeared on the dusty roads that crisscross Samaria and vanish in the desert beneath the fickle sands, a man whom his disciples called the Magus and his enemies derided as "the Borborite." Some claimed he had come from a miserable Samarian village named Gitta, others that he was from Syria or Anatolia. It cannot be denied that he himself contributed to the confusion, answering the most innocent questions about his origins with a wave of the hand broad enough to take in both the neighboring hamlet and half the horizon.[2]

The paragraph uses a particular diction through a repetition of consonant sounds. The original includes a series of proper names: Simon, Samaria, Syria. Starting from this feature of the original, Heim then saturates the paragraph with "ess" sounds: dusty, sands,

---

2   Heim's translation of Danilo Kiš, *The Encyclopedia of the Dead* (Northwestern University Press, 1989) 3.

miserable, vanish, even Jesus. In addition to this network, the paragraph also includes a pattern of hard "kay" sounds: miraculous resurrection, fickle, contributed to the confusion, questions.

These two patterns intersect in the word "crisscross," a word that appeared above in the revised account of Prague Spring. Yet this item from the Heimian lexicon appears in the service of the text, imbuing the translation's musical rhetoric with crucial thematic importance. The word is a version of "Christ's cross," just as Simon is a version of Christ. Simon's two fates also cross like the dusty roads of Samaria: one goes up, the other down. And Simon's rivalry "crosses" Christ's authority, and God, "the greatest of all tyrants," takes revenge by killing Simon, a man killed for crossing Christ who was killed on a cross. No other word will bring so many themes together. When I read this type of find, I shake my head and smile. The entire story becomes this word. By following out the rhetorical possibilities of English, Heim has created a text that displays the complicated themes of the original story.

We read these interviews, then, not only for what they tell us about Heim, not only to hear again the voice of an old friend. It seems utterly characteristic of Heim's modesty that we would not rest finally on his personality, however amply it appears in the pages that follow. Following his "personal diction" leads us to ways of paying renewed attention to the texts he translated. This approach becomes all the more important when considering a polyglot translator like Heim. Where will someone be found to compare his translations to their originals in Czech, Russian, Romanian, Hungarian, German? The list goes on too long. We have to notice that, even when talking about himself, Heim helps to find ways of reading his English that will open avenues into translation.

—Sean Cotter

A HAPPY BABEL

Adriana Babeţi: When you arrived at Timişoara, you were sweaty, hungry, and thirsty: your train had come to a standstill on the tracks for two hours, in an open field, under a forty-degree sun. A railway strike. Yet when you stepped out of the train, your face had a smile I couldn't understand. You explained that sitting opposite you was a young man who bore an unbelievable likeness to yourself, at age seventeen. How would you describe your seventeen-year-old self?

Michael Heim: I was a more or less typical American in that I was extremely naive: I had never been outside the U.S. and knew nothing of the world. It was 1960. I had just finished high school, a public high school in the semi-rural borough of Staten Island, a true anomaly, administratively a part of New York City, but tranquil, provincial even. Imagine, many of the residents had never been to "the city," as they called Manhattan, which was only a thirty-minute ferry ride away. (I made the bus, ferry, and subway trip to Manhattan every Saturday to take piano and clarinet lessons at the Juilliard School of Music preparatory division.) I felt a little foreign to the place, having come there from California. We had moved because my mother remarried after my father's early death.

9

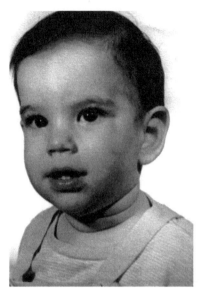

Heim as a toddler.

Adriana Babeți: Where were you born?

Michael Heim: I was born in Manhattan, as it happened. My father was a soldier, stationed in the south, in Alabama. I was supposed to be born there. But at the last moment my mother got cold feet: she was worried about the conditions in the military hospital and decided to give birth in Manhattan, where her mother was living at the time. Barely a month after I was born, however, we moved to Texas, where my father had been transferred. Then, toward the end of the war, we settled in California, in Hollywood, because my father wrote movie music.

Adriana Babeți: Who was your father?

Michael Heim: He was, of course, a Heim, Imre (Emery in English, which is what my mother called him) Heim, but he

composed under a pseudonym, Hajdu, a common Hungarian sur-
name. My father was Hungarian. It's possible that Hajdu was his
mother's maiden name; it's possible he used Hajdu to highlight
his Hungarian origins, Heim being of course a German—or, in
my family's case, Austrian—name. My father was born in Budapest, as were his parents. My grandfather's name was Lajos, my
grandmother's Sárolta. Unfortunately, I know nothing definite
about my paternal great-grandparents except for a hint from my
grandmother that one of them was a Gypsy. Most Americans of
my generation and earlier had scant knowledge of their forebears.
Nor did my mother and her mother, both of whom were born in
the U.S., take much interest in their ancestry. Our family lore is
limited to the following: my grandmother was the last of sixteen
children and the only one born in America. The rest came from
Kovno in what was then the Pale of Settlement. My mother was
Jewish, my father Catholic.

Heim, age 6.

Adriana Babeţi: Could you retrace your father's footsteps and put his biography together? What do you know? What do you remember?

Michael Heim: I remember listening to what I later learned was classical music, and I remember that the first piece of music to stick in my mind was Stravinsky's *Petrushka*. I couldn't have been more than three, but when I heard it again much later I perked up immediately. Superimposed on the music is the image of my father. I have photographs and an elegant charcoal portrait, so I know I resemble him closely. So much so that one day, a friend of mine, seeing a picture of my father as a soldier, asked me how I came to be wearing a uniform, since he knew I'd never served in the army. When my grandmother in Budapest (my mother and I always referred to her as "Grandma-in-Budapest") saw me for the first time, she cried and cried. She said it wasn't her grandson visiting; it was her son. My father was born in Budapest in 1908 and studied piano at the Royal Conservatory with Bartók, but—on my grandmother's insistence—also apprenticed to a master baker in Vienna. Baking was the family trade. My grandparents ran four pastry shops in Budapest.

Adriana Babeţi: What were Viennese baking schools like?

Michael Heim: Very rigorous, I imagine. But I knew nothing of Viennese or Hungarian cuisine. I didn't eat my first *palacsinta* until I visited my grandmother. By the time my father left Europe, he had gained a reputation as a composer of popular music, the Irving Berlin of Budapest, my mother used to boast. One of his specialties was reworked Gypsy melodies. Once in a Budapest restaurant, the musicians learned I was Hajdu's son and immediately struck up one of his hits. But he was also one of Hungary's best-known film composers. A few years ago a friend

brought me a videotape of a Hungarian film from the thirties
scored by my father. It was very much of its time and quite good,
actually. I had been told he also provided the score for the classic
Czech film, *Ecstasy*—classic, because it purports to be the first
film to show a woman in the nude, the famous Austrian beauty
Hedy Lamarr, running through the woods. Given my later fascination with things Czech, I was naturally intrigued but also a bit
skeptical. How could I have missed a reference to my father? But
five years ago I managed to view the film and everything fell into
place. It features a twenty-minute scene in which the hero visits a
Gypsy tavern. Aha, I thought, so that's why my father had been
called in. The on-screen credit went to the man responsible for
the rest of the score. My father would also do some ghostwrit-
ing later in Hollywood, where he was getting a new start and
completely unknown.

Adriana Babeți: When did your father go to America?

Michael Heim: In 1939, for the New York World's Fair. As a
pastry chef in the employ of Gundel, then, as now, one of the
most sought-after restaurants in Budapest, one my grandparents
provided pastries for. As it happened, Gundel handled the food
concessions at the Hungarian pavilion and needed skilled pastry
chefs. The war had broken out in Europe, and America was a
safe haven, but it was very hard to get a visa. Not for my father,
though. He went as a pastry chef, not a refugee.

Adriana Babeți: Would he have left Hungary if it hadn't been for
the Fair?

Michael Heim: As I say, it would have been all but impossible. He met my mother in 1939 or 1940 through friends who

recommended him as a piano teacher. She had taken piano lessons as a child, and her friends knew my father was looking for
work. That's how they met. My mother was five years younger
than he was. Her family was relatively well off. They had had a
lumber business in the old country. They were Ashkenazy Jews,
but completely assimilated.

Adriana Babeți: What was your mother like?

Michael Heim: Her name was Blanche. She was beautiful and
intelligent. But like many middle-class American women at the
time, she made less of her life than she could have. She finished
college during the Depression and longed to study English literature. She was the perfect anglophile: she enjoyed English tea,
English novels, the English lifestyle. But she had to do what she
could in those hard times, and she went into marketing. More
precisely, copywriting with a little modeling of hats on the side.
It wasn't particularly thrilling, but it enabled her to make her own
way. Then she got married. At that time when a woman of a
certain means married, she gave up going to work. My mother
read five or six novels a week; she cooked, gardened, crocheted,
and did charitable work. (My wife Priscilla characterized her
as "comfortingly normal.") She played tennis regularly, and we
occasionally played together. She had been Westchester County
Women's Junior Champion for a year, and I have a feeling she
and my father, also an avid player, bonded more over tennis than
piano lessons. Of course she also raised a child, me. She was
a good mother, very hands-off. She simply expected me to do
well in school and so never made anything of it. Some assumed
I would follow in my father's footsteps and become a musician,
but soon my true passion came to the fore: practicing scales on

the piano at the age of eight or nine, I would prop a novel on the stand and read away.

By the time my parents married, Pearl Harbor had brought us into the war. My father immediately joined the army and became a proud American citizen. When I was born, they named me Michael, not because there was anyone on either side of the family by that name but because in my father's mind Mike was the quintessential American name. He served in the entertainment corps, playing for the troops and composing battalion marching songs and the like. But then a freak accident occurred—we never found out what it was exactly—and in 1946 he died of cancer from the consequences. I long puzzled over what connection there could be between physical trauma and the growth of abnormal cells in the body until I found an answer in Tolstoy's *The Death of Ivan Ilyich*, where death comes about in an analogous manner.

In 1966 I was drafted to fight in Vietnam. I was against the war, but not being a Quaker I was ineligible for conscientious objector status. If it had to be, it had to be. But when the draft board went over my background, they discovered I was the sole surviving son of a soldier who had died in the service of his country. Drafting me was illegal. They immediately kicked me out of the office, cursing me for wasting their time.

Adriana Babeți: What kind of contact did you have with your father's parents in Budapest?

Michael Heim: My father had invited them to come to California, but they refused, claiming old age. When my father died, my mother determined to visit them. But by the time she'd gathered the necessary papers, it was too late: the Cold War was in full swing, and the Communists had taken over. My grandparents experienced difficulties under the Communist regime. They belonged to the bourgeoisie: they owned an apartment building and a building that was bombed out during the war, and they had a private business. Everything was confiscated. My grandfather died some time in the fifties, but I did get to know my grandmother when, in 1962, I went to Europe for the first time.

I found her wonderfully engaging. She had even managed to maintain a sense of humor throughout the disasters of her life: the loss of her son, the loss of her husband (by all accounts a jolly old soul), the loss of her very living space. She was forced to share her apartment first with a family of strangers, then with two, and was eventually moved into an old age home. We would send her monthly packages. During our visit together she brought out a leather jacket of mine we had sent when I was ten. She was so shrunken she could still wear it. My mother and I would write to her in English, and as a child I had no idea she didn't know the language. Only after getting to know her in person did I learn that she had paid to have our letters—and her own—translated. But by then I was studying German, the second language of all educated Hungarians of her generation, and we had been corresponding in German for some time. And if she wept when she first laid eyes on me, it was not merely because I was the spitting image of her son but also because she couldn't believe I'd actually learned German: she assumed that we, too, had hired a translator. She and I talked non-stop for a week, then maintained a regular correspondence until her death in 1965. I've kept a bundle of moving letters from her. The salutation was inevitably *"Mein heissgeliebtes Mikykind"* (My Dearly Beloved Mickey).

At the time I was passionately interested in Chinese philosophy, which to my mind held the key to a conundrum I later discovered has plagued many an adolescent, namely, whether man is born good, evil, or a *tabula rasa*. I hoped the answer would guide me through life. As a Columbia undergraduate I accordingly majored in Oriental Civilization (which encompassed the history, philosophy, and literature of China, Japan, India, and Islam) and studied Chinese for two years. But I was crushed when I learned that as an American I would not be permitted to travel to "Red China" to study at the source. I took my advisor's advice and started Russian. "You will never want for employment," he told me, "if you have the two major languages of the Cold War." Since my advisor, F. D. Reeve, a prominent Russianist and poet, also happened to be the father of Christopher Reeve, the most recent Superman, I like to say it was Superman's father who put me on to Russian.

In the end, I double-majored in Oriental Civilization and Russian Language and Literature, the latter taking over in the guise of Slavic Languages and Literatures when I went on to graduate school at Harvard. Although Grandma-in-Budapest accepted my original Chinese orientation with equanimity, I can imagine how thrilled she would have been to know that I eventually learned Hungarian ("Don't forget you are Hungarian" she kept telling me) and translated some of the finest contemporary Hungarian writers including Péter Esterházy, scion of the noble Esterházy line.

•

Adriana Babeți: If I remember correctly, the first foreign language you learned in school was French. Why?

Michael Heim: Because it was the international language, the language of a great culture. Then came German, to write to my aunt and grandmother in Vienna, who sent me a birthday present every year on behalf of my Hungarian grandparents, whom the state kept from sending anything.

Adriana Babeți: Did they ever send anything special?

Michael Heim: Yes, more than once, and I still have some things. A leather bag, for one, and something even more unusual, a camera. It was a very complicated device for me at the time, and it came with a German manual that I couldn't read. I was eleven or twelve, and hadn't begun any foreign language at all. The gift irritated me. What was I supposed to do? It was the first time I encountered, as an idea in itself, a foreign language. I started to take pictures. I tried to do a lot of different things, most of which did not work because there was no one to read the manual for me. I decided to become a photographer; I even set up a darkroom. I took it very seriously. I probably could have made a career out of it. When I went to Budapest for the first time, I wondered what I would have become if I had been born there, under communism. It's hard to say. Maybe a piano teacher, or a photographer, because those fields weren't political.

Adriana Babeți: You said you have your father's gift for music.

Michael Heim: When I was eight, I took piano lessons from a magnificent teacher. Later, I went to Julliard, the famous music school. I took lessons every week: piano, flute, and clarinet. Plus theory. I played in a wind quartet.

Adriana Babeți: And yet, you didn't go into music or photography. Why did you choose literature?

Michael Heim: I didn't follow through with a music career because it was clear to me that I didn't have enough talent. Music was very demanding. Next I wanted to become an architect, because we lived in an apartment and I dreamed of buying or building a house. I loved to look at plans and architecture magazines. They fascinated me. But I couldn't draw. So I was left with literature, which was how I spent all my time, anyway. I read and read, just like my mother. Even when I took an hour break from practicing the piano, I read.

Adriana Babeţi: What did you read?

Michael Heim: Novels, classics, English literature especially. But also adventure stories. Everything. I read even while I was doing my arpeggios. But I didn't want to specialize in literature, I just wanted to read. When I went to college, I purposely did not choose to study literature. I didn't want to ruin the pleasure of reading, to turn a pleasure into a job. It was an interesting field, but too dry.

Adriana Babeţi: Where did you study?

Michael Heim: My first four years of college were at Columbia, in New York. I stayed in New York to continue at Julliard, no other reason. At Columbia, I became interested in Asian studies. Then I moved to Harvard, where I started to study linguistics. That was interesting, but also dry. I thought I would get bored. And I was still reading as much as I could. In the end, after my master's, I surrendered: I decided to dedicate myself to literature. In 1970, I finished my doctorate in Slavics. At Harvard, I studied with Roman Jakobson, and his wife suggested I focus on literature. She was my Czech professor.

Heim, 1974.

•

Daciana Branea: You are an excellent storyteller. Did you ever think of writing, yourself?

Michael Heim: I'm often asked that question. My answer is simple: There are so many wonderful books that need to be translated, and this is what I know how to do best—I'm not being modest, just honest. As long as there are untranslated books in the world, I know that this is where my duty lies. I have some ideas I could write about if I ever started to, but I prefer to work on those books that I already know can change people's lives. I still have some time.

Adriana Babeți: Today, when you are more than fifty-five-years old, do you still believe in literature? Do you believe it can change anything, to repeat a well-known question?

Michael Heim: Do you mean now?

Adriana Babeți: Yes, now. Can literature make a difference?

Michael Heim: Oh, yes, it can do a great deal. I believe literature is enormously important today. But I didn't at the time. I just loved it. I do believe in its enormous importance, precisely because it is ignored: it is not a practical field. We could say it's a lie. But a lie that can go far, very far: all the way to a truth. Not Truth, but a truth that we've forgotten. A truth somewhere beyond us, not within, but one that may become part of us if we accept the idea that outside of ourselves are worlds and people who feel in different ways.

Adriana Babeți: Who needs literature today? Even here, in Romania, where people read a lot before '89 (for reasons we all know), belletrist literature seems to be in retreat.

Michael Heim: It's true, things here were different than in America. But your situation was artificial. You read a lot because you had no choice. You read the best literature from the rest of the world, just because it was so difficult to get to that world or even talk about it. It was a kind of sublimated revolt against the political order. Once other forms of action appeared, once people had a chance to make a real choice, they began to forget literature. In the West, this decline has been going on for more than a hundred years. And yet literature still exists, because there will always be a small group of people who cannot live without it, people for whom it still means something. I am bothered by the fact that, in American society, it almost seems someone is making a special effort to keep people from reading literature. It's a kind of false democracy. We're afraid literature is too elitist, too difficult for most people. Of course, everyone in America has heard of Shakespeare. But far fewer have heard of Goethe, Dante, Flaubert. And this is true even in the academic world. It means that people haven't been given the chance to learn that these great writers exist. Maybe some know that Cervantes is a great Spanish writer, but they probably heard about him from a grammar exercise in Spanish, a language many of us study.

Adriana Babeți: Is it possible to live without *Don Quixote*?

Michael Heim: It's possible, of course it's possible. But what kind of life is it? Perfectly quiet and flat. You can live without *Don Quixote*, especially if you don't even know it exists. What upsets me is the fact that there are thousands and thousands of people in the United States who are deprived of *Don Quixote*. Or *The Divine Comedy*. Or *The Human Comedy*. They don't know these things exist, simply put. They don't know what literature there is to read. I have students at the university who have never read a novel.

Adriana Babeți: How is that possible? Don't high schools teach world literature? Or any literature?

Michael Heim: They teach what is called "English," and which for most means spelling and very practical exercises: how to write an essay with an introduction, conclusion, etc. The teachers don't even know about literature, because they were only born thirty or forty years ago. They don't even know what they are missing.

Adriana Babeți: But what about those who study literature at college?

Michael Heim: That is a very small group, as I said. Of course, there will always be such a group. Parents read literature, children see their parents read literature, or they have a professor to convert them, to send them to the libraries—the many, immense public libraries in America—and make them read novels. The number of passionate readers remains tragically small. What can we do? As a professor, I for one know what I have to do. How can I make students fall in love with literature? Instead of talking about sophisticated theories, I get them going with a simple question, such as: why did you read this book, what can a classic work say to you? What does literature mean *to you*? How can it change your life?

Adriana Babeți: Did a book change yours?

Michael Heim: I'd just as soon say no particular book changed my life, but *books* did. What would my life be like without books? Absolutely bland and uninteresting. I can't say this is true for everyone. Just that many, many people in the United States live flavorless lives, and they don't even know it. Maybe they sense something is missing, but they don't know what. They watch television, work, stay home, see a movie, most often they simply lead empty lives. Many people believe they can fill their lives by shopping. This is truly a disease for us. For some, going to the mall is the highlight of their week. I don't believe that literature is for everyone, but it can offer everyone a more meaningful existence. Still, people don't know this, because we didn't tell them when they were children. The French novelist Daniel Pennac wrote a fantastic book about reading and the way literature should be taught. It's called *Comme un roman*. Pennac holds that every child, every person has an almost physical need for stories. The stories that children watch on TV are colorless, repetitive, and stereotypical. Unsatisfying. All it takes is the plot of one good novel, or reading a fragment aloud, to win an entire class of children over to literature.

Heim and his granddaughter Jenny, 1995.

Adriana Babeți: Do you have any children?

Michael Heim: I have three stepchildren, my wife's children. Twin girls and a boy. I even have grandchildren. Seven. I am a grandfather already. We are a large, mixed family, in every sense. For example, one of the twins is married to a Chinese man who grew up in Thailand. Except for the boy, I haven't been able to attract any of them to literature. My wife has a principle that I share: we stand alongside our children, we don't tell them what to do.

Cornel Ungureanu: We've been pleasantly surprised by your calmness and serenity. Is there anything that upsets you?

Michael Heim: I am worried by the enormous amounts of garbage we produce. Every day, when I walk to the university—not always a pleasant walk, but even so, I've done it for seven or eight years—I collect empty bottles and cans in large plastic bags. I take them home to some Mexican workers, and it's probably enough material for them make a living by recycling. I collect 60 or 70 every day, so I have probably helped recycle millions of bottles and cans. But I don't feel any more optimistic for doing it.

Adriana Babeți: You wrote me once about books you've lost while doing this. Which ones? Tell us about the lost books, because what you said sounded almost supernatural. We couldn't understand what garbage you were carrying, what bags of scrap metal you collected . . .

Michael Heim: It's ridiculous. There's so much waste in America . . . If you've never been there, you can't imagine it. There are vending machines every hundred meters where you can buy juice or mineral water. They are restocked every three hours. No one packs a lunch. All the restaurants sell food in plastic containers, which are then thrown away. Mounds of cans are thrown into plastic garbage bags that, in turn, are thrown away. I read somewhere that if we didn't use plastic bags, we would save six million barrels of oil per day. And you can't do anything about it, because people refuse to think. In fact, you don't need any of it. You can make a sandwich and take it to work in a box that will last you forty years.

Adriana Babeți: When we were in kindergarten, we had little metal lunchboxes . . .

Michael Heim: Made of sheet metal, yes, that was the way to do it.

Daciana Branea: You've been reading too much Hrabal!

Michael Heim: You may be right.

Adriana Babeți: Or Klíma, *Love and Garbage*. Have you read *Love and Garbage*? It's a book about the author's time as a garbage collector.

Michael Heim: You asked how I lose my books. On my way to school, I study foreign languages. I did this with Romanian. It's not part of my research, so I study while I walk. But when I read while I'm picking up garbage, sometimes I put my book in the trash.

Adriana Babeți: You wrote once that, perhaps at the same moment you were writing me, the lost book was being recycled.

Daciana Branea: How long ago did you lose your Romanian book?

Michael Heim: Not long. I got another copy, but I had to promise I wouldn't take it out of the house. I didn't, and so I never finished it.

Ioana Copil-Popovici: Michael, do you have any other obsessions besides recycling?

Michael Heim: Yes, I do. What I'm about to say might make you think I'm a little odd. I've noticed that, in the last twenty, thirty years—I've been teaching at UCLA almost three decades—people have become obsessed with photocopies. I remember when I was in college and I bought a book from the bookstore, I would feel, subconsciously, that owning the book was as good as reading it. Obviously that's not true, but I kept the book on my shelf and I could open it whenever I wanted or needed to. Photocopying today creates the same sensation, but much worse: when you make a copy, you feel you know that book. In Germany I once saw a sticker over a Xerox machine that said: "*Kopiert is nicht kapiert*," that is, "copying is not understanding." For us, the problem has another, more pernicious side: in college, rather than have the students buy books, many professors use photocopied anthologies. Let's say you are teaching a course on the Russian novel. You make a course pack that includes the ten novels you will cover. It seems like a good idea, because the students will have the material, and it's cheaper than buying six or seven books. But in my opinion, it's very dangerous. In the first place, the students will never buy those books. This means they will never have those books on their bookshelves. Even if they don't read all that many stories by Chekhov or Pushkin in the class, when they have the books on their shelf, they can always come back to them, loan them to their friends . . .

Ioana Copil-Popovici: But books, at least for us at this moment, have become too expensive for students to use.

Michael Heim: That may be. When we talk about Central Europe, we have to put the question differently. We all know there were no Xerox machines under the totalitarian regimes. Because, in general, copy machines were considered subversive: you could make hundreds of copies of a manifesto, pass them out, and disappear. So Xerox machines were few and well guarded. (In 1980 I did a summer course at the College of Letters in Moscow. The sole copy machine was kept under lock and key.) So you are going through a real Xeroxing euphoria, when you can make copies of anything at no cost. You are in fact in the same situation we are, maybe it's even more serious for you, since here the copy machine is a novelty. But we tell ourselves the same thing: students don't have money for books, because they cost a lot for us, too. Books are not any more expensive than they were, relatively speaking, in my time. But think how much money your generation spends, for example, on cassettes, CDs—goodness, on batteries! Why don't you spend it on books, if you're a student? A student reads books. That's his job. Maybe I'm just old-fashioned, and the truth is that today's students don't read originals, only copies.

Still, I believe that something is lost if they never own these books. When you are done with a course pack, you throw it away. It is not a beautiful thing, something you want to keep. In a way, course packs feel like ID cards, documents, bureaucracy.

•

Marius Lazurca: If you don't mind, I'd like to ask you a more personal question. You said once, before we started recording, that Dostoyevsky appeared in your life in a certain moment, that he made an impression in this moment, but later you moved away from his vision of the world, toward a different cultural sphere. Would it be correct to say you traveled from a period of belief toward one of atheism?

Michael Heim: No, I wouldn't say that.

Marius Lazurca: Or, to put it another way, from a period of unknowing piety to lucid atheism?

Michael Heim: Not at all. I would love to answer this question, I don't mind at all. When I was 16 or 17, I was searching, like all young people, I wasn't any different, but maybe I thought I was, at the time. This is why I like to teach Dostoyevsky to young people. I know that this author may become very important for them, that they need a point of reference for their ideas, and Dostoyevsky seems like a good choice. I enjoy his books to this day, but I do so from my students' perspective. Chekhov never mentions God, but he seems to show a world in which imagining God is possible. It is much subtler, a veiled way of speaking about the divine, an approach that later became stimulating for me, as much intellectually as spiritually. I found something like it in works by Central European authors. They don't try to fix my problems, don't offer solutions or try to make me their disciple, but instead, their texts suggest new ways to think about the ideas that interest me, ways I would have not discovered on my own. This is why I believe that literature plays an extremely important role for those drawn to study the spiritual side of existence. For me, as a twentieth-century person, Havel's words are extremely important—perhaps even more important than Dostoyevsky's theology. We are part of a world in which we, the human race, are not alone, but connected to a power above us, which we can call whatever we like, but which calls on us to take responsibility for our deeds. If we don't think reality is above us, but within us, then perhaps there is no real reason—this is going to sound like Dostoyevsky—why we shouldn't kill each other. Responsibility for our freedom—words that again sound like Dostoyevsky, but I think that Havel's way of putting it is more appropriate for the twentieth century—comes from the sense that we are not the sole or supreme beings in this world.

•

Cornel Ungureanu: There is a great Hungarian author who wrote a *Cultural History of Human Stupidity.* Have you read it?

Michael Heim: No, unfortunately.

Cornel Ungureanu: I'm wondering what signs of stupidity you see in the world . . .

Michael Heim: I wouldn't want to list one stupid thing or another, but you asked before what bothers me. In general—and I'd like to write about this sometime—it bothers me that people rush about without thinking, especially without thinking ahead. As a joke, I'd say that this is our contribution to the world, our Californian or American contribution. California is a good example: it only rains in two or three months out of the year, so when you leave home in the morning, you don't have to wonder whether you need to take your umbrella with you, or if you will be able to have your picnic. You don't have to think ahead, and from this, of course, many things follow. Almost all the stores are open non-stop—this is capitalism: you believe that if you stay open an hour later, you can make another dollar. But it also encourages people not to think, but to act impulsively, instinctively. We lower ourselves and reduce our lives through our refusal to think. I'm not saying you have to be serious, or even rational, all the time—I don't want to give that impression—but the fact that we neglect cause and effect just because it's simpler to do so . . . American capitalism profits greatly from this commodity. Thousands of things get thrown away . . . Someone put it well: we are not just a consumer society but a throwaway society. If you throw a bottle away, you don't have to remember to take it to the store to refill it. That's simpler. This means, on the other hand, that billions of these bottles are lost every year. This is just one example, but it shows how people waste their lives.

Sorin Tomuţa: I've heard the same thing about Germany.

Michael Heim: I wouldn't believe it. Germans are, in fact, much better off than we are, as least as far as recycling goes.

Sorin Tomuţa: People don't have to think and are encouraged to avoid doing so.

Michael Heim: Yes, they find it convenient. We Americans export this idea and the whole world welcomes it with open arms. Even if, on the one hand, it is a kind of American cultural imperialism, fashionably called "globalization," on the other hand, it's nothing we force on people. Take music, for example. I read somewhere that all types of rock have the same rhythm: the heartbeat. The music is meant to hypnotize you, in a way, keeping you from thinking. People who walk down the street listening to rock music on Walkmans look like they've been brainwashed. But this is just what they want: a type of music that doesn't tax their brains. I don't know what can be done about this, maybe we can try to show people that there are more useful things than short-circuiting their brains. Things that could help them find life more interesting. I don't think it's natural for people to do nothing, yet people do so little. I am sure you've read that in the United States, people spend on average six to eight hours per day in front of the television.

Cornel Ungureanu: What do you think of Clinton?

Daciana Branea: We were wondering about your politics . . .

Dorian Branea: Are you a Republican?

Michael Heim: No, Democrat.

Cornel Ungureanu: We only asked you that as a goad.

Michael Heim: I liked him at first, and I've tried to stay true to my first impressions. Yet, Clinton has made so many mistakes. And now, this scandal, so ridiculous . . . A friend in Washington says that his real problem is that he's provincial and has never been able to shake it off. Bill Clinton comes from Arkansas and still has not learned that, if you want to do great things, you can't allow yourself to get tripped up with small things. His sexual issues are a kind of small thing.

Sorin Tomuţa: It's interesting that this Sexgate incited such a huge political storm. There are conspiracy theories . . .

Michael Heim: There's no conspiracy, it's just a small-time provincial who took advantage of his circumstances. This caused a ridiculous and embarrassing situation for everyone. We keep seeing how the European press makes fun of Americans for being so naïve. But in America, on all the call-in shows, people protested the nonstop coverage. There are much more serious and urgent things to talk about. And, in the end, the pressure of public opinion brought the scandal to an end. I was proud to see it. Up to now, I've been saying ugly things about Americans, but I have to admit that I was proud when this situation was cleared up. It is interesting that the scandal gave rise to a large number of political jokes, a genre I associate more with Communist Europe than America. For example, a poll was taken of all American women, asking if they would sleep with President Clinton. Twenty-five percent said no, forty percent said yes, and the rest: "Even if you paid me, I'd never do that again."

·

Adriana Babeţi: How did you come to study the languages of Central Europe?

Michael Heim: I was still interested in Russian and I wanted to visit Europe. It was difficult—now everyone travels everywhere, it's normal, but then people didn't have so much money. Furthermore, I had only just turned eighteen, and my family wouldn't let me go by myself. For me, going to Europe in a young people's tour group was degrading, I refused. I tried to preserve my independence, but I couldn't make it work, so I split the difference. At the time—1962, when I was nineteen—the first student trips to the Soviet Union were being organized. Before then, it was impossible, you couldn't go. So there's the solution. A trip to the Soviet Union was still adventurous. Even dangerous. I showed I was no coward. But to prepare, I had to study Russian. So Superman's father, my adolescent pride, and last but not least, Dostoyevsky drove me toward Russian. Then there was another story, somewhat . . .

Adriana Babeți: Romantic?

Michael Heim: That, too, but I was thinking of something else. In Leningrad, I went into a large bookstore for Eastern Bloc countries, a so-called "Friendship Bookstore." I wanted to buy some German books, since they were cheaper there. I was thinking I'd buy Goethe, Schiller, maybe Brecht. But I found a Chinese salesperson. I realized I could buy books in Chinese, too. I began to copy the book titles down in a notebook. At the time, I knew about two thousand Chinese ideograms, not enough even to read the titles, so I planned to copy them down and look them up later. When the Chinese clerk saw me, she was shocked. For two reasons: because I was an American, of course, and also because it was the first time that she had ever seen someone write left-handed, and in Chinese, no less! And the first time she had seen a ballpoint pen! This was '62. It was too much for her, so she came over and spoke to me in Russian. Her Russian was even worse than mine. I responded in Chinese and she told me—today, I can't believe I understood, but then I did—she told me the story of her life, married to a Russian who beat her, and other things. She wanted to go back to China. We met again the next day and she gave me some of her books, and I gave her my pen—a Parker—and left right away. She was scared to be seen with a foreigner. I knew I would not be able to go to China; it was impossible for an American to visit Red China. I was in Russia and told myself that I would never see China. But I could come back to Russia. It would be difficult, but possible. So I decided to major in Slavics.

Marius Lazurca: So, you gave up on China because of a pen?

Michael Heim: Not the pen, but the Chinese woman. Yes, we could say that was the turning point.

Adriana Babeți: And then?

Michael Heim: I went back to the United States and continued to study Russian. So I had a double major: Oriental Studies and Russian Language and Literature.

Daciana Branea: Did you ever go back to Russia?

Michael Heim: I've been back a few times, but only on short visits. I was in Russia in 1970, while I was writing my dissertation.

Daciana Branea: What was your dissertation topic?

Michael Heim: Eighteenth-century Russian literature, and more precisely, the first translators of French and German into Russian. Trediakovsky, Sumarokov, Lomonosov. Lomonosov is wonderful, a genius. Trediakovsky and Sumarokov are important in Russian literary history, but that's all. I compared their translations and discussed the role of translation in the development of literary Russian. I told my dissertation chair . . .

Daciana Branea: Was he Russian?

Michael Heim: Yes, most of our professors were Russian. But he had left Russia during the Revolution, when he was eleven or twelve, and grown up in Germany, so he was more German than Russian. I translated his history of Russian literature from German into English. About my dissertation, he said to me, "It's an interesting subject that I know nothing about. See what you can do. You have two years." I did what I could.

One day while I was working, I answered the phone and heard a man's voice: "Mike?" Who could it be? I thought it was my uncle. So I answered, "Hi, Uncle Leonard!" "I'm not your uncle," the voice said indignantly. "Then why did you call me Mike?" I asked, also annoyed. The conversation continued anyway. The man wanted me to go to the Soviet Union, East Berlin, and Prague as the interpreter for a group of American sound engineers. Three weeks. I wouldn't make any money, but I wouldn't have to pay for anything while I was there. I said no, since I was busy with my dissertation. Then I thought I could speed up my research before leaving and be okay missing three weeks. It turned out that the man was the head of an organization named, strangely, the Citizen Exchange Corps, a group that arranged trips to the Soviet Union and meetings with local people. It was very political. Typical 1970s. What was the big danger? Nuclear war. This group thought that if enough Americans came to know enough Russians, no one would ever launch a bomb. At the organization's office, a few hours before departure, I saw a rare object: the second half of the Leningrad phone book. For years and years, it had been impossible to find a phone book for any Soviet city.

Daciana Branea: Why just the second half?

Michael Heim: I don't know, but I needed letter Ю, the second to last letter in the Cyrillic alphabet. Because the best scholar of Russian translation history lived in Leningrad, a man named Etkind. So I wrote his number down, and the first thing I did when I reached Leningrad was to prepare what I had to say, in the best Russian I could—since I didn't want my accent to reveal that I was a foreigner. I called, he answered, I said what I had to say, as clearly and practically as I could: who I was and what I wanted. He invited me to his house right away, we talked for three hours. I explained what I had done up to then, he showed me what was and wasn't good in my work and recommended a bibliography. These were the three most important hours in my academic life. I returned to the Soviet Union in 1980 and 1981, for three or four weeks. In 1984, I took 60 American students. It was awful. On the first day, one of the students came to me and said, "I have to tell you something very important. Everyone in my family has died of cancer, and I think I have it, too." He was very upset, he had never travelled abroad, or anywhere, and he was sure he had to see an American doctor. I took him to the embassy and he came back with an aspirin. He was perfectly healthy.

Adriana Babeți: And how did you come to Central Europe?

Michael Heim: As I've already said, when I finished college—this was 1964—I decided to study linguistics; I had studied Russian, Chinese, German, and French. I also spoke Spanish, because I had worked as a guide while in college, to make a little money, and there were many tourists from Latin America. They needed people to accompany the tourist groups, so I had a good reason to learn the language quickly and speak it fluently.

Daciana Branea: How quickly can you learn a foreign language?

Michael Heim: Spanish was not too hard; you'll remember what they used to say about Spanish. We looked down on it. As you know,

Spanish has many dialects. Foreigners learn a standard version that, in fact, does not exist. You had to speak the same language with people from Cuba or Puerto Rico, and you didn't understand one iota of what they said. They understood us but could not understand why we didn't understand them. But Spanish became important for another reason: my Hispanic Literature professor would become the most important translator of Latin American literature.

Daciana Branea: Who?

Michael Heim: His name is Gregory Rabassa. He translated *One Hundred Years of Solitude*, all of García Márquez's novels. He translated Jorge Amado, and another six great writers who . . .

Daciana Branea: Who translated Borges?

Michael Heim: Not him. The American translations of Borges are very problematic. All of his work has been translated, of course, except for the essays, which a friend of mine is working on at this moment. But Borges, who chose his own translators (and spoke perfect English), didn't start off with the right people and let himself be led astray by under-prepared translators. One of them—an impostor—called on Borges once, just so he could later claim they were friends.

Daciana Branea: How have American perceptions of foreign languages changed over time?

Michael Heim: Not at all. Or yes, actually, now we think no one needs any foreign languages . . .

Daciana Branea: Except English.

Michael Heim: Americans think everyone in the world should know English. In California, if you want to talk with the housekeeper or gardener, maybe you should know five words in Spanish. No more than five. You can buy special dictionaries: Housekeeper Spanish, Gardener Spanish.

Daciana Branea: Is this *politically correct?*

Michael Heim: No, but neither are the people who make them.

Adriana Babeți: And still: Central Europe?

Michael Heim: I began to study linguistics in graduate school because I had learned such different languages, and I liked theory. The same thing happened with music: I was a musician, I liked to play the piano and to study music theory. But after the first week of my linguistics career, I realized I had made a mistake. In the second week, you could still drop a course and add a different one. When people ask why I went to the Slavics department, I laugh and tell them, because it was on the third floor. The French department was on the second. French was—and still is—the foreign language I speak best. I asked for information about their program, but they didn't give me a second glance, because they already had too many students. The library was on the first floor, Slavic languages the third, and the fourth was German.

Adriana Babeți: But you never made it to the fourth.

Michael Heim: No, because the secretary on the third was very . . .

Adriana Babeți: Reserved?

Michael Heim: Worse, blasé. She said something like, "If you're good enough for us, we'll know." So I ended up there. I had majored in Russian, at least on paper, and even if Oriental Studies had been my real specialty, I had worked a lot on Russian. But, back to Central Europe. In the Slavics department you studied Russian literature plus an East European one. If you specialized in linguistics, you studied Russian and two other languages. Russian is an Eastern Slavic language, and the other two had to be Western Slavic (Polish or Czech) and Southern Slavic (Bulgarian or Serbo-Croatian).

Daciana Branea: Did this seem like a more comfortable choice than literature?

Michael Heim: As I've said, I didn't want to study literature because I liked it too much. The same reason I didn't study music. I thought literature meant so much to me that it would be a mistake to approach it professionally. Work is one thing, affinity another.

Daciana Branea: Maybe we should change our specialties, too . . .

Michael Heim: You shouldn't make something you like into your job, or so I thought. I studied Slavic linguistics, which was completely different from general linguistics. I could do a little literature, too. I chose Czech. Why? Two reasons. I had heard the Czech professor was very good—when I tell you who it was, you'll understand. Then, I remembered something my mother had told me about Czechs. When my father was a Hollywood composer, there was a kind of Central European mafia: they wrote the music, directed the films, they did everything. There were many in the business, but you don't hear about most of them. For example, my father, a newcomer, wrote music for films without ever receiving credit. This happened with everyone starting out, until you rose up the hierarchy. My mother remembered the Czech women, she said most were beautiful, intelligent, good cooks, elegant dressers. But back to my professor. You've heard of the linguist Roman Jakobson. Well, my professor was his wife. And Jakobson was our linguistics professor, a wonderful man, he loved . . .

Daciana Branea: . . . his wife.

Michael Heim: He loved her, but they had just divorced. I never saw them together. I was her student, and his. She taught Czech and was a wonderful woman. She was a true Central European—just like my mother had described—not only cultured and refined, but she had traveled widely, knew everyone. So that's how I ended up studying Czech and learning what espresso was. With that language, it seemed a whole new world opened up in front of me. I decided to go to Prague. My professor was so interesting that I thought all Czechs would be like her. Of course, it wasn't like that. But that was a good time to visit Czechoslovakia. I got there in '65, when things were beginning to open up. The Soviet Union in 1962 and Czechoslovakia in 1965 were like night and day.

Daciana Branea: Is that when you met Havel?

Michael Heim: Yes, and this was how it happened. My aunt and uncle visited me that year, I was very close to them. This was the Uncle Leonard I confused for the head of the Citizens Exchange Corps. I told them I was studying Czech. As it turned out, everyone else I told this to thought it was a silly idea. Why would anyone want to learn Czech? No one had heard anything about Czechoslovakia since 1938 and Munich. But my aunt, instead of saying it was strange, said, "Oh, a good friend of mine from school is a journalist and lives there with her family." So I had a place to stay in Czecho-slovakia. That family's children introduced me to their friends. There weren't too many Americans around, and I was an American who spoke Czech, so people wanted to meet me. Two weeks after I got to Prague, I was taken to the premiere of one of Havel's plays. And now I think it was one of his best works, *Memorandum*, a satire of bureaucratic language, but also an allegory of the entire Commu-nist system. I hope it's been translated into Romanian. Afterward, I was introduced to Havel as an American guest. But I have never met him again. I admire him immensely, I wrote a detailed study of *Letters to Olga*, I translated his address at UCLA a few years ago, and I teach his plays to my students (they work very well because they help young people understand how the regime functioned). But I can't say we are friends.

Adriana Babeţi: How did you come to Serbo-Croatian?

Michael Heim: That happened much later.

Adriana Babeţi: So, in order, what language came after Czech? Hungarian? Why?

Michael Heim: Hungarian, but not for sentimental reasons. I said earlier that my grandparents were part of the respectable bourgeoi-sie—not upper, not lower—they had a few bakeries. They also had a house that my father had placed under my name. And because I was an American citizen, born in America, when they national-ized the houses, no one could touch it. And so, when I visited my grandmother in the same year, 1962, she told me about his house. She said, "You are Hungarian," (she was a great patriot, that's why she didn't want to come to America), "and this is your house. You can come here whenever you want." I went to a lawyer and asked him to send money to my grandmother. I sold the house. When she found out, she started to cry, so I went back to the lawyer. Because I was only 19, not 21, it turned out the sale had not been legal, so the house had never been sold. Later, many years after my grandmother died, I did sell it, and not understanding how business works, I lost all the money. So. Since I had to do business with Hungarians, I began to study Hungarian . . . At that time, I had already started to work as a translator. I had to stay in Hungary a few weeks to resolve some legal problems, and there I met a woman from the state literary agency—another Central European woman who matched my positive stereotype—and we talked about literature; this was my interest. She asked me who my favorite author was. I said, Chekhov. (He still is.) She gave immediately me a novel by Örkény, which I translated right way. Word for word, the title is *Exhibition of Roses*. I don't know if it was translated in Romanian, but it is a superb book, really great. A TV reporter wants to film three people in the throes of death, to capture the moment when life passes into death. He finds three people about to die, and he follows them . . . step by step. The novel (actually, more of a novella, a hundred something pages) is a study of the ways art changes life. The moment something is made into art, it is no longer the same as it was before. It is an extraordinarily refined story. I tried to find someone to make a version for television. The text still feels current, not confined to the Communist period. There are some political references, but they aren't the most important part. It's about art—television as an art form—and art's influence on life. I spoke once with the author, and he told me that the idea for the novella came to him in New York, while he was watching a show on a similar theme, and he re-set the story in Hungary.

Daciana Branea: How would you describe your knowledge of Hungarian?

Michael Heim: Every time I translate something from Hungarian, I have to re-learn the language. It's hard, because Hungarian is very different from the other languages I know, and I began to learn it rather late. I was about forty.

Daciana Branea: So, you know the language more passively.

Michael Heim: Not passively, exactly. A translator must have a more than passive understanding of the language he translates. That's why I am here. If I want to learn Romanian well enough to translate, I have to know how people talk and to be able to reproduce what I hear. I can do this in Hungarian. I could say in Hungarian everything I am saying now, without it seeming too forced, but it would take a little time to form the sentences, to get used to the language. I have to start from the beginning every time, and every time it gets easier. Still, it is the most difficult language I speak.

Adriana Babeți: What came after Hungarian?

Michael Heim: Serbo-Croatian, and for a very simple reason: money.

Adriana Babeți: Like Spanish?

Michael Heim: No, I didn't make a penny from it. My university was low on money when the person who had been teaching Serbo-Croatian retired. If there had been money, the university would have hired someone else. But at about the same time, I met a Serbian film director, Vida Ognjenović—she taught with us for a semester—who commanded me, "You must learn our language." I didn't understand at the time why she had said, "our language." It was, in fact, a way to avoid saying "Serbian" or "Croatian," something people still do today. This was in 1984, and it was a problem even then. A deep-seated one, even if no one would have admitted it. Today, it is not possible to use the term "Serbo-Croatian." We could talk about this, but it is a very delicate subject. At that time, you could still say some things, it wasn't such a serious issue. So I decided to learn the language. Vida was a good friend of Danilo Kiš, who was looking just then for a translator for *The Encyclopedia of the Dead*. This was the first book I translated from Serbo-Croatian. I met the writer once in Belgrade and another time in Paris.

Adriana Babeţi: Was there anything after Serbo-Croatian? You're scaring us already.

Michael Heim: I decided after Serbo-Croatian not to study any more languages. I promised my wife. Because studying a new language meant spending time away from home. And here I am in Timişoara! This is a little personal. I promised my wife I would put a stop to it. But in 1992, I was at a conference in Newark where I met three Romanians: Mircea Mihăieş, Ioana Ieronim, and Adriana Babeţi. I realized there was a gap in my knowledge. I knew nothing about Romania. You asked me about Polish. It would be very difficult for me to learn Polish and to use it, actively, because of Czech, because the two languages are very close. If I picked up a text in Polish—not literature, but an essay or newspaper article—I could understand it. Once when I had to do it, I could. I had to read a book quickly, and I managed. I can read Polish, but only quickly, not slowly. I can understand the topic when I hear it spoken. But with Romanian, even though it is a Romance language, things are not as simple. You can't read Romanian by knowing French, the way a Czech would read Polish. Whatever they say, no French or Italian or Spanish speaker can read Romanian without some preparation.

Daciana Branea: But can't they understand spoken Romanian? Can't Italians, for example?

Michael Heim: Can they? Maybe because Italians want to feel at home in any company. Or it's their innate optimism. I understand why they might be able to do it more easily than others. But not even Latinity can work miracles, or erase two millennia. So I realized there was an entire area I knew nothing about. Judging by the people I was talking to, it was a fascinating world. I knew nothing about Romanian literature, but with such people . . . Another motivation was that, at that time, a colleague and I had decided to form a working group for Central European literatures and to make a list, to get a clear idea of what was translated into English from this area, what was well translated, what was poorly done and needed to be re-done, what had been done well but was no longer available. In each case, I asked two people for their opinion: someone whose native language was English, and another whose native language was the one under discussion. I had no problems finding people for any of the languages except Romanian. There was no one born in the United States who studied Romanian and Romanian literature. The Romanian person involved was wonderful—Virgil Nemoianu—but he had to do the work of two people. It's true that there are American specialists— Daniel Chirot, Keith Hitchins, Gail Kligman, Katherine Verdery— who knew Romanian very well, but they are all social scientists.

So I hadn't found anyone to translate from Romanian literature. This was the second reason, as I later realized. The third was that we had an excellent lecturer, from Bucharest.

Adriana Babeţi: Georgiana Gălăţeanu.

Michael Heim: Yes, Georgiana Gălăţeanu-Fărnoagă. She was in our department, and I could ask her questions. This project took several years. In the meantime, I spent a month in Italy, where I had to give a paper in Italian.

Adriana Babeţi: In Bologna?

Michael Heim: Yes, Bologna, then Padua, in the north. I was glad to learn the language, since I wanted to read a wonderful book, *Magic Prague* by Ripellino. He created a new genre of literature, also used by Claudio Magris. The book is called *Magic Prague* and subtitled *romanzo saggio*, novel-essay. It was a fascinating book. It includes about 150 fragments of cultural and personal history. The book may also be read as an elegy for the past. It was written in '71-'72, the darkest period of recent Czechoslovak history. I am proud that I ended up translating it.

Dorian Branea: It would be interesting to hear how you choose the novels you translate . . .

Michael Heim: I would *like* to choose the novels I translate. I make suggestions, of course, but, at least recently, publishers are very concerned with finances and target profitable books. Usually, I have very little say. So whenever I propose a book, I try to use a different approach, but my approach consists in telling publishers why the book is important to a particular tradition and why the English-language public will appreciate it. Quite often, publishers will send me a novel for an evaluation, which I am glad to write—sometimes positively, sometimes the opposite. I think this is a very important side of my work, the "secret" side. The responsibility is enormous. No one has ever published a book I rejected . . . but I cannot say that all the books I recommended were published. The problem is, whenever I recommend a book myself, people think I want to translate it too, even if this is the furthest thing from my mind.

Dorian Branea: What, then, attracts you most about a book?

Michael Heim: The first thing is the language. I don't want to say that the ideas are completely unimportant. For me, at least, it's not the ideas in the text that count, but its literariness. What is literature, in the end? I was trained as a structuralist and I think this has given me great freedom of movement.

Dorian Branea: Do you believe that the structuralists were able, as they dreamed, to create "a science of literature"?

Michael Heim: I don't think that's the question. I don't think we need a science of literature. In any case, we don't need the word "science." If you want to say science, just do so. The fact that I claim that what I do is "scientific" doesn't help me at all to read a book. Probably, for those who are in the social sciences it is important to believe they are a branch of science. I don't care. One example: Bakhtin. His theory helped me to see things in some books—especially *Švejk*—that I would have missed otherwise. And yet, Bakhtin cannot be applied everywhere, he is not universal. But we don't need universal answers in literary criticism.

Dorian Branea: Vasile Popovici, in his book *The Character's World*, makes a persuasive critique of the dialogical; looking at a series of Romanian and foreign novels, he decides that this term is insufficient, too restrictive, and he offers instead the trialogical, a term drawn from ancient Greek tragedy, where the epic event is viewed from three perspectives at the same time.

Michael Heim: I met Vasile Popovici yesterday, but we didn't have a chance to speak about this. I will have to ask when I see him next. In any case, it's true that, in literary criticism, no theory excludes— or should exclude—any other. Marxist criticism, for example, in its ideological form, is awful. Like feminist or psychoanalytic criticism. At the same time, there are many valuable things in each, as long as they don't claim to be exclusive.

Sorin Tomuța: Part of your academic career has been dedicated to the study of translation. You are, likewise, a well-respected translator, working from languages that most Americans would consider exotic. Is a successful translation a personal version of the original?

Michael Heim: Anyone who has tried to translate a full literary work, not just a few pages, knows that translation is interpretation. You must interpret in order for the translation to come out well. I could give thousands of examples. Yes, certainly, translation is interpretation, and you can see this best if you compare two translations of the same text. You can tell right away that there are two minds at work on the same problem, each from a different point of view. Two people never translate the same sentence the same way. This claim leads to a part of your question: how can a future translator be taught? In the first place, the translator must be a careful reader of literature, which means he should study not only the history of the literature in which he wants to specialize, but also various techniques of researching or analyzing text, *explications de textes*.

In my literary translation seminar, I try to bring together students with different maternal languages. I don't work separately with those who know French or Spanish or German. If you work like that, you tend to focus on what translators call the source language, the language from which you translate. The seminar becomes a language class, rather than one on translation. For me, the target language is much more important in training a translator, the language *into which* you translate. This is the language that will be read, what really counts. This doesn't mean that the other language is not important. Of course it is. But only as "a technical detail." You have to know the language from which you translate, you have to know it well enough to know how much of it you don't know. In my seminar, students have to bring, every week, a fragment from a literary text they have translated, fragments that we discuss together. We discuss, more exactly, the literary nuances of different English choices. It is amazing that, even though not all the students know the original language, they can find the mistakes exactly, just because the English text is unclear or makes no sense. The one doing the translating can't see it, because he is too immersed in the source language. So it's not a problem to work with people who don't necessarily know the original language. Often I don't know it, myself. This past spring, for example, students were working from Arabic and Armenian, languages foreign to me, and yet my comments and those from the other students were just as relevant as what we said about texts from French or Spanish. And this method can be used anywhere. In our university, each trimester is ten weeks long, and of course you can't make someone a translator so quickly, but what you can do is to show someone the work is worth doing more of, in the future. I often see students surprised to discover that they can be translators, even publish. All of the seminars up to now have produced translators who publish translations of major works. I think it is important that all over the world there be a sustained interest in translation, since with this kind of training you create a team of active people, that is, people who will not wait for the publisher to sign a title that has to appear. If every university with a strong Comparative Literature department began to produce qualified translators, they could start to work immediately, and then there would be more opportunities for foreign authors to reach their audience. This is true everywhere, not just in our country.

•

Adriana Babeți: Dear Mike, I don't even dare ask you my next question. If you tell me there are people in your country who haven't heard of Dante or Balzac, what can we say about Hašek or Kundera, Kiš or Esterházy? What is happening with Central European literature in the United States? How is it regarded?

Michael Heim: I have said that in this immense mass of people are smaller groups, of tens, hundreds, or even thousands of readers. All it takes is for the works to be translated. Even if they are not read by hundreds of thousands of people immediately—so I tell myself when I translate, to quiet my fears—they will be in the libraries. I once met someone who, on hearing I was a Slavics professor, told me he had just taken a great novel out of the library, by the Serb, Crnjanski: *Migrations*. He wanted to know if I had read it, and if I hadn't that I should. You can't imagine how happy it made me. Or I might see someone on an airplane reading a book I have translated. I'm moved. It's not every day, but still, it's happened a few times. Even if the novels sell poorly (an average print run is no more than two thousand, in a country as large as the U.S.), I don't think this matters. There will always be that loyal "gang," people who aren't even aware how exceptional they are. I do what I do for these people. I know that it is important for them to read Hrabal, Esterházy, Ugrešić, Kiš, or Crnjanski.

Adriana Babeți: How many books from this part of Europe have you translated?

Michael Heim: I couldn't tell you unless I went home and counted. I haven't kept track. Over twenty, I think. But I've also translated from Russian. A different cultural area.

Adriana Babeți: Of all Central European authors translated, who are the best known in the United States?

Michael Heim: Kundera, Kundera, Kundera. By far. All intellectuals have heard of him. Whether they've read him is a different story. But they enjoy playing with the title of his best-known novel *The Unbearable Lightness of Being*, going on about the unbearable lightness of this and the unbearable lightness of that. I laugh when I run across newspaper headlines adopting the formulation. The editor who commissioned me to do the translation first heard the title over a bad transatlantic phone connection from Kundera in French. All he could make out was that it consisted of three abstract words. I realized a title consisting of "three abstract words" would be a hard sell in the US but was surprised the initial opposition to a literal translation came from Kundera himself. "I realize that for you Americans the title will be a bit hard-going," he told the editor, "so we can try something else." And he suggested one of the chapter titles: "Karenin's Smile." I protested. "We're not children," I told the editor. "If *The Unbearable Lightness of Being* is the title, so be it." And so it stayed. I'm glad I pushed for it. Even the film based on the book adopted it. Unfortunately, the film, though a box-office success, failed to take advantage of the cinematic structure inherent in the novel.

Cornel Ungureanu: How would you describe Kundera's relationship with the Czech spirit?

Michael Heim: Kundera now calls himself a "European writer." And that's what he is. He wrote his last two books directly in French. But for me, he is still a Czech writer. And he is extremely conscious of his roots. He wrote a study of Vladislav Vančura, a great Czech novelist, unknown abroad, because he is very hard to translate. His material is very Czech. Maybe one day I'll attempt a translation.

Cornel Ungureanu: Czech writers have a strong relationship with Czech directors . . .

Michael Heim: Yes, Kundera himself didn't teach at a school of letters, but at the well-known Prague film school. He taught French literature there. Film is extremely important in this relationship. It has helped me personally to promote Czech literature in the American market. Czech culture had already impacted the public through Menzel or Forman. I remember the Oscar for Menzel's film *Closely Watched Trains*. Because of it, I was able to win the battle for the novel on which it's based. Also important were the events of 1968.

Cornel Ungureanu: Is that when you met Hrabal?

Michael Heim: No. I met him in 1965 when I was in Czechoslovakia and he was introduced to me as the most important living Czech author. I'd like to go back for a moment to Kundera's Czech roots. In that study of Vančura, Kundera also admits he owes a great deal to Čapek. Whoever has read *The Joke* can see it. Čapek argues in most of his novels, including *An Ordinary Life*, that there are no mediocre, banal, indistinguishable lives, that each one has its own purposeful biography, and thus its own point of view, its personal vision.

Cornel Ungureanu: How did Hrabal strike you then, in 1965?

Michael Heim: He was my true introduction to Central European literature. Through him, I discovered a completely new universe. In my opinion, Hrabal is the incarnation of Central Europe. Because his works have all the major themes of this area, but not in an elevated, highbrow way—quite the opposite. Everything Hrabal does is extremely popular, but it is clear also that he is a very cultivated person. He knows German literature and philosophy very well, especially Schopenhauer, Nietzsche, and even Hegel.

Daciana Branea: Which Central European literature is the best known in the U.S.?

Michael Heim: Certainly Czech literature, because of Kundera.

Daciana Branea: Was his article, "The Tragedy of Central Europe," as important as they say?

Michael Heim: It was extremely important, only because it came *after* Kundera was already celebrated as an author. Kundera became known in the States as a writer first, for *The Book of Laughter and Forgetting*, at the beginning of the '80s.

"The Tragedy of Central Europe" was an important explanation of "the other Europe." Earlier, Philip Roth had started a series of translations from Central European literatures, called "Writers from the Other Europe." This became the place to go to find all these authors. You, an ordinary American reader, not knowing which books to choose, you could let Roth judge for you. He could be your guide . . . and so he was for many people. And his name was on the cover of every book, printed just as large as the name of the author. I'm sure the publishers did this on purpose, because they knew it was much more likely that the American reader would buy a book with

Philip Roth's name on the cover than one with a name no one could pronounce and no one had seen before.

Daciana Branea: You were saying that Czechoslovakia enticed you because you had heard so much about its beautiful women. Were you disappointed?

Michael Heim: I came to Czechoslovakia for the first time in the summer of 1965. I was 22, and the quality to which you refer was very important . . . and I was completely satisfied [laughter] . . . by what I found. I don't mean only the women, but everyone my age. I learned something that surprised me about myself: they taught me how "American" I was.

I had been in the Soviet Union three years before. This was 1962, my first trip to Europe, and I was very naïve, in the best sense of the word. I didn't have any preconceived ideas. I was simply horrified by all I found there: the lack of freedom, the fear . . . When I came to Czechoslovakia, everything was different. I met people my own age who knew how to stand up to the system, how to manage within it, and who were not at all afraid. They weren't afraid, for example, to have a conversation with a foreigner. While in the Soviet Union, you planned your meetings far in advance, and if you met someone in the street, for example, you could only say a few words because you knew you could make trouble for them. In Prague there were no such problems.

Daciana Branea: What were the major differences between Czechoslovakia and the USSR?

Michael Heim: The most important was the fact that there, in 1965, people trusted each other. And they could say whatever they wanted. Even if they didn't do it in public, they were as free as possible with each other. For me, the most important thing was that I learned you shouldn't believe everything you read, and my friends were much more sophisticated readers than I was. Readers of magazines, but by extension, readers of everything, including literature. I had been schooled to believe that everything I read was, more or less, true. And more or less, everything I had been reading *was* true. My Czech friends were used to questioning everything, while I tended to accept it.

Daciana Branea: What did they read?

Michael Heim: They read everything they could. They also translated, here and there. But Czech literature was becoming more and more interesting. I constantly asked them who were the best writers of the moment, because there were some exceptional young writers. The first time I was in Czechoslovakia, I had only studied the language a year, so of course I wasn't ready to read literature. But I went back the next year, in 1966, and again in 1968, and I learned a lot about a group of authors that now everyone knows about, today they are a part of world literature. The most important names were Hrabal, Kundera, Škvorecký. At the time, completely unknown outside of Czechoslovakia. My first summer there, 1965, I met Havel. As I have mentioned, we didn't become friends, but I shook his hand at the premiere of *Memorandum*.

Daciana Branea: Who was the first Czech author you translated, and why?

Michael Heim: The first author I *tried* to translate into English was Škvorecký, whom I had met. Škvorecký knew English, it was his professional specialty. I decided to translate one of his stories, and when I got back to New York, I sent it to a publisher. It was one of his detective stories. This translation was an important lesson for me. The publisher said that he had read the story and he liked it, but . . . the translation had some slips. He showed me one mistake: I had translated a word meaning "tanned" as "sun-burnt." A huge mistake, one stemming not from a lack of knowledge of Czech, but negligence of my English. I realized I could never let that happen again, that I needed to pay close attention to my own language. I learned that a translator is a writer in his native tongue, and the language from which he translates is nothing but—as I like to say, in exaggeration—a "technical detail." Of course, *you must* know the language you translate from, but if you don't understand the text well enough, the game is not lost, because you can ask a native speaker for help. The most important thing is to master the language you translate *into*.

Daciana Branea: When you began your career as a translator of Central European literature, was there already significant interest in the United States?

Michael Heim: Not a trace.

Daciana Branea: So you were a kind of pioneer.

Michael Heim: I was a lost pioneer. First, because my first translation was not good—the publisher was right—then because I was very young and no one took me seriously. Between 1966 and 1968 I practiced with prose fragments, trying to catch the attention of American publishers. I was sure that these authors were very good. But again, I couldn't find anyone to listen to me. Then came 1968.

Daciana Branea: How were you received, as an American, at that time? It was the Czech "Jazz Age" . . .

Michael Heim: Yes, the Czechs at the time were fascinated by American music and literature. The same could not be said of the USSR, where the propaganda was so powerful that people either believed it absolutely or thought it was completely false and, as a result, thought the U.S. was a kind of inaccessible paradise. The Czechs were much, much more sophisticated. Most of their parents were middle class, bourgeois, from the time when "bourgeois" was a neutral term. Many had suffered during early Communism. Yet, one way or another, they managed. I was born in 1943. If my friends were born, let's say, in 1943, it means they started school in 1948, the first year of the Communist regime.

Daciana Branea: So they grew up with it.

Michael Heim: Yes, they were the first generation schooled completely by this regime. But of course, they all knew that you heard one thing at school and another at home. In the Soviet Union at that time it was very hard to live, because two or three generations already had grown up under the Communist regime, and many people came from illiterate families. The Soviets taught them to read, then they gave them the only books they were allowed to have. They controlled them mentally, spiritually, intellectually. In Prague, where the people were 100% literate, this couldn't happen. Everyone knew that they had to hide what they thought. They had had a lot of experience, they had just come out of the Protectorate under Hitler. They knew, therefore, how to deal with the system, and they had learned things from *Švejk*, as well. They were very interested in America, but I never felt like a museum piece or zoo animal. I was a normal person, with the interests and desires of a twenty-two year old, the same as them. I had just been born in a different world and could teach them a little about it. In turn, they could teach me many things. We developed a very natural, symbiotic relationship.

For the same reason, it was interesting for me, as an American, when I came home, to talk to my Czech professor about Prague. She asked me, "What seemed different to you about Czechoslovakia?" What had surprised me most of all, in comparison with the Soviet Union, was how free these people were when it came to sex. In Russia, I never heard anyone mention sex; it was a very Puritanical society. In contrast, people in Prague talked about sex all the time, it was completely natural. They used four-letter words all the time. I learned them right away, no problem. I told my professor how surprised I was by the sexual openness, and she said, "Of course, it's a Catholic country . . ." This surprised me too, quite a bit, because I grew up in a neighborhood that was 75 or 80% Catholic. An Italian neighborhood. I told my professor, and she replied, "Oh, but there's no Catholicism in America. American Catholicism is just Protestantism with a pope." All these things shaped me . . . provincial American that I was.

But to come back to the question of literature—the United States had no interest in this literature, no one had heard of the authors, no one had head of the country—Czechoslovakia—for a long time . . . It may seem hard to believe, but then, we were only dimly aware of the differences between "the Communist countries." More sophisticated people called them the "countries of the Eastern Bloc" or "the Soviet sphere." Eastern Europe was a solid black spot—misery symbolized by the gray apartment blocks where people lived. Everything looked the same. And all the countries looked the same. They had simply disappeared from our awareness. They were an imaginary extension of the Soviet Union. And there I was telling the people around me: you're wrong, where we only see gray and more gray is a vibrant, colorful world. I was speaking, of course, about Czechoslovakia, I couldn't speak for other countries, I couldn't yet explain the diversity. But I knew something was happening. Beginning in 1966, a number of Czech films began to become known in the West. They had been preceded by some Polish films. The more sophisticated people immediately caught on that there was something there.

Daciana Branea: This means that the West first discovered Central Europe through film.

Michael Heim: Yes. The first Czech directors to become successful in the West were Miloš Forman and Jiří Menzel. The first films I saw were *Loves of a Blonde* and *Closely Watched Trains*, both masterpieces. Then came others . . . But the political situation was the most important part. At the end of 1967, in October, the Writers' Conference took place and censorship was abolished. Can you imagine? A writers union in a Communist country abolishes censorship, all by itself! Then, in January 1968, when Dubček came to power, the newspapers wrote about Czechoslovakia again. And this counts for something in the States. For example, the literature of the Soviet Union wasn't well known, either. Even though they were our main enemies, we knew very little about the Soviets for a long time. But when there was a scandal and the newspapers began to pay attention, *Doctor Zhivago* became a best-seller. The first time I was in the USSR, in 1962, *A Day in the Life of Ivan Denisovich* became a best-seller in the States, because of Solzhenitsyn's politics.

Daciana Branea: You mean that Czech writers became known in America only after 1968?

Michael Heim: Yes, afterward. But it took a while, because we weren't ready, we didn't have the translators, we didn't know who the important authors were. I was lucky, because I was there. Suddenly, people started to listen to me.

Prague, 1968. Photograph by Michael Heim.

Daciana Branea: So you were there, in '68 . . .

Michael Heim: Yes, I was there when the tanks rolled in. By then
I was comfortable with Czech. My major literature was Russian,
but I developed a strong interest in things Czech during the three
summers I spent there, '65, '66, and '68. During the summer of
'68 I worked on an English-Czech dictionary, providing Czech
equivalents of American slang, and was employed as a translator by UNESCO in Prague. I translated scholarly articles, not
literature. It was good practice, a good apprenticeship. It left me
plenty of time to go out with friends to meetings and demonstra-
tions. I had made friends among some of the leading filmmakers
and actors and went to a film or play nearly every evening. It was
fantastic: there was so much going on. Prague was second only
to London.

By chance it was during the summer of '68 that the International Congress of Slavists took place in Prague. Ironically, the gathering of scholars coincided with the invasion of armies from the scholars' countries. Just before the first session I went to the barber's. It was the era of long hair, and mine was much too long for an event as staid as an international conference. The barber had read about the conference in the papers, and since barbers like to chew the fat as they work, I regaled him with human interest stories about the star of the conference, the structuralist Roman Jakobson, a world-renowned linguist whose biography I knew well because I had studied with him. He had fled his native Russia after the Revolution ("and a good thing, too," the barber interjected) and come to Prague ("and a good thing, too"), where he helped to found the famous Prague Linguistics Circle ("didn't know we had one"), and after the Hitler's invasion he fled to America, where he still lived ("smart guy!").

Chatting with my Czech teacher, Jakobson's wife, I learned that after she made a brief visit to Czechoslovakia in the late fifties (the first time she was allowed back since she and her husband had fled), her sister, a perfectly innocent Czech housewife, was picked up by the secret police and interrogated. All they wanted to know was: "What is structuralism? What is structuralism?" They must have thought it was a plot against the regime. But by '68 the political situation had changed to such an extent that Jakobson could receive an honorary doctorate from Masaryk University in Brno, where he had once taught.

My Czech teacher, myself, and a few other Czech professors had dinner together at a Prague restaurant on what turned out to be the evening before the invasion. It was in the air, of course, but we all agreed it would be counterproductive on the part of the Soviets. It would tarnish an already tarnished reputation, and what would it gain them? Dubček, the symbol of the Prague Spring, called for "socialism with a human face," not the reinstatement of capitalism. Most of my Czech friends were not particularly enamored of capitalism either; they wanted to reform the system from within and set an example for the other Warsaw Pact nations and even the world: a third way. No one knew how far the current changes would go, but that was an internal Czech affair. "No, the odds were against it," we concluded and went home.

I was holed up in the empty apartment of some American journalists who were vacationing on the Adriatic. At about four in the morning the phone rang. It was my Czech teacher. One of her friends had called to report the invasion was underway. I quickly turned on Czech radio. It had gone off the air, a bad sign. Then I switched to the German station Deutsche Welle, and suddenly things were clear. A half hour later I saw the tanks. The street where I happened to be living was Czechoslovak Army Street, and the apartment was only a few blocks from the Ministry of Defense.

In the week that followed, I constantly crisscrossed the city interpreting between Czechs and the soldiers. Czechs were all supposed to learn Russian in school, but they had such antipathy to the language that even though Czech and Russian are closely related they could not communicate with the invaders. No Czech ever asked me who I was. They were just grateful I could help them convince the Soviet soldiers what a mistake they were making. The soldiers were mostly naïve kids and mostly non-Russians, that is, members of the national minorities. I suspected they had been singled out as a demonstration of the possible consequences of trying to strengthen their national identity, which is after all what the Czechs were after.

Daciana Branea: So they simply didn't know what they were doing there.

Michael Heim: They thought they knew, because they believed the propaganda they'd been fed, namely, that they were to give "brotherly aid" to a Warsaw Pact country invaded by capitalists. As proof *Pravda* published a front-page article showing a cache of "West German weapons" and bemoaning the threat of German invasion. The irony was that Germans had in fact invaded, but East Germans not West Germans.

In this connection I encountered an interesting instance of false linguistic friends. When the Czechs told the soldiers, "We didn't ask you to come," some of the soldiers admitted they'd been surprised when the populace greeted them with—using the Russian word—"fists" (*s kulakami*), while they'd been told they would be welcomed with open arms. The Czechs did not understand; the Czech word for "fist" is *pěst*, and they thought the Russians were talking about "kulaks," the supposedly rich peasants Stalin annihilated as a class in the thirties. "But we have no kulaks!" the Czechs protested through me. The Czechs were not armed and couldn't protect themselves, so they resorted to the ruses they so pride themselves on as a nation. One of the things they did, which took on a great deal of importance for me in the days following, was to paint over the street signs, to prevent the Soviets from locating the people they were out to arrest. There were, of course, some Czech traitors who guided them around, people who went on to occupy high positions in the new regime.

Daciana Branea: So the majority chose a non-violent strategy consistent with their traditions.

Prague, 1968. Photograph by Michael Heim.

Michael Heim: Right, and it worked. Permit me a digression. One day, as I was making the rounds to say good-bye to my friends, night began to fall. Because the invaders had placed the country under martial law, it was illegal to walk the streets after dark. I could easily have been arrested. So I ducked into a hotel, thinking I could sit it out in the lobby until morning. As it happened, a West German television crew had put up there, and I joined them. We worked together for several days. Despite the painted-over street signs I knew the city well enough to get them where they needed to go to warn potential victims that Soviet agents were after them. And since I also spoke both German and Czech, I could help them find ordinary Czech citizens to interview. (German was still the most commonly spoken foreign language in Czechoslovakia at the time, and several of the Czechs I interviewed lamented over the "good old days," by which they meant the Austro-Hungarian Monarchy of their youth, and one made a telling slip of the tongue: "It was awful when the Germans—I mean the Russians—invaded last week.") I also recall a graphic example of the non-violent strategy you referred to, a hand-painted poster depicting, on the top, a little girl offering a flower to a tank decorated with the hammer-and-sickle coming to liberate the city from the Germans dated 1945, and on the bottom, the same little girl with her flower crushed under the same tank dated 1968.

Prague, 1968. Photograph by Michael Heim.

The television crew eventually drove me to Vienna and delivered the interviews, and I not only saw myself on TV but was stopped by numerous passersby, congratulated on my courage and quizzed about the latest developments. Celebrity for a day. But we were in little danger. When the television audience saw a tank veering around the corner, the image looked much more dramatic than it was.

Once home, I was loaded down with a stack of invasion-related documents crying out for translation, but I was more interested in translating literature. Even so, my first translation from Czech literature did not appear until 1975. It was a collection of wonderful, surrealistically tinged stories by Bohumil Hrabal. My objections notwithstanding they were published under—and are still available under—the misleading title *The Death of Mr. Baltisberger*, which makes the collection sound like a novel, and a downer of a novel at that. Nothing could be further from the truth: each of the stories exudes a zany joie de vivre. I fervently hope they will attract the audience they deserve once they appear with the title I envision for them: *Romance, and Other Stories*. They are among my favorite works of literature.

Daciana Branea: After August of '68 came Kundera, with "The Tragedy of Central Europe" . . .

Michael Heim: That was later. Milan Kundera was around before that, he was an excellent writer before 1968, he had published *The Joke* and a collection of superb short stories: *Laughable Loves*. *The Joke* appeared in English in 1969, without anyone noticing . . . It had excellent reviews. I wrote one of them, full of high praise, but even though it was in the *New York Times*, it didn't help. No one knew *how* to read this novel. *The Joke* was first published in England, in a version with Communist-style "abridgements." The chapter on folklore was completely removed, you probably remember . . .

Daciana Branea: "Jaroslav's Story"

Michael Heim: . . . which was essential to the context. The weaving together of the kings and the history of Czech folk music disappeared. The publishers thought that Western readers would be confused and get bored. It's clear it was the editor's decision, not the translator's, but the fact remains that the English version of *The Joke* omits this chapter. I decided to translate it myself and send it to the most important scholarly folklore journal in the United States, published at Indiana University. I included an introduction describing the novel and placing Kundera in the context of contemporary Czech literature. It seems that a few years later, someone sent a copy of the article to Kundera, just after he moved to France. Kundera sent me a letter inviting me to visit him whenever I liked. A few years after that, I was in France for some months. This was 1979. I couldn't make myself visit him. I didn't know what to say, I'm not a "star-hunter." Maybe because I live in Los Angeles, where you see a celebrity every other block . . . In any case, I didn't do anything about it. Through a strange coincidence, Kundera himself came to the building where I was living, for French lessons, and my wife often saw him on the street.

Daciana Branea: Did you meet him later?

Michael Heim: On my very last day, I said to myself, okay, it's the last day, I'll call him and see what happens. He invited me over right away, and he told me that his most recent novel, *The Book of Laughter and Forgetting*, was going to be translated into English, and would I do a sample. I said I would, I did, and I became the book's translator. I translated *The Book of Laughter and Forgetting*, then *The Unbearable Lightness of Being*, and I retranslated *The Joke*. I also translated Kundera's play, *Jacques and His Master*.

Daciana Branea: What impact did these translations have on the United States?

Michael Heim: *The Book of Laughter and Forgetting* was the first to catch on. A few Czech authors had been translated, and by then everyone had heard about Czechoslovakia. There was already an audience for Czech literature. In the '70s, something else happened that made things easier for people like me to promote foreign literature in the States: Latin American literature became extremely popular (beginning with Gabriel García Márquez). Suddenly, it wasn't unusual for English-language readers to read translations. A lot of things were translated in this period. Latin Americanists call it the Boom. I think of it as a boom for all foreign literatures.

Daciana Branea: Are there any similarities between Central European and South American literatures? We have the impression that when *The Unbearable Lightness of Being* appeared, critics compared Kundera with Márquez, as "two masters of magical realism."

Michael Heim: I can't say the two literatures have all that many features in common, but it's clear that both are very different from Anglo-American literature. Both look at things from a different perspective, and I think, at that moment, we were ready. We were at least open enough to accept a new way of looking at the world. One of the characteristics of Latin American literature, as you well know, is magical realism, while the principle feature of Central European literature is, I believe, an interest in the intimate connections of public and private life. Here is something that does not interest American literature. Someone once defined the difference between English literature and Russian (not Central European) literature like this: you read an English novel to find out whether or not the heroine will marry well, but you read a Russian one to find out whether or not the hero will commit suicide. Central European literature is intellectual, a literature of ideas. Russian literature is also a literature of ideas, but extreme ideas. Central European literature seems to me to present its ideas more subtly, as incarnated in its characters. It is more ironic, more cynical in many ways, and because of this, very modern. And it's this modernity that has appealed, I believe, to the American reader. Also, it offers a way to understand what happens in "the other world," to know how the Communists think. Except that it actually means much more. It expresses, if you will, the Zeitgeist, the spirit of the time, what happens in the world in general.

Daciana Branea: Is this part of the world still interesting to you?

Michael Heim: To me personally, yes. Generally, interest has waned, but it's cyclical. The West believes it has less profit to make here than elsewhere on the globe. I fear this is the explanation.

Dorian Branea: How have these translations affected American literature?

Michael Heim: The translations have greatly affected American literature. Not the best-sellers, of course, those don't change very much. But I have read a string of authors who I can say were very influenced by, say, Kundera. I don't think they are among the best, because you can sense the imitation right away. Still, in general, I think that our literature—that is Anglo-American (not just American) literature—is at the moment very healthy. There are tons of excellent authors and you can sense that they have read Central European literature, and as a result, their perspectives are much broader. I am happy to discover, in a good writer, the subtle influence of Czech or Polish or Hungarian writers. I know he has read them and emerged the richer for this literary experience. Certainly, our literature only stood to gain from these translations.

Dorian Branea: I think Kundera has been such a success because he found a way to combine popular taste with extremely sophisticated ideas. You can read Kundera on more than one level . . .

Michael Heim: Also, he does something, consciously, that makes him attractive to many readers. He teaches his audience what he wants them to read or to understand; he says, for example, *this* is *love* or . . .

Daciana Branea: He gives you certain key terms, his characters embody a word and he guides their fates toward a particular moment, an epiphany . . .

Michael Heim: Exactly. I for one am a little suspicious of all these definitions. I believe that, in a sense, Kundera tries to flatter his readers: you have just read *such* a deep book, because I write about *ideas*.

Daciana Branea: My book is more than a beautiful story, it is an essay on the theme of . . .

Michael Heim: Yes, this is a very Central European way of putting

things. Still, Kundera is a fabulous writer, I'd stake my name on
it. But I am not sure any more if I, a passionate reader, like to be
lectured to and theorized. Yet Kundera has found his audience, not
only in America, but many countries. Readers like to feel they are
reading a deep book.

•

Michael Heim: Literature, in general, was extremely important under
the Communist regimes, for two reasons. First, because the regime
itself considered it important and promoted it, as an ideological tool.
Second, because literature taught its audience to read between the
lines, so that any allusion, any subversive idea, any protest could be
decoded.

Daciana Branea: What does this kind of literature offer a foreign
reader? What happens if he doesn't have the key?

Michael Heim: Of course, the foreign reader is at a disadvantage,
but I believe the translator can lend a hand, transposing the text
into his language not only well but also in a manner that helps the
reader understand certain nuances, sometimes clarifying points. He
can also write a useful introduction. I don't like footnotes at all,
because they transform a literary work—something very different
from research—into a scholarly article. I often tell my students that
I like to read the notes to a translation, but only because this is my
profession and I have to know as much as possible about the text.
I think however of the real audience, the real reader, who deserves
the same book its first reader read. And that work had no footnotes.
Furthermore, it is too easy to explain things in footnotes. A translator should be more creative.

Priscilla Heim and Bohumil Hrabal, visiting the Heims, 1989.

Daciana Branea: How has Hrabal been received in the United States?

Michael Heim: Unfortunately, without much excitement. He has had little influence, so far.

Daciana Branea: Don't you think that, in spite of the difference in popularity, Hrabal is a more important writer than Kundera?

Michael Heim: Kundera has a broader appeal than Hrabal. Hrabal needs an "initiated" audience. An audience that has read more or already feels at home in the Central European context. You remember, when we were speaking about Kundera, I said he teaches you how to read his books. Hrabal doesn't. He just says what he has to say.

Daciana Branea: Hrabal can also be read on different levels . . .

Michael Heim: Of course, but this makes him even more difficult, in the sense that you have to realize on your own that the book is more than just a crazy narrator going on for ninety pages without using a period. But if you don't understand that, you might wonder why you should keep reading. "It's so strange, I've never read anything like it . . ." If you have read Hašek, for example, you are prepared. But even if you don't have the right background, you can pick up a Kundera novel and say, "Oh, okay, I see what he wants to tell me . . ." Kundera is much more accessible. Hrabal has a foreign readership too, but a much smaller one, a select group.

Daciana Branea: What can you say about Ivan Klíma, in comparison with the other two?

Michael Heim: Klíma became known more after the change in regime, after 1989. Klíma had written wonderful books before then, he was one of those recommended to me in 1965 when I asked about the best Czech writers. In the '70s and '80s, his books were banned in Czechoslovakia, they were read in samizdat, and this helped him in the West. But Klíma was only truly discovered when his country was in the news again, and he seemed to be the one to tell us what was going on in the new regime and how things had gotten to that point. He had the language and vision to communicate what was going on. I think this is his niche, the position he discovered for himself.

Daciana Branea: Have you translated Klíma?

Michael Heim: The only thing I've translated from him—even though I love his work—is his introduction to a collection of Jan Neruda stories, classic Czech short stories from the nineteenth century. But I met Klíma a year ago. He spent about six months at Berkeley, and during his visit, he was part of a roundtable on "Literature in Post-Communist Societies." I was asked to moderate a conversation between Klíma and Czesław Miłosz (who was a professor at Berkeley). I was afraid no one would come, that there would be three of us at the table and two in the hall. Almost two hundred people came. It was overwhelming. The discussions could have gone on forever because the listeners were interested and well informed. The questions could have run for days.

Daciana Branea: How often did you visit Hrabal? What kind of person was he?

Michael Heim: I spent a few days at his house, outside of Prague, talking. He was a wonderful person, open, communicative . . . A real intellectual, which might be surprising to those who picture him through his works. There were moments when he resembled the works, but we have to remember he had read a great deal of German philosophy. Then, Hrabal spent a day with me at my house in California, in the spring of 1989. It was the first time he had been allowed to leave Czechoslovakia.

Daciana Branea: Hrabal was banned in his own country.

Michael Heim: He was offered the chance to publish a few books in censored versions, and he took the deal, because he wanted to give people something better to read than what they had had up to then. The concession made him unhappy, however, and he even wrote a short essay on fear.

Daciana Branea: What is happening now in Czech literature?

Michael Heim: It's hard to say. It is not a propitious period. Immediately after freedom came, there were many light novels, superficial, even pornographic. There was a frenzy to write what could not have been written before. Content was all that mattered. This period has exhausted itself, and writers are trying out other things. There are quality books being written, experimental ones especially, such as the novel *City Sister Silver* from the young writer Joachim Topol.

Daciana Branea: How would you describe the Czech sense of humor? We use a certain phrase to describe their particular humor, and it makes us laugh every time: "the grotesque Czech."

Michael Heim: First of all, it is a humor based on irony and self-irony. Then, there is the great love for the Czech language, puns and other plays on words. This is true not only in literature but in everyday life. I speak from experience.

Dorian Branea: I understand you met Danilo Kiš.

Michael Heim: I did meet him, several times. First in Belgrade, then in Paris.

Dorian Branea: Have you translated from Serbian, too?

Michael Heim: Yes, a bit. As I said earlier, I learned Serbo-Croatian to take the place of the professor in our department who retired. There was no one else to do it, so I made the sacrifice. Of course, I had read Danilo Kiš already, and it happened that he had a book ready to be translated when I finished studying. It was one of his masterpieces, *The Encyclopedia of the Dead*. I just finished the first part of his trilogy, titled *Early Sorrows*. I also translated some of his essays.

Dorian Branea: When were you first in Belgrade?

Michael Heim: 1984.

Dorian Branea: How did Belgrade compare to Prague? It must have been another world.

Michael Heim: Oh yes, it was very different. My first night in Belgrade, I went to a play called *Marx, Public Enemy*. It was a unique play, a great introduction to Yugoslavia, because it let me see how alive and vibrant this culture was. I don't remember the name of the playwright, or whether he was a Serb or Croat. It was only an hour long, performed as part of the Godot Festival. In the play, a girl practices scales on an out-of-tune piano, over and over, for the entire hour. It becomes clear that this is Marx's daughter. Then comes Marx himself, complaining to his wife that he can't finish *Das Kapital* because he is surrounded by so many distractions. You don't need to know any more, the idea is clear: Marx was a normal person, he had his everyday problems and this must be reflected in his work, somehow. Maybe we shouldn't found a society on the works of a man who was hassled by his daughter practicing the piano, or had to write fast to make enough money to pay his taxes . . .

Dorian Branea: In the '50s or '60s, Prague was the center of avant-garde theater, but then Belgrade became the place, with the BITEF festival.

Michael Heim: I was in Belgrade for the festival. In fact, I saw a "dissident" Czech play, which could not have been staged in Prague, *Maria's Struggle with the Angels* by Pavel Kohout. I translated it later, because I liked it so much. I was lucky to be in Belgrade at that time. Unfortunately, as we know too well, things changed later on.

·

Michael Heim: From Crnjanski I translated the first part of *Migrations*, a wonderful novel. I was completely fascinated by this book because it finds a way to combine two movements that don't usually go together: the historical novel and modernism. The first part was written in 1929 and offers a good reflection of its period.

Dorian Branea: Crnjanski is known as the founder of the modern Serbian novel. From a linguistic point of view, *Migrations* is quite provocative.

Michael Heim: You're right. When people ask what makes me want to translate a novel, I have to admit that, above all, it's the language. I don't want to say that the "message" is not important, but I can imagine translating a novel whose message I disagreed with. But I can't imagine translating a novel with uninteresting language and a message that was actually dangerous. In the case of Crnjanski, I was attracted by his language, so rich, dense, and sensual, and his Central European themes: the novel takes place under the rule of Maria Theresa. The plot you can put in two or three sentences, but you haven't said anything, you have to read and savor every page. Reading Crnjanski is like eating Turkish Delight: you chew slowly and enjoy every mouthful. You shouldn't eat so much, but your hand constantly goes back to the plate. It was a great delight to translate Crnjanski, because it allowed me to read him more slowly than anyone else ever has.

Adriana Babeți: Let's turn to Hungarian literature. What authors have you translated?

Michael Heim: I've translated István Örkény, Péter Esterházy, and György Konrád. The first two, a novel apiece, and from Konrád, an anthology of his essays—an exception, since usually I only translate literature. Konrád is of course a novelist, but at the same time, he is a great essayist. The collection is titled *Melancholy of Rebirth*. Not the European Renaissance, but the reawakening post-communism. I selected the essays from almost 2,000 poorly photocopied pages, printed on old presses, pinned together: keynotes, letters, articles, everything. Each piece had a different style. Literarily speaking, it was quite a production. I also wrote an afterword, happily it was well received by the critics. I was especially happy that Vladimir Tismăneanu called *Melancholy of Rebirth* the best book he'd read about the post-communist transition.

Adriana Babeți: What is the melancholy of rebirth?

Michael Heim: First we should ask, why "rebirth"? Because something comes back to life, and because this true life existed before, between the wars. So you awaken, you remember how you were before, you see how things now are not going well, not changing as quickly as you would like. Thus, melancholy. Konrád is speaking about the period between '89 and '94. This is the first part of Hungarian post-Communism. I waited for the elections, I found his last essay and put together the anthology only then. I am very proud of this book. It will grow in importance in years to come because Konrád understood and captured everything. It is an important witness to a crucial period in the history of Central Europe. Konrad never stopped believing in Central Europe and he continues to argue for its importance.

Adriana Babeţi: We also translated a text of his for our group's first anthology: *Central Europe: Neuroses, Dillemas, Utopias.*

Cornel Ungureanu: Were you in contact with Konrád when you translated the essays?

Michael Heim: Yes, all the time. I kept him current on the selections.

Cornel Ungureanu: What was he like: indifferent or involved?

Michael Heim: Completely indifferent. I don't know where that came from. I would like to think he had faith in my judgment. But I think he was working on other projects at the same time. He didn't mind whether the book came out one way or another. He was a completely different kind of author than, say, Kundera, who wanted control over every page.

Cornel Ungureanu: How long did Konrád's book take?

Michael Heim: I should explain something, first. In America, there is no such thing as a professional translator. Of course, there are people who translate mechanical manuals and the like. But there is no job as a literary translator. You can't make a living at it. So everyone has to have another profession, as well. I am a university professor. Everything I translate, I do in my free time. Sometimes I don't translate anything for five or six months, because I have to prepare my lectures. When you're on stage, you have to have something to say. Then, there are also dissertations to work on. These have to be read chapter by chapter. What you say is very important to a student, it's his life in there. When I work on dissertations, I do nothing else. In the summer, I have some peace and quiet, and I work well. This is why I travel so little. I stay put and translate. People say to me, "but

you made a lot of money off of Kundera." I tell them quietly that I
didn't make anything. The author decides the rights a translator has.
The translator receives a modest sum from the publisher, but if the
writer doesn't feel like sharing his royalties with the translator, he
doesn't and that's that. In most cases, though, it doesn't matter: the
book sells so poorly there are no royalties. I usually say, with a little
irony: translating is a very profitable profession. If you translate, you
don't have time to go out to eat or see plays. When you translate,
you don't spend any money. You sit in front of the computer with
your books.

Cornel Ungureanu: Did you know Örkény? Were you friends? And
Esterházy?

Michael Heim: I only saw Örkény two weeks before his death, when
I was translating *The Flower Show*. I know Esterházy well. He comes
to Los Angeles often. I have to admit I was a little nervous the first
time I met him. First, because of his name. He's a descendant of the
famous Esterházy family, a real-live count. In the second place, he
has a reputation for being extraordinarily intelligent. He's not only a
writer, with a famously limpid and caustic attitude, but also a math-
ematician. In the third place, I was embarrassed that my Hungarian wasn't exactly fluent. I tortured myself for no reason. Esterházy
turned out to be a true aristocrat, meaning that he knew just how to
put us all at ease. He is a brilliant conversationalist, but he doesn't
intimidate. And he speaks German as well as he does Hungarian.
I translated *Helping Verbs of the Heart*, which I think you have also
translated, and a very funny story he wrote in homage of Hrabal,
for his seventy-fifth birthday. I agreed to do *Helping Verbs* because
it was proposed to me, by coincidence, two or three weeks before
my mother's death. It's a 100% postmodern novel—on each page
the narrative is accompanied by a text from an author Esterházy

admires, Bernhard or Borges, say—but it's a postmodern novel with heart. It was a very difficult book to translate.

Cornel Ungureanu: Do you read a lot of Hungarian literature?

Michael Heim: Not as much as I'd like. I relearn the language with each translation. I don't read Hungarian as easily as I do other languages.

Ioana Copil-Popovici: You have translated many authors from Central Europe, including some women. Does women's writing from this area bear any distinguishing features?

Michael Heim: Yes. The prospect of translating women authors made me very curious: I wondered if it would be more difficult for me. After the first few pages, I realized there was no difference at all, because I don't become any of the people I translate, neither the men nor the women. What counts is the text itself. The text may be difficult, but the difficulties are not connected to the gender of the author.

I have a student who wrote a very interesting thesis on three translations of Flaubert's *Un coeur simple*. It is the story of an ordinary woman. Using the word "simple" is dangerous, because it has many layers of meaning. In French or English, it can carry a pejorative sense, but not necessarily. Isn't it the same in Romanian? The student compared versions of the woman in the three translations, and she determined, surprisingly, that the oldest one—from the 1920s—was the best, or as translators say, the most adequate. The first translator was the best (I don't know if he was a feminist or not), because he was able to avoid signs of prejudice toward the woman. The more recent translations, which we expected to be ideologically correct, instead contained many negative insinuations toward the woman, insinuations that did not exist in the French version. All three translators were men.

So what really counted was translation technique, not the gender of the translator. In the past five years, I've translated three women, two Czechs and a Croat, each very different from the others. Two I would consider Central European, one more generally European: Sylvie Richterová. I translated a short part of an oneiric novel from her that seems to take place after some kind of nuclear disaster. It wasn't exactly clear to me what she wanted to say, but the language was very beautiful, very poetic, with a self-analytical bent, or self-deconstructive, if you like. I hope to continue the translation. It was an interesting experience, because I felt lost, often, and I was forced simply to trust the author and her words.

The other Czech writer I translated is Daniela Fischerová, a play called *An Unexpected Unpleasantness*. It seems typically Central-European to me, because it is a play of ideas, and it assumes a fluent knowledge of European culture. It's a political allegory about two characters—Job and Niobe—so it refers to the Bible and Greek mythology. The characters argue, but we know that they are in a Czech mental asylum and are arguing because of their relationships with their fathers. Job let his father, that is, God, dominate him, while Niobe rebelled against her father, Tantalus. She symbolizes the dissident, and he is the good and patient Czech. This debate is constant in Czech society: should we rebel or not. It appears in literature—in *Švejk*, for example—and in real life, in the discussions that followed the Soviet invasion. The author addresses contemporary Czech issues, in a very intellectual and, I believe, successful way. The play was performed by a student company in New York, but no one I've met since then seems to understand what the play was about. I sent the play to a director who had just finished working on *Waiting for Godot*, and though there is a lot of Beckett in the play, she declined, saying it was too intellectual, even for her taste.

The third writer is the Croat, Dubravka Ugrešić. Dubravka, who has become a good friend, had problems in Croatia and now lives a little bit everywhere. She was not forced to leave her country by the threat of arrest or being sent to a camp, but because she was not nationalist enough and thus did not match the spirit of her time. The book I translated, *Fording the Stream of Consciousness*, is a very literary work—another Central European characteristic—and very funny. (Is this another Central European trait? I don't know.) This typically postmodern novel takes place at a pre-1986 literature conference, so it's not connected with the events after '89 or the war in former Yugoslavia. The writers symbolize, hilariously, the characteristics of each nationality. But to get it, you have to know what these are, you have to have read Flaubert, to know what the situation was in Czechoslovakia at the time, what the previous 10 or 15 years were like in the Soviet Union, etc. That's a lot to expect, at least of American readers. I'm not saying the book is not read. But it's hard to convince a large group of readers that they might find it interesting.

I have also translated some of Dubravka's parodies of Russian plays. And here, the potential readers of the translation encounter a problem. How can you understand a parody, if you haven't read the original? You don't necessarily have to have read it in the original language, but you have to know at least who wrote it, or that it exists! And, especially in a society where, unfortunately, literature is not considered a priority, it is very difficult to find people who will read something like this. In Central Europe, it's a different story.

Yet, I would not want to idealize the position of the writer there. As I said, Dubravka has had a lot of troubles. She was named one of "the five witches of Zagreb" in one of the big newspapers. All the victims of the "witch hunts" were accused of "Yugo-nostalgia," the most serious crime possible in Tudjman's Croatia. I did all I could to protect her. I event went to an international PEN Club meeting in Dubrovnik, which many members of the organization—whose principal purpose is to stand up for persecuted writers—boycotted because the Croatian PEN members had stayed silent regarding these absurd accusations of "witchcraft." My public protest had no effect. Dubravka is a nomad. A year in one country, another in another. The concept of exile, also a Central European idea, seems to be still current.

·

Cornel Ungureanu: Do you feel at home in Europe?

Michael Heim: Yes, because I have spent so much time studying European literature and thought. I don't think anyone can doubt it. I am not a typical American.

Daciana Branea: That's obvious.

Michael Heim: But I'm not typical of any nation.

Daciana Branea: You're a typical Heim.

Cornel Ungureanu: I asked whether you feel at home in Europe, because you have an absolutely extraordinary level of insight into European culture, great insight and sensitivity. And the question could be this: what affinities bind you to European writers?

Michael Heim: I wouldn't say that I feel closer to European writers or American ones. (I feel at home in America, too!) I am bound to literature, in general. Three or four years ago, Salman Rushdie published a wonderful novel for children, called *Haroun and the Sea of Stories*. The antagonist is a tyrant who hates stories. He wants to rule the world, but fiction constantly creates other worlds, alternatives, rivals he cannot control. We need literature precisely because we need these alternative worlds. And I believe in its power to enrich our lives (however clichéd that may sound), in its power to give us, not new answers to difficult questions, but resources to give them life. Not European or American literature, but literature, plain and simple. I don't think that literature can do everything, but we must give people the chance to profit from all that literature can offer.

THE THREE ERAS OF MODERN TRANSLATION

MICHAEL HENRY HEIM

(edited and annotated by Esther Allen)

This talk was delivered on September 15, 2011, at the Center for the Art of Translation, in San Francisco, during a program in celebration of the Center's achievements and its move into a new space. A year earlier, Heim had been diagnosed with Stage IV metastatic melanoma.

I'm terribly proud to be here because this is such a wonderful occasion. I first heard about this fantastic organization two years ago when I met Olivia[1] in Salzburg, Austria. She is a powerhouse, as you all know. I'm so glad that things are working well here and you are moving forward in these times when nothing seems to be moving forward, everything seems to be moving back.

What I wanted to do, rather than give a reading, was to talk about the translator's new visibility, from reactive to active to proactive. I'm going to try to be positive. We're moving in a vector toward something that I think does exist, and we want to keep it existing. The ears of many of you will prick up when you hear that word

---

1   Olivia Sears, founder of the Center for the Art of Translation.

"visibility," if you've read Lawrence Venuti's *The Translator's Invisibility*, which came out in 1995.[2] It was a revisionist history of translation. Instead of going through all kinds of technical innovations, he tried to show why translation has been swept under the carpet, basically. What I thought I would do here is talk about what I have seen translation *do* in the years I have been involved in it.

I start with the Cold War because that's when I began thinking about translation. That is what I call the reactive period, in which basically—I'm exaggerating, of course—but basically a work was translated because there was an event that took place, and the work was either part of the event itself or was reacting to the event.

Let me give you two examples. First is *Doctor Zhivago*, by Boris Pasternak, which came out in 1958,[3] and it was a sensation—twenty-six weeks on the *New York Times* best-seller list. I won't go into the personal story, but I did meet Max Hayward, the book's British translator, and he told me exactly how he was forced to work when he was translating that novel, which was a sensation because it was the first time a work had been exported, smuggled out of the Soviet Union, and by Isaiah Berlin, of all people. All of a sudden this novel was front-page news. It was extremely important for the translation to come out as fast as it possibly could because the publishers wanted to cash in on the publicity. Apparently what they did was lock Max Hayward in a hotel room with his collaborator, and they wouldn't let them out. Literally, they would not let them out until the entire translation was done. That's how important it was. But that certainly is reactive.

A few years later a similar work came out of the Soviet Union. This one *was* actually published officially, but it was published only

---

2 *The Translator's Invisibility: A History of Translation* (Routledge, 1995; second edition, 2008).

3 *Dr. Zhivago*, trans. Max Hayard and Manya Harari (Pantheon, 1958). In 2010, Pantheon published a new translation by Richard Pevear and Larissa Volokhonsky.

once and then disappeared: Solzhenitsyn's *One Day in the Life of Ivan Denisovich*, a work that mentioned the labor camps for the first time. Until that point, nobody was allowed to mention the fact that these camps existed. Millions of people who had been affected by the camps saw their lives justified for the first time because of this book. It was a big sensation and it was published as fast as it could be published in all the languages of the world, and in English—three times in three different translations. This is 1963. And, yes, best-seller lists again, but this time it's even more interesting because there were three translations, which meant the reviewers *did* have to deal with the translation. So all of a sudden we're getting a little bit closer to the next category that I'm talking about—the active period. All of a sudden, people began having to read about translation in the daily press, and that made a big difference. Three translations came out at the time and later two more came out, so it was an ongoing kind of thing.[4]

Now let's move on to the active period. Once again we're still political, but now semi-political. This next category I want to talk about is also connected with the Cold War, but the Cold War is now at a different stage. In 1974, Philip Roth inaugurated a series with Penguin Books called "Writers from the Other Europe." He edited it and he gave his name to it; he gave his cachet to it. I laughed and said that his name was bigger than the author's name on each book. But maybe that wasn't so bad because people trusted his name, and that would make them trust a name they couldn't pronounce, these foreign names, Central European names, like Kundera and Schulz, Tadeusz Borowski, and Danilo Kiš, and so on. These works

---

4   There are now, in total, six English translations of *One Day in the Life of Ivan Denisovich*, by Ralph Parker (Dutton, 1963), Ronald Hingley and Max Hayward (Praeger, 1963), Bela Von Block (Lancer, 1963), Thomas P. Whitney (Crest, 1963), Gillon R. Aitken (Farrar Straus Giroux, 1971), and H.T. Willets (Noonday/Farrar Straux Giroux, 1991).

introduced a whole new kind of mentality to the West, and Roth's name made them perfectly acceptable. This went on from 1974 to— well, you can imagine what year: 1989. After that things moved into a different vein and we'll be talking about that.

But first I wanted to move onto the next phase of this period; now we're getting a little bit closer to *proactive*. There was a movement away from political reasons to be translating, and that was the Latin American Boom, which took place at more or less the same time, except that it wasn't political. Or rather, I'm sure it was very political for the Latin Americans, but we didn't view it that way. We viewed it simply as fine literature. Not only that, but we started to have what I would call, though I hate to use the word, "superstar" translators. You had writers from various countries, and that was important, too, not just one country, but various countries: Cortázar from Argentina, García Márquez from Colombia, Fuentes from Mexico, Vargas Llosa from Peru. And enter star translator Gregory Rabassa. He translated most of these authors, not all of each one, of course. And he also made a kind of headline news. García Márquez made a very big push in his favor, saying that Rabassa's translation was better than the original. And what does that mean? You can interpret it however you like. On the other hand, it did bring visibility to the translator.

I'd like to include in this active category something that is, let's say, an anomaly, something completely *sui generis,* and that is a single author who became a worldwide best-seller: Umberto Eco. And he also had his Rabassa, who was William Weaver. His *Name of the Rose* was an absolute sensation. It came out in Italian in 1980 and was translated in 1983.[5] Notice that there is a gap there, but it finally did come out.

5   Umberto Eco, *The Name of the Rose,* trans. William Weaver (Harcourt Brace Jovanovich, 1983).

There's a wonderful writer—I've translated several of her novels—a very literary, clever, *brilliant* Croatian writer named Dubravka
Ugrešić, and she once said that when she went to the nude beaches
on the Dalmatian coast she could always tell the nationality of every
person, even though they didn't have a stitch of clothes on, because
she could see what translation they were reading *The Name of the
Rose* in. It was really something.

At about that time, or maybe a little later than that, I was asked
to be on an Australian cultural program called *Friday Night Live*—I
don't know if they were playing on *Saturday Night Live* or if the title
had anything to do with that. I had to stay up until three o'clock in
the morning to talk to the presenter, who was interviewing me in
Los Angeles and Weaver in Italy, where he was living. The interviewer asked me where I was sitting, and I said in my kitchen. Then
he asked Weaver where he was, and he said, "In the echo chamber."
And what was the "echo chamber"? The Eco Chamber was the
building he had built, a separate building, from the profits he had
made basically from that one book (though of course he translated
many other books as well). That's how important that phenomenon
was at the time.

Let me move on now to the proactive period. We are moving on
in time and we have different kinds of situations to talk about. I can
only say that the Center for the Art of Translation, the enterprise we
are all celebrating tonight, is unique. It's one of the first examples of
this proactive moment. When did you begin, Olivia? 1994. That's
just unheard of. Nothing was happening then. That took *real* vision.
That didn't just happen. Somebody had to have real perspective—
which nobody had at the time. And then *to keep it going all this time!*
I mean, do it once: okay, fine. If you'd started in 1994 and ended in
1996 that doesn't leave very much behind.

I won't go through all the wonderful things the Center has done
that all of you here know about. Instead, I want to point out why I

think that what Olivia did was so important. Lots of things have happened since then and they're good things, I'm not saying they're not, but most of them are connected with academics. And there's nothing wrong with that. I'm an academic, and I don't want to talk down my colleagues. But there were certain things that happened because of the new field called Translation Studies, for example, the 1995 book by Venuti I talked about. What happened was that all of a sudden you had a field in the university. It was the use of "studies," especially—you had that wonderful "studies" word, and you can make anything into a field with that. "Cultural Studies," of course, and "Gender Studies," which really mean something, but I've heard people claim that now you can major in things such as "Baseball Studies." In any case, the word "studies" is important. What happened was that now you could say that this is a legitimate field. It isn't just something that a few people are doing in a back room somewhere.

Recently, a few of us got together. It just so happens that the last three presidents of the Modern Language Association, the MLA, were all either translators themselves or concerned with translation. We had long, long meetings about how to make the academic world really accept that translation is both a creative act and a scholarly act, and that members of various literature departments should be able to get credit for doing this kind of work. That automatically means—I hope it's going to mean—that academics who had literally been told before by their university tenure committees, "Don't translate; if you translate you're not doing your own work, and your own work is more important than translation . . . ," won't hear that any longer. The argument that we raised was that, let's face it, how many of those thousands and thousands and thousands of articles that get churned out are so important? Aren't you giving more to the field by translating, let's say, one of the articles by somebody who really has something to say, rather than recycling for the third or fourth

time what many, many people have already said? This is something
new to say! And the same is true of literature. The argument that we
made there was that a translator must deal with every single word. If
you're writing an article about, let's say, *Death in Venice*,[6] you can forget about some considerable percentage of the words there and just
concentrate on your own idea. But if you're translating it, you've got
to deal with absolutely every word; every word is part of an integral
interpretation.

We've made some headway. There are quite a few programs now
in various universities. For a while there were MA programs but no
PhD programs, and now there are PhD programs at SUNY Albany,
at Kent State, at Urbana-Champaign. There's even an undergraduate
program at Princeton, which, it being Princeton, is extremely well
funded. And I must say that I know the people there and it was a
fantastic coup. It's an undergraduate program and they call it the
Princeton Program in Translation and Intercultural Communication.
And "intercultural communication" is *in,* so that takes care of that
strange first word. And it has done a lot of good for the field.

Several of the departments that have fostered translation have
also fostered a press to go with translation, and that was a brilliant
idea. The first one to do that was John O'Brien at Dalkey Archive
Press—you know, I'm sure, its work—and what he did was to negotiate, very cleverly, a position for himself as a professor of English
and then use three-quarters of that time to run the Press. His university allowed him to do that. And hundreds, or I think hundreds,
but certainly a hundred new translations have come out of that press
by now and it's going strong. Chad Post, one of his former minions,
then moved on to do a similar, courageous program at the University

6   Heim's translation of *Death in Venice* (Ecco Press, 2004), with a preface by
Michael Cunningham, was awarded the 2005 Helen and Kurt Wolff Translator's
Prize.

of Rochester. It's now going very strong—Open Letter Books, it's called—so we have all kinds of new translations coming out of there.

I'm very curious about what's going to happen with something I just found out about. It's called AmazonCrossing—has anybody heard of it? It's Amazon.com's attempt to enter the book publishing field, but in translation; all of the books it puts out are books in translation. I tried to find out what its criteria are, and the only thing I could figure out was that its selection is done by algorithm. They know who their audience is, and so they decide ahead of time that's what they'll sell. That may be a bit of a nasty thing to say, but Amazon has done some very good things. I also want to mention a wonderful, I guess you could call it, institution, the only one that is close to what Olivia has done, and that is *Words without Borders*. It's an entirely online institution, and that's what I want to talk about in connection with Amazon. *Words without Borders* has done enormously interesting work presenting translations from various literatures that have been largely ignored. It also does extensive thematic issues, so it's a wonderful step forward. It's definitely a part of this proactive situation that I've been talking about.

I want to conclude now with just two other important proactive additions to the translation landscape in this country in the last few years, let's say the last five years or so. PEN—that's P, E, N, for poets, essayists, and novelists—PEN American Center established a PEN Translation Fund. It started in about 2005,[7] and I was on the board—together with Esther Allen, some of you know her, I'm sure—that tried to decide how best to use this money. The whole point was not to give money to people who have already proven themselves. You have the National Endowment for the Arts (NEA)

---

7 The PEN Translation Fund's first round of grant-giving was in 2004. See http://www.pen.org/content/penheim-translation-fund-grants-2000-4000

grants in translation and the National Endowment for the Humanities (NEH) grants in translation, but that was always a catch-22: oh yes, you can get some money if you've already shown you can do something.

The idea of this Fund was to throw the floodgates open. Anybody could present any kind of translation at all. There isn't much money, but we hoped that it would encourage young translators with no background whatsoever to try their hand at translation. The $2,000-$3,000 grant really was a pittance. But what we found was that it worked. We had to read a hundred and fifty or so translation projects a year.

And we also found something very different, and I want to leave you—well, not quite, because I have one more point—to leave you with this insight that we had. We thought that we were helping these people, the new translators, get started, but we didn't realize how much we were helping. We realized after the first year that about 35-40% of the winners of the grants found that they had a lot of interest among publishers. And by now, six years along the line, I think it's 75% of the works funded that have been published or are forthcoming.

Why? Well, we finally figured it out—and this is a real lesson, I think, for everybody, especially everybody in publishing and in translation. Why do we have so few translations, or *had* so few translations, in this country? Our editors are Americans; they're all Americans. And we don't study foreign languages. We don't know what a foreign language is. If you are an editor who has only had your two or three years of high school Spanish, and you receive a translation from the Czech, for example, what you do? You have absolutely no way of knowing whether it's decent. But if you receive a translation that has won a PEN Translation grant, you have two ways of vetting that translation. The first is that it's been approved by an advisory board of seven people who supposedly either know the language or have found someone who knows the language, so you don't have to worry: you're covered. The other thing is that the grant is awarded not to the translation only, but to the work itself. In other words, there's no point in having a great translation of an uninteresting work or a bad translation of a good work; they've both got to be equally good. So what happens is that these editors are therefore vindicated. They can say, "Look, it's not me. I didn't choose it. It's these people who chose it." And I think that's made an enormous difference.

Let me just conclude with another part of this proactive statement I want to make. There are now quite a few books that deal with translation and that have stirred interest among the general public. Eco wrote two of them in the early 2000s, *Experiences in Translation* and *Mouse or Rat.*[8] And there are a few others that I think are more relevant to our interests here. One of them is a wonderful memoir by Gregory Rabassa.[9] I mean, think of it: a *memoir* by a translator! What does a translator do? He sits and translates! And how is that going to turn into a book of memoirs? But this book, which came out in 2005, was just that, and I'm proud of it for two reasons. It was a *Los Angeles Times* notable book of the year for 2005; a book about translation! And I'm proud of that because I wrote the review for the *L.A. Times*, but also because I'm an Angeleno, and everyone pooh-poohs us—oh *those* people. I should point out that another best-seller the *L.A. Times* listed about that time was a re-translation of Stendhal's *Charterhouse of Parma* by Richard Howard.[10] That was an *L.A. Times* best-seller, which was really something.

---

8 Umberto Eco, *Experiences in Translation,* trans. Alastair McEwen (Toronto Italian Studies/Emilio Goggio Publications, 2008); *Mouse or Rat: Translation as Negotiation* (Phoenix, 2004).

9 *If This be Treason: Translation and its Dyscontents* (New Directions, 2006).

10 Stendhal, *The Charterhouse of Parma,* trans. Richard Howard (Modern Library Classics, 2000).

And then there are two other books that you may know of. The first is by Edith Grossman, another master translator, titled *Why Translation Matters.*[11] And there's a new book now, by one of the people involved in the Princeton program, David Bellos—a British translator who does a lot of Oulipo work, a very difficult kind of French writing—called *Is That a Fish in Your Ear?*[12] That one hasn't come out yet, it will soon. But this is the kind of thing that we are now able to show the world and I think that is important.

We're on a roll. Let's put it that way. And how do we keep the translator, and more importantly, of course, the *translations* visible? The translator, I think, is less important. I don't agree with Larry Venuti so much about that. First, of course we have to publish more translations, keep it going. But not everybody can be a translator, and so what we want to do is something that each one of you *can* do, and that is read more translations and talk them up, and, especially if you're a teacher, *assign* translations. Don't only assign—here I'm talking against myself—don't only assign Chekhov's plays and *Death in Venice.* Assign those, too, but make sure you assign at least one contemporary work of translation that students wouldn't have heard of otherwise. I think that's going to make a big difference. Otherwise, the progress that we've made toward the translator's new visibility can fade or, even worse, turn from the translator's new visibility to the Emperor's new clothes.

---

11 Edith Grossman, *Why Translation Matters* (Yale University Press, 2011).

12 David Bellos, *Is That A Fish in Your Ear? Translation and the Meaning of Everything* (Faber & Faber, October 2011).

MICHAEL HENRY HEIM
(1943-2012)

CHRONOLOGICAL BIBLIOGRAPHY: BOOKS AND PRODUCED PLAYS

(compiled by Esther Allen)

*2015. Blecher, Max. *Adventures in Immediate Unreality.* Trans. from the Romanian. Forthcoming from New Directions. 128 p.

2010. Chekhov, Anton. *Easter Week.* Trans. from the Russian. Illustrated with engravings by Barry Moser. Los Angeles: Shackman Press. 35 p. "Easter Week" and "The Student," trans. by Heim, are included in Cathy Popkin, ed. *Anton Chekhov's Selected Stories* (Norton Critical Editions, 2014).

*2009. Claus, Hugo. *Wonder.* Trans. from the Dutch. Archipelago Books. 338 p. Winner 2010 PEN Translation Prize.

*2008. Schlink, Bernhard. *Homecoming.* Trans. from the German. Pantheon. 260 p.

*2007. Konrád, Gyorgy. *A Guest in My Own Country: A Hungarian Life.* Trans. from the Hungarian by Jim Tucker. Edited by Michael Henry Heim. Other Press. 303 p.

---

* Indicates that the work, though not necessarily the first edition listed, is in print.

*2007. Grass, Günter. *Peeling the Onion*. Trans. from the German. Houghton Mifflin Harcourt. 423 p.

*2007. Mora, Terézia. *Day in Day Out*. Trans. from the German. Ecco-HarperCollins. 418 p.

*2006. Heim, Michael Henry and Andrzej W. Tymowski. *Guidelines for the Translation of Social Science Texts* (also published in French, Japanese, Russian, Arabic, Vietnamese, Chinese, and Spanish). American Council of Learned Societies. 28 p.

*2005. Chukovsky, Kornei. *Diary, 1901-1969*. Trans. from the Russian. Eds. Elena Chukovskaya and Victor Erlich. Yale University Press. 630 p.

*2005. Ugrešić, Dubravka. *The Ministry of Pain*. Trans. from the Croatian. Saqi. 254 p.

*2005. Ugrešić, Dubravka. *Lend Me Your Character*. Trans. from the Croatian by Celia Hawkesworth and Michael Henry Heim. Revised by Damion Searls. Dalkey Archive Press. 200 p.

*2004. Mann, Thomas. *Death in Venice*. Trans. from the German. Introduction by Michael Cunningham. Ecco. 142 p. Winner 2005 Helen and Kurt Wolff Translator's Prize.

*2003. Chekhov, Anton. *The Essential Plays*. Trans. from the Russian. With introduction and notes by Michael Henry Heim. Modern Library Classics. 263 p.

1999. Heim, Michael Henry. *Un Babel fericit*. Iaşi/Bucharest: Polirom. 212 p.

1999. Matvejevic, Predrag. *Mediterranean*. Trans. from the Croatian. University of California Press. 218 p.

*1999. Enzensberger, Hans Magnus. *The Number Devil: A Mathematical Adventure*. Trans. from the German. Illustrated by Susanna Rotraut. Metropolitan Books. 263 p.

*1999. Günter Grass, *My Century*. Trans. from the German. Harcourt. 280 p.

*1998. Kiš, Danilo. *Early Sorrows (For Children and Sensitive Readers)*. Trans. from the Serbian. New Directions. 118 p.

*1998. Tišma, Aleksandar. *The Book of Blam*. Trans. from the Serbian. Harcourt Brace. 226 p. Reprinted 2014, New York Review Books Classics.

*1997. Hiršal, Josef. *A Bohemian Youth*. Trans. from the Czech. Northwestern University Press Writings from an Unbound Europe. 85 p.

*1995. Kiš, Danilo. *Homo Poeticus: Essays and Interviews*. Trans. Frances Jones, Ralph Manheim and Michael Henry Heim from the Czech. Text editor, Michael Henry Heim. Introduction by Susan Sontag. Farrar, Straus & Giroux. 300 p.

*1995. Hrabal, Bohumil, *Dancing Lessons for the Advanced in Age*. Trans. from the Serbian. Harcourt, Brace & Co. 160 p.

*1995. Karel Čapek, *Talks with T.G. Masaryk*. Trans. from the Czech by Dora Round, ed. Michael Henry Heim, with foreword. New Haven: Catbird Press. 198 p.

1995. Konrád, György. *The Melancholy of Rebirth: Essays from Post-Communist Central Europe.* Edited and trans. from the Hungarian, with afterword. Harcourt Brace & Co. 176 p.

1994. Ripellino, Angelo Maria. *Magic Prague.* Trans. from the Italian by David Newton Marinelli. Ed. Michael Henry Heim. University of California Press, 1994. 352 p.

1994. Crnjanski, Miloš. *Migrations.* Trans. from the Serbo-Croatian. Harcourt, Brace & Co. 274 p.

1993-1994. Fischerová, Daniela. *Sudden Misfortune* (play). Trans. from the Russian. Production: Juilliard Drama Division, New York.

1993. Uspensky, Èduard. *Uncle Fedya, His Dog, and His Cat.* Trans. from the Russian. Illustrated by Vladimir Shpitalnik. New York: Knopf Books for Young Readers. 136 p.

*1993. Neruda, Jan. *Prague Tales.* Trans. from the Czech. Introduction by Ivan Klíma. London: Chatto & Windus. 368 p.

1992. Ugrešić, Dubravka. *In the Jaws of Life and Other Stories.* Trans. with Celia Hawkesworth from the Croatian. Foreword by Andrew Wachtel. Virago. Northwestern University Press Writings from an Unbound Europe series. 252 p.

*1991. Roziner, Feliks. *A Certain Finkelmeyer.* Trans. from the Russian. Norton. Reprinted 1995, Northwestern University Press. 362 p.

1991. Ugrešić, Dubravka. *Fording the Stream of Consciousness.* Trans. from the Croatian. London: Virago. 225 p.

1990. Esterházy, Péter. *Helping Verbs of the Heart.* Trans. from the Hungarian. Grove Weidenfeld. 128 p.

1990. Sokolov, Sasha. *Astrophobia.* Trans. from the Russian. Grove Weidenfeld. 385 p.

*1989. Kiš, Danilo. *The Encyclopedia of the Dead.* Trans. from the Czech. Farrar, Straus & Giroux. 201 p.

1988. Čapek, Karel. *The White Plague* (play). Trans. from the Czech. Production: Northlight Theatre, Evanston, IL. Published: *Cross Currents*, 7, 1988, pp. 429-504. *Plays in Progress*, 9, 1 (Theatre Communications Group).

1987. Aksyonov, Vassily, *In Search of Melancholy Baby.* Trans. from the Russian. by Michael Henry Heim and Antonina W. Bouis. Random House. 227 p.

1987. Lyubimov, Yuri. *The Master and Margarita* (play). Trans. from the Russian. Production: American Repertory Theater, Cambridge.

1986-87. Lyubimov, Yuri. *Crime and Punishment* (play). Trans. from the Russian. Production: Arena Stage, Washington, D.C.

1986. Troyat, Henri. *Chekhov.* Trans. from the French. E. P. Dutton. 364 p.

*1986. Hrabal, Bohumil. *Too Loud A Solitude.* Trans. from the Czech. *Cross Currents* 5, pp. 279-339. Reprinted 1990 Harcourt Brace Jovanovich. 112 p.

*1985. Kundera, Milan. *Jacques and his Master: An Homage to Diderot in Three Acts.* Trans. from the French. Harper and Row. 96 p.

1984. Heim, Michael Henry and Olga Matich, editors. *The Third Wave: Russian Literature in Emigration.* Ardis. 303 p.

*1984. Kundera, Milan. *The Unbearable Lightness of Being.* Trans. from the Czech. Harper and Row. 320 p.

*1984. Ageyev, M. *Novel with Cocaine.* Trans. from the Russian. Dutton. 204 p.

1983. Aksyonov, Vasily. *The Island of Crimea.* Trans. from the Russian. Random House. 369 p.

*1982. Kundera, Milan. *The Joke.* Trans. from the Czech. Harper and Row. 336 p.

*1982. Örkény, István. *The Flower Show.* Trans. from the Hungarian, with introduction. Published with *The Toth Family*, translated by Clara Györgyev. New Directions. 169 p.

*1981. Kundera, Milan. *The Book of Laughter and Forgetting.* Trans. from the Czech, with afterword by Philip Roth. Penguin Books. 228 p.

*1980. Chekhov, Anton. *The Cherry Orchard* (play). Trans. from the Russian. Production: Cincinnati Playhouse in the Park, Cincinnati.

1979. Heim, Michael Henry. *The Russian Journey of Karel Havlíček Borovský*. Slavistische Beiträge. 194 p.

*1979. Chekhov, Anton. *The Seagull* (play). Trans. from the Russian. Production: Pittsburgh Public Theater, Pittsburgh. Published, 1992: Woodstock: The Dramatic Publishing Company.

1978. Roščin, Mixail. *Echelon* (play). Trans. from the Russian. Production: Alley Theater, Houston.

1978. Heim, Michael Henry, Zlata Meyerstein and Dean S. Worth, eds. *Readings in Czech*. Trans. from the Czech. University of California Los Angeles, Dept. of Slavic Languages. Revised second edition, 1985. 147 p.

1977. Ganschow, Gerhard, ed. *An Anthology of Ugric Folk Literature: Tales and Poems of the Ostyaks, Voguls and Hungarians*. Trans. from the Hungarian, with Charlotte Rogers. Selected and with introduction by Marianna D. Birnbaum. Veröffentlichungen des Finnisch-Ugrischen Seminars an der Universität München. 239 p.

1976-78. Arbuzov, Aleksei. *Tales of the Old Arbat* (play). Trans. from the Russian. Production: Pittsburgh Public Theater, Pittsburgh.

1976. Heim, Michael Henry. *Contemporary Czech*. Michigan Slavic Materials. Reprinted 1982 and 1988, Slavica. 271 p.

*1976. Chekhov, Anton. *Uncle Vanya* (play). Trans. from the Russian. Production: Pittsburgh Public Theater, Pittsburgh.

*1976. Chekhov, Anton. *Three Sisters* (play). Trans. from the
    Russian. Productions: Mark Taper Forum, Los Angeles;
    Shakespeare Festival, Stratford, Ontario, Canada.

*1975. Hrabal, Bohumil. *The Death of Mr. Baltisberger.* Trans. from
    the Czech. Doubleday. 216 p.

*1973. Chekhov, Anton. *Letters of Anton Chekhov.* Trans. from the
    Russian. Edited and annotated by Simon Karlinsky. Harper
    and Row. Reprinted 1975 as *Anton Chekhov's Life and Thought*:
    Selected Letters and Commentaries. University of California
    Press. 494 p.

COMMUNITY

THE MASTER AND HIS PETS

DUBRAVKA UGREŠIĆ

(translated from the Croatian by David Williams)

Michael Heim was my role model. Although little separated us in terms of age, in his presence I always felt like a little girl, hence the reason that even now, at my age, I use the somewhat inappropriate term, "role model." Michael was a "good American," he was "Superman." Of course he wouldn't have agreed with me; I don't always agree with myself, and I'm not even sure what "good American" is supposed to mean. Maybe it's just the product of an imagination overflowing with Hollywood images. Michael always reminded me of the good guys in American films, of the very *idea* of goodness. During one of my stays in Los Angeles, Michael took me for a walk around Paramount Studios, where his father, a film composer, had often worked. It was a Sunday, everything shut up and deserted. The absence of external attractions only served to inflame my imagination. There are few things that could erase the image I remember: of me, walking the production lot of a dream factory with a "good American."

Michael was the most humble man I knew, always in the background, always at the service of a student, the text he was translating, always in the shadow of the good deeds he did. "To do good deeds" is a phrase from an old-fashioned primer, my socialist one, among others. Michael made the phrase ring true, he brought it to life, the type of hero who would help an old lady cross the street, the type who would surrender his bus seat to the elderly. *He is truly a good man*—who can say that of someone they know today? And who still cares about goodness!

Michael was a renaissance man, a scholar, and master translator.[1] He was a maestro, juggling words like a juggler's balls. I never met anyone able to juggle as many words in as many different languages as he could. Although I first met Michael long ago—back when Yugoslavia, today a non-existent country, was still whole—I didn't discover his trick for learning languages until much later, when he and I were guests at an American academic conference. It was one of those "After the Fall of the Wall" events, ubiquitous for the time. While old warhorses polished their dusty Cold War chestnuts (the war had recently ended, yet the old boys were obviously struggling to junk the fantasies of the era), younger participants tried to break down stereotypes. Michael sat quietly beside me, and appeared to have switched off completely. Under the table, so no one would see, Michael flipped a bundle of cards with Romanian words written in his own hand. As the old boys gave their all to make Eastern Europe conform to their stereotypes, Michael was learning Romanian, because in the rich collection of East European languages he knew—Czech, Russian, Serbo-Croatian, Polish, Hungarian, and who knows what else—Romanian was missing!

Languages were Michael's passion. He knew and understood

---

1 Michael translated two of my novels, *Fording the Stream of Consciousness* and *The Ministry of Pain*. He also translated two of the short stories from *Lend Me Your Character*, which was first published in English as *In the Jaws of Life and Other Stories*.

more languages than he admitted to. Chinese, Italian, French, Dutch, German, Russian, Czech, Croatian, Hungarian . . . All these languages swam in Michael's head, jousting for his attention. Languages were his pets, and he attended to them daily, pulling a random Czech or Croatian phrase out from somewhere, picking up cards of Chinese and Japanese words that had fallen from a drawer, stroking the spine of an English-Albanian dictionary as if it were a cat. From the shelves in Michael's home and university offices, books in multiple languages peered out.

There are different kinds of translators. Michael was the rarest kind. I don't know anyone to rival Michael's range of expertise: he was a scholar of language and literature, a savant, an educator, a literary "activist"—an enlightener in the best sense of the word. The list of authors he translated is as impressive as it is long: Anton Chekov, Milan Kundera, Bohumil Hrabal, Vassily Aksyonov, Danilo Kiš, Karel Čapek, Sasha Sokolov, Péter Esterházy, Felix Roziner, Jan Neruda, Eduard Uspensky, Miloš Crnjanski, George Konrád, Bertolt Brecht, Josef Hirsal, Aleksandar Tišma, Hans Magnus Enzensberger, Günter Grass, Hugo Claus, Thomas Mann, and many others.

For Michael, translation was a delight, yet it was also a secret mission to connect different worlds. Michael really believed that with the books he translated, American readers would become better educated, would become better, period. Because the only capital Michael acknowledged was the capital of knowledge. Relationships were everything to him—with languages, with books, with his students, with people . . . He loved introducing people he was fond of to each other. "She'll be a friend for life," he said, when long ago introducing me to Marina Warner. And he was right, Marina has become a friend for life.

Heim in his garden, 1994. Photograph by Dubravka Ugrešić.

Given the nature of our profession, Michael and I would often
catch up in different points of the globe—in Zagreb, in London, in
disparate American college towns—yet I remember him most fondly
at the home he shared with Priscilla in Los Angeles. Priscilla and
Michael put me up on a number of occasions, and I loved their company. On waking, I'd stumble out of "my" room and wander into the
back yard. The yard was small—with a view out onto a steep rock
face, a giant slab laced with climbers and other vegetation—all in
their own way a wonder. Michael would step out of his office, which
overlooked the yard, and march off to a corner. Judging from his
movements he imagined the yard ten times bigger than it actually
was. Seeing there was nowhere to go, that the space was rather tight,
he'd tend to a plant, watering it gently, before returning to his desk.
Then Priscilla would suddenly appear from somewhere, heading
out into the yard with the same spatial ambitiousness in her head.

Confronted with the fact for the who-knows-what-number-time that the yard was smaller than she imagined, she'd also tend to a plant, water it a little, pick a tomato or two, or a sprig of basil, and return to the kitchen to prepare breakfast. I think it often happened that they watered the same plant a few times in a day, even though in their household they were always careful about their water usage. Although tiny, the yard exuded a sense of freedom: plants grew every which way, and Michael and Priscilla looked after them as best they knew how. Their garden plan seemed chaotic to me, but it grew on me with every visit, which perhaps just goes to show that the yard was the real heart of their home. A bench and table in the garden, a piece of big blue California sky above our heads, the scent of eucalyptus in the air, conversations at the garden table in the morning and evening, just the three of us, or with other guests, these are the cheerful and joyous images I remember.

In the Heims' garden, 1989. Photograph by Dubravka Ugrešić.

In the Heims' garden, 1989. Photograph by Dubravka Ugrešić.

Michael walked from the house to the university campus for the love of another unusual mission or mania—it depends on your point of view. Along the way he'd gather empty cans and bottles, plastic and glass. He'd haul a bagful to the university and set it down in his office, and then in the evening, on his return home, he'd again collect whatever he found along the way. On his front porch he'd sort the trash: cans in one pile, plastic bottles in another, glass bottles in a third. By the morning the trash was gone. Young Puerto Ricans would spirit it away in the night. It was Michael's way of giving these kids—whom he never saw or met—a little daily pocket money. The kids would return the cans and bottles for small change. Michael kept it up for years (neither missions nor manias last twenty-four hours), one of his ways to improve this imperfect world. Michael had an almost "religious" streak in him: he truly believed that each of us was capable of making this world a better place if we only wanted to. Teaching (at the university and outside it), translating, his auto-didacticism (learning languages)—these were all forms of his enlightening mission, as was his belief that in each of us crouched a miniature Superman, a little repairer of the world. Michael and Priscilla were definitely such people. I once heard a story about how they used to volunteer in impoverished neighborhoods of Los Angeles, teaching kids Latin and Old Greek. With Priscilla's classical training, I'm sure she managed better than Michael. Being as modest as they were, the story was one they never confirmed.

I, an East European cynic, thought of Michael as a "saint." The reality is that he wasn't an entirely convincing one, lacking a certain saintly severity and seriousness. Instead of discretely wearing his saintly aureole, he'd scampishly cock it like a country hat, or wear it backward like a French beret, or brush it from his head as if it were an annoying bee. I think he probably regretted that the halo wasn't made of gold, so he might sell it and give the proceeds to someone who really needed the money.

I've kept one of Michael's letters, and I read it every time my faith in what I'm doing is on the wane. I hope Michael will forgive me for citing a passage without his permission:

> *Although I'm an absolute pessimist about minor things like the possibility of a viable life on this planet in a hundred years, I am optimistic about major things like literature. You see the book fairs as a last gasp, an attempt at shoring up a dying institution, whereas I see them as a sign that many people (and it's never been more than many) really do incorporate literature into their lives. You see literature as a doll in an amusement park booth, a doll boys throw balls at to hit off the shelf, but I see it as a doll in the next generation of amusement parks, a doll attached to a bar (so the booth owner doesn't have to bend down and pick it*

up). The boys still throw balls at it, but each time they hit it, it
bounces back. Keep writing.

Love from us both,
Michael

When the people we love die, we do a little processing: we try
to choose how we're going to remember them. Unconsciously we
choose what to forget, or moreover, what we're going to remember.
If we don't make this effort, the person risks disappearing from our
memory, vanishing without a trace. That's why we build a little
pyramid, a personal miniature window display, a little coffin, a story,
an image, a metaphor—so that we might commit it to memory. I
loved my father very much, but I was young when he died and didn't
respect this process of elimination. That's why today, some forty
years after his death, I can hardly remember what he looked like, let
alone anything else.

We like people who display genuine passion, and the more they
have for something, the more we like them. I guess it's because we
like sources of energy, and Michael was an energy source. I guess
it's also because we like the idea of goodness in people, and Michael
was the embodiment of goodness. Michael adored his languages like
pets. Michael spoke the softest Croatian I've ever heard, and Croatian was neither his first foreign language, nor was it an important
one. It was just one of the handful of Slavic languages he knew.
While he spoke Croatian quite rarely, he used the words so gently,
as if there was a lurking danger of harming the very essence of the
language; as if he were taking a newborn kitten in his hands, afraid
that if he were not gentle enough, he might crush its spine. The
result was the softest and most tender Croatian I've ever heard.

In June this year I was invited to the Dublin Literary Festival,
as a guest speaker in an annual series of talks where writers present

their favorite books. I chose Bohumil Hrabal's slender *Too Loud a Solitude*. I opted for this "unusual" selection for a number of reasons. Firstly, because all the English and American writers who had gone before me had spoken about their favorite English and American books as if this were the most natural thing in the world, as if other books, writers, and languages didn't even exist; secondly, because *Too Loud a Solitude* really is one of my favorite books; thirdly, because Michael Heim's translation of the book is simply brilliant; and finally, because of a little peculiarity: an archival photo showing Hrabal, the old Czech maestro, drinking beer in a Dublin pub, seated below a photo of James Joyce that hangs on the wall. I wrote to Michael telling him of my intention. I knew he'd love hearing about it. And he did, very much.

When picking an image as a coffin in which I am going to bury my friend and translator, a "Hrabalian" one seems most appropriate: Michael—like a *yurodivy*, like Haňt'a from *Too Loud a Solitude*, a Master—is sitting in the sun surrounded by his translations, as if they are his pets. The pets adore the Great Master, and he adores them; they slink their bodies against his legs, eat from his hand, and he scratches their loins, strokes their fur coats, pulling their tails in jest, teasing them playfully. This is an image Michael himself would like, one in which he wouldn't mind being buried: the Great Master with his favorite pets, his translated books.

MY FRIEND MIKE

HENNING ANDERSEN

In 1989 I joined the faculty of the Slavic Languages department. I had a new set of colleagues to get to know. But Mike and I were on the same wavelength from the first day.

I would often be one of the last to leave the office in 115 Kinsey Hall. If Mike's office door was open, I would call out a "Good night, Mike." Or, if there was time, drop in for a chat.

Mike and I would talk about everything under the sun. Often, of course, mundane concerns like the department's direction or the preparation of our students. But also loftier things like literary theory and linguistics. Perhaps more often linguistics.

As the sensitive translator he was, Mike was keenly aware that the target language of his translations—English—was actually a moving target. I have a sort of professional interest in language change and have been observing the changing usage of English for a long time. Here we had an area of shared, abiding interest.

There was one more topic that would come up every now and again: family.

Here, I have to explain. Actually the foundation of Mike's and my friendship was not laid at UCLA in 1989, but way back in the 1960s.

Let me offer you a selective timeline.

1967, spring semester. Mike is enrolled in my course on the History of Russian at Harvard University. A remarkable student who knew not only French, German, and Russian, but Spanish as well. And then he had an undergraduate background in Chinese!

1967, fall semester. Mike is appointed TA in first-year Russian. I was the coordinator. We had a terrible textbook, actually a textbook without any text, a grammar with sentences. Without much discussion Mike and I started creating a course in spoken Russian, based on actual texts that followed the progression of grammar, and utilized the vocabulary, of our assigned textbook. The bulk of the texts—known locally as "the Vera stories"—was made up by Mike.

During this time Mike became a friend of my family. He had dinner at our place several times and invited us in return. He offered to babysit, and the children loved him. Karen, whom I talked to the other day, still remembers how she woke up late one evening and went to the living room. And Mike took her hand and led her back to bed.

We were a bilingual household (Danish/English), and Mike decided to learn—Danish!

1970, summer. I go to Ukraine as an exchange scholar. Back in Cambridge, Mike would look in on Kerstie and the children. Sometimes he would play ball with the children in the yard. One day he took the three of them on a day trip in his car. He was into photography then and took some of the loveliest pictures we have of the children, ages six and three at the time.

In the 1970s our ways parted. Mike went west to Los Angeles, and a few years later I went east to Copenhagen. But we continued to meet from time to time, as I would lecture at UCLA every couple of years.

1976. On my way to LA for a lecture, I am delayed two hours in Tucson. On my arrival, Mike comes to the rescue, picks me up at LAX and rushes me to UCLA and the Bunche Hall Conference Room in record time. I'm one hour late, but the room has a large, expectant audience hosted by Professor Robert Stockwell (another friend whom I have recently lost).

That evening at a reception at Mike and Priscilla's place, Mike introduces me to Mary. She is not just the manager of the Slavic Department but, amazingly, a speaker of Danish! Eventually, in 1987, Mary becomes my second wife.

I spend 1980–1981 as a visiting professor at UCLA. Many good talks with Mike. At the end of December 1980, the children come to visit from Denmark, and we spend New Year's Eve with Mike and Priscilla.

1983–1987. Karen is an undergraduate at UCLA. She has fond memories of running into Mike on campus from time to time, typically reading a book as he walks along. Mike has grown-up, scholarly conversations with her about literature, often terminating in a book recommendation or the loan of a book.

1984. Mike passes through Copenhagen on his way home from Moscow. We are celebrating my mother's 85th birthday. Mike comes along to my brother's house, meets the guests, talks music with my brother, who was a musicologist, and surprises my mother by addressing her in, you guessed it, Danish.

Then in 1989 Mary and I move to UCLA.

I have already mentioned the many good hours I have spent with Mike since then. The last couple of years we continued to have our occasional academic conversations in the newfangled Humanities Building, although our minds were dominated by concerns of a non-academic sort.

But then—2011. Karen is visiting with her daughters, Ingrid and Asta, twelve and five. Mike, who has known Karen since she was five, is eager to meet her children. Mike and Priscilla invite them with Mary and me. A wonderful, sunny afternoon in their back yard. The children are quite taken with their hosts. They will never forget Mike.

Some time ago I thought of Mike's and my friendship, how we have met time and again over the years, often after an interval of years, and each time have engaged with each other not as if nothing had happened in the meantime, but with an implicit confidence that *we* had not changed.

Some time ago I thought of comparing our lives to two vines—each with its own path of development—that intersect and at times intertwine as they grow their separate ways.

But this simile leaves out the remarkable fact that over the years we each expanded our circles of acquaintances and friends enormously, Mike probably much more than I did, and this never affected our friendship. Mike's personality was remarkably spacious, but his loyalty to his friends was adamant.

He will remain in our hearts.

FROM MIKE TO MIKE

MICHAEL FLIER

(remarks for Mike Heim Memorial, UCLA, Nov. 29, 2012)

In the fall of 1972, his first year at UCLA, I met Michael Henry Heim, our new assistant professor, our specialist in Czech and Russian literature. He was a couple of years younger than I, but we shared Jewish New York backgrounds—his direct, mine indirect—and a great love of both languages and music. During one of those long, early conversations strolling around the campus, Mike was delighted to learn that I knew the words to the fight song for Columbia University, his alma mater, and we harmonized "Roar, Lions, Roar" in full voice as heads turned in astonishment. He seemed a long-lost younger brother. Instant bonding. This year marks the fortieth anniversary of my relationship with Michael Heim, a camaraderie of deep affection that I will cherish for the rest of my life. We Michaels hit it off right away and instantly switched to Mike and Mike. We were ever thus.

Apart from his obvious intelligence, what struck me immediately about Mike was a fierce intellectual passion manifested in the gentlest of souls. Mike was a true *mensch*, a feeling, caring human being in every sense of the word: honest, straightforward, direct. He said what he meant and meant what he said—a man devoid of pretense and guile. He was a superb teacher and mentor, as witnessed by the many testimonies of former students and colleagues who have profited from his wisdom and guidance. Mike was one of the least pretentious people I have ever encountered, someone who cared deeply about people and the world around him. He detested waste in any form, and abstained from anything he considered frivolous or extravagant. If we consider the great works of world literature he has made accessible to speakers of English everywhere, we understand globalization in the best sense of the word.

As we all know, Mike went on to become an international champion of translation and translation studies, promoting translation workshops and (as now revealed) providing an endowment to generate grants for translators of literature through Mike and Priscilla's generous gift to the PEN Translation Fund.

Mike's love of language was patent, especially his fascination with gradients of meaning, style, and cultural reference. He was never without scraps of paper, peppered with lists of vocabulary items, more material to learn and master, especially when he found himself waiting in lines, capturing five free minutes between appointments, or preparing to fall asleep. He loved the quirkiness of idioms, those collocations that often break the rules of logic or association: *a bee in one's bonnet; shooting the breeze; cutting the mustard.* After I met his mother, Blanche, a New Yorker through and through, I understood where this penchant came from, for she too loved the *bon mot*, the turn of phrase, the ironic retort. I learned this in no uncertain terms when I once responded to something Mike had said with "Well, well, well!" and he immediately shot back with "Three holes in the ground," a treasured Blanche-ism. No surprise that one of the primary tools on Mike's translation bookshelf was Longman's *Dictionary of English Idioms.* Through this intersection of language and narrative, Mike developed his tremendous capacity as a story teller. A Mike Heim story among his friends became a generic term for a 5- to 10-minute narrative with as many twists, turns, and exotic characters as a Gogolian tale, usually with some sort of moral at the end.

In 1974 Mike wrote from Harvard that his book project on Havlíček-Borovský was falling into place, and delighted in reporting that he was "milking [Widener] library for all it's worth." He stopped off in Austin, Texas, to visit his dear friend and colleague, Svatava Pírková-Jakobson before returning home to his new apartment in my building on Midvale in Westwood. "You have no idea how comforting it is to have an address to come home to." I mention our apartment building because of a marvelous letter Mike sent from Aarhus, Denmark, in the summer of 1975: "Isačenko came up to my place after pizza last night to watch the news (very spottily interpreted by yours truly), and what did I find waiting for me but a telegram from Los Angeles . . . All kinds of dire predictions ran through my mind as I tore it open. And what was it? Mrs. Schenk [our landlady] telling me that my September check had not been sent in by the guy who sublet the apartment! Now she knows perfectly well that I'll be back on the 21st and that I've never failed her before, yet she asks whether the check is on its way. Well, it isn't, and for two reasons: I don't carry her address around close to my heart, or my checkbook either. Please call her and relay all this to her civilly . . . There is one side effect to the telegram that I hope won't annoy you. You see, I figured that as long as I felt I had to write you about something else I thought I might ask you to come pick me up at the airport. If you can, fine. If not, no problem . . . [But] I hope to see you there. It will feel great to be whisked home after two straight days (but more than forty-eight hours) of travel. [Signed] Mike. P.S. I'm homesick."

It was right about this time, in 1975, that Mike married Priscilla Kerr, the love of his life, his true helpmate, fervent supporter, and believer in all the causes and projects that captured his passion. He also gained an instant family in Priscilla's three children—Becky,

Jocie, and Michael—who provided great joy to Mike as he contemplated the tenure decision four years down the road.

Whenever possible, Mike spent time away from Los Angeles during holidays and summers, conducting research on all his many projects. From Priscilla in Berkeley 1977: "Enclosed are warm greetings from Mike, shouted as he ran past on his way to the many projects that never seem to diminish . . ."

From Mike in Berkeley, 1978: "The big social event of our season has just come and gone: the Symphony here . . . had a KCET-type auction, and Simon [Karlinsky] bid for and won . . . a day on the Bay in a thirty-six foot yacht. And last Saturday—it was the most beautiful weather we've had yet—a party of six of us . . . cruised past Alcatraz, Angel's Island, Tiburon, Belvedere, Sausalito, in and out of Fisherman's Wharf, and back to the St. Francis Yacht Club for drinks and dinner. Fantastic! In the process we missed Gleb Petrovič's [Struve] eightieth birthday party at the Hughes's, and Simon is afraid it may take another eighty years for G.P. to forgive him, but other than that the day was perfect."

From Priscilla in Berkeley, 1978: "Various people are still reading Mike's book, so keep your fingers crossed. And the last Tolstoy lecture is in the works—what a quarter! (Mike would be mortified if he knew I had switched to black ink in the middle of this letter, but here I am in the library with a dry blue pen. So don your colored glasses. It's the thought that counts, right? [My contribution to the form/content controversy].)"

In 1972, feeling the emotional pull of his Hungarian-born father who had died when Mike was four years old, he abandoned his stepfather's name, Berman, for his original birth name, Heim. His fascination with things Hungarian developed full bloom at UCLA as a result of his intellectual interaction with a major literary soulmate and good friend, Marianna Birnbaum, whose deep knowledge of European literatures and cultures provided him with an exciting forum to explore his ideas on language and literature in a Central European context. Determined to learn his father's native language in depth, Mike spent a month in Budapest in the winter of 1979. But apparently learning Hungarian is at a far remove from learning Slavic, Germanic, and Romance languages. In Mike's words: "Never again will I presume to embark upon so humiliating a venture as learning a foreign language. No one will be more sympathetic in front of the classroom next fall."

Michael Heim, Priscilla Heim, and Michael Flier, Santa Monica, 1991.

Mike came up for tenure in his seventh year, in the spring of 1979, my first year as Department chair. This was no open-and-shut case. Mike had a monograph in press, *The Russian Travels of Karel Havlíček Borovský*, and a number of articles, but his primary activity of late was translation. UCLA and the Slavic field were in a very different place in 1979 as compared to now. The traditional bases for promotion to tenure at the university were research and teaching. Translation was considered a secondary activity, something scholars engaged in to earn extra money or to make particular foreign publications accessible to monolingual American students. Fortunately for me, Mike had some powerful ammunition—the final manuscript of his translation of Milan Kundera's *The Book of Laughter and Forgetting*. I had talked with Mike many times about his philosophy of translation, but I needed to convince myself that a case could be made for translation in preparing the department's rationale for tenure. I took the original and compared it with Mike's translation to evaluate his achievement. I would read a paragraph of Kundera and then review Mike's rendering. I was blown away, seemingly moving between a text in Czech and a Czech text in English! It was magic, even though Mike himself would describe the feat with the self-deprecating term *legerdemain*. Now I truly understood what Mike meant when he said that he was not creating a new text, but rather creating the same text again, only in English. It was this phenomenal ability to reproduce the same atmosphere, the same setting, the same tonality of discourse as the original that marked Mike's true brilliance in translation. Having this appreciation of his skill, I was somewhat put off by the opening statements in the *New York Times* obituary, in which Mike was lauded for his active mastery of six languages and his passive mastery of six more, as if that were his major accomplishment. I personally have known many people who have collected foreign languages like postage stamps, but who have nothing significant to say in any one of them. Fortunately the final paragraph ultimately revealed, in Mike's own words, what was truly extraordinary about his translation technique: "The reader must believe he or she is reading a work in French or Japanese and yet be reading it in English," he said. The description captures the essence of Mike Heim's work—he was not a translator of words; he was a translator of worlds. That insight gave me the key to make his case, both in the department itself and in the Committee on Academic Personnel, which would recommend for or against tenure.

At that time, there were two complementary criteria for promotion in addition to teaching: original research or other creative activity. The latter term was used for cases in the performing arts, painting, sculpture, music, theater. The Department agreed to extend "other creative activity" to include translation of the highest caliber. Weeks turned into months that passed in an eternity until mid-May, when word finally came back from the Chancellor's office that Michael Henry Heim had been promoted to associate professor with tenure.

But Mike and Priscilla were in Paris at the time and in 1979 there was no email, SMS, or Skype to communicate the glad tidings. A telegram seemed so 1930s (Dear Mike and Priscilla STOP. Good news STOP . . .). I decided to splurge on the department budget with a person-to-person call, something of an extravagance in those days. With an eleven-hour time difference, I woke Mike and Priscilla up in the middle of the night, Paris time. Mike's letter back conveys the vibe: "The excitement of a transatlantic call (remind me to tell you the saga of my call to Mother in Budapest) and the excitement of the message have combined to make our actual conversation quite hazy in my mind." We were all excited beyond words and eager to celebrate properly with French Champagne when they returned to Los Angeles.

I leave you with one of my most vivid memories of Mike, telling his favorite joke. Naturally it would involve language. It seems a Frenchman was visiting New York City for the first time and was naturally fascinated by the differences between Paris and Gotham. He was overwhelmed by the lights, and the hustle and bustle, all the while staring at the skyscrapers above so intently that he wasn't watching where he was going. He stepped out into the street, only to be hit by a taxi careening around the corner. He flew through the air and crashed onto the pavement in a heap. Speaking virtually no English, he struggled to get up but pedestrians simply ignored him, castigating him and climbing over his bruised and bloody body.

"Anybody here speak French? Anybody here speak French?" he cried, staggering to his feet. Brushed aside, he crashed against a door, hit a garbage can, and stumbled down a staircase into a large basement hall where some sort of union meeting was going full blast. "Anybody here speak French? Anybody here speak French?" The room suddenly grew silent as all eyes turned toward him in wonderment. "Anybody here speak French? Anybody here speak French?" Finally a little man made his way from the back of the room, raised his hand, and proudly proclaimed, "Je!" Mike's eyes lit up, that toothy smile flashed across his Lincolnesque physiognomy, and we all roared with laughter. Mike the Storyteller in fine fettle!

One final quote from Mike, just to give him the last word:

From Mike in London, 1986, following his promotion to full professor: "Dear Mike, Because both winter and spring have been the coldest in fifty years, we haven't seen as much of London itself as we planned, but we're trying to make up for lost time. Mother's arrival last week has spurred us on. This Friday we will celebrate her seventy-fifth birthday. The Hoskings are coming to dinner and Priscilla and B[lanche] will spend the afternoon at an international antique show (I will spend the afternoon proofreading). See you soon."

BLED – PARIS – SHANGHAI – SALZBURG – OSLO: MEETINGS WITH MICHAEL

BENTE CHRISTENSEN

It was during a PEN conference in Bled, Slovenia, in 2005, that I first met Michael, at a session of the Translation and Linguistic Rights Committee. Representatives from different countries were sitting around a large table, discussing writers' issues. Suddenly a tall thin man asked for the floor and said, "But what about the readers? Should they not be taken into consideration?" The question astonished the assembly, and nobody seemed to want to follow up, but it had started to work in my mind. After the meeting, I went up to him, got to know his name: Michael Henry Heim, a specialist in Slavic languages, working at UCLA. We started to talk, and after five minutes I knew that I had met a person I wanted to stay in contact with. I mentioned to him that there was an organization in Norway called "*les!*" ("read!"), and that I would have liked to send him more information about it, if it had not been for the fact that this information was in Norwegian. "That's okay," he said. "I can understand a little Scandinavian." At that moment I was really impressed, and I started to wonder if he would want to stay in contact with me, since he obviously was such an extremely learned person.

Luckily for me, he did, and we continued our discussions and our cooperation until his much too early death. In Bled he told me about his project "Guidelines for the Translation of Social Science Texts," organized by the American Council of Learned Societies, with Michael and his colleague Andrzej W. Tymowski as principal investigators. They worked together with French, Chinese, and Russian colleagues, and they met in the respective countries of the source languages to develop the project.

It is a fact that English is a hegemonic language in the world, and that the Anglophone countries have a tendency to consider themselves as independent from cultural impulses from abroad. The rate of translation in the U.S. is very low, both for fiction and non-fiction, and Michael and his colleagues, being multilingual, were very aware of the disproportion between output and input in the American cultural sphere. They started with the social sciences, where so many important texts are written in languages other than English, and they had a double goal: to produce quality translations into English of the most important social science texts, and to develop quality translators who could take up this task. A more detailed description of the project can be found in the booklet, "Guidelines for the Translation of Social Science Texts," published in 2006 by ACLS.

I was very interested in this project and found it very important, so I was pleased to be invited to the "*Séminaire sur la traduction et la diffusion des textes de sciences humaines*" at L'Institut d'etudes politiques in Paris in July 2006 (in which French was the principal working language). The seminar was meant to work as feedback on the pre-publication formulation of the project, and professional translators like myself were asked to use their expertise to comment and make recommendations.

This was more than a translation project; it was an epistemological project. Translation is often a difficult, slow, and expensive process, and nowadays it is a common sentiment that everybody should write in English to avoid all the fuss. More and more often doctoral theses and articles are written in English in universities all over the world. The English used is not always very good, and in the humanities this means that it limits the scope of thought, as we are thinking through language. Consequently, everybody must learn better English. This is where Michael's project is so important, by pointing at the necessity of multilingual thinking. I cite from the project: "The forms of thought and argumentation in the Anglo-American social science community have become a Procrustean bed to whose dimensions all conceptualization must fit. The result is an increasing homogenization and impoverishment of social science discourse."

To hear these words from the users of the hegemonic language is very important for users of other languages, small or not so small, so I asked Michael and his colleagues to present the project at the World Congress of the International Federation of Translators in Shanghai in August 2008, which they did, with great success. I chaired the session, so I witnessed it. Michael was asked to send copies to several persons interested in running similar workshops in their countries, and he told me later that this contact with people from different parts of the world was "what conferences are for." And he would not have been Michael if he had been content with the congress sessions; he also found time for some Chinese studies, and told me that his "budding Chinese" was "moderately improved."

The next time we met was in Salzburg, in February 2009, at a seminar called "Traduttore Traditore? Recognizing and Promoting the Critical Role of Translation in a Global Culture." Michael was talking about the role of the academy in promoting translation, and he was the chair of the working group on the same question. The goal was to draft two documents, one aimed at governmental stakeholders, the other at academic institutions and cultural and translation centers. Its function was, according to Michael, "to educate the administration of the universities and centers about the scholarly and creative value inherent in the act of translation; in other words, it is meant to open the eyes of those who might otherwise view translation as a mechanical process. The sections dealing with possible uses of translation in the classroom are meant to give them an idea of how fruitful the teaching of translation can be, not to prescribe what or how to teach."

As always, Michael asked for feedback, and as always he was very open to discussion. But we saw during the sessions in the working group, and we can also see from the citation above, that there is a long way to go in the United States when it comes to the general understanding of translation. European colleagues noted, for example, that the idea of having to underline the necessity of introducing the theory and history of translation in university-level courses would be almost offensive, so a proposal to do so could not really be part of a text presented to a European audience. The discussion was lively, and I have thought about it afterward, and have understood that Michael in his work was up against more conservative and immovable forces than I had been able to imagine.

I also invited him to participate in a symposium at the University of Oslo in March 2011, "Aspects of Translation," where he presented the Guidelines project and took part in numerous discussions. I could then see his pedagogical side, the way he approached the students, and the patience he showed with all their questions, informed or not. And I saw his willpower. Because of his duties at UCLA, he could not stay for a long time in Oslo, so he must have been suffering from severe jet lag, but nobody could see it. When I asked, he said that he simply told himself the jet lag did not exist, so then it did not. This was in the beginning of March, and still cold, but he came with a tweed jacket and a scarf and absolutely refused to borrow a coat. He was not cold, he said, so he was not. Of course, this willpower and stamina might mislead one to think that somebody is invulnerable. I had the impression that Michael would always be there, for me and for so many other people who loved and admired him. Now he is gone, and I feel very sad at the idea that I will never again be able to talk to him, discuss things with him, and learn from him. But his memory stays vivid in my mind, and he has left traces of his work that I will do my best to continue.

MICHAEL HENRY HEIM, A UK PERSPECTIVE

CELIA HAWKESWORTH

I am forever indebted to my friend and colleague Ronelle Alexander of UC Berkeley for having brought Mike into my life. As everyone who knew him will know, Mike had an extraordinary capacity for being wholly, generously present, warm, open, and accepting so that although, sadly, we did not meet all that often, the mark he made in my life was huge.

When we met, I was teaching at the School of Slavonic and East European Studies in the University of London and he came to my office in Russell Square. Standing in the rather dingy corridor, he made, of course, an instant impression, with his height and that wonderful face, all lucid, wise eyes, and broad smile. We had arranged for him to talk to students interested in translation. I remember vividly the quality of that talk, so different from much of the prevailing academic discourse. Its essence was a passionate concern with communication, embodied in Mike's way of being in the world and articulated with typical, and typically modest, clarity. That concern with communication, combined with his uniquely wide interest in and knowledge of the way different languages work, was of course the springboard of his involvement in translation. What impressed me then and continued to do so in all the conversations we later shared about translation was that his approach was so rooted in his practice. While everything he did was deeply thoughtful, Mike's practical account of the process of translation was refreshing. He described the method he adopted in his own work of first "prepping" the source text. This involved reading carefully for potential stumbling blocks, technical difficulties or cultural allusions that would need to be accommodated or resolved in a way that would not interfere with a smooth reading of the translated text. Once these problems and solutions had been identified, he would be able to enter fully into the original text, as he worked through it, making it his own and finding the most appropriate formulations to give his version the fresh authenticity that is his trademark.

A frequent topic of discussion over the years of our friendship was inevitably the question of varieties of English. I remember him beginning to talk many years ago about his conscious favoring of "Mid-Atlantic" as a solution to the potential jarring of words or expressions that could be distractingly marked with either UK or U.S. associations in the other cultural context. This had always seemed to me, instinctively, desirable, but it was very helpful to have the issue highlighted in Mike's usual practical way. Our most recent professional exchange of emails was over his essay "Varieties of English for the Literary Translator," which he sent to me, asking that I check some of his assertions about British English usage. The essay includes a list of potential solutions to some recurrent pitfalls and some typically creative suggestions for avoiding over-marked expressions. His whole concern with this topic is of course typical of his inclusiveness, his desire to communicate as fully as possible across all kinds of linguistic divides, including those between English-speakers in different parts of the world. This essay, covering also different registers, colloquialisms, slang, and the importance of using vocabulary appropriate to the age of the source text typifies Mike's meticulous approach. It reminds his readers of the daunting truth that translators can only do full justice to the texts before them by paying vigilant attention to all the varied nuances of their own language.

He was meant to deliver a course to a group of students from the University of East Anglia's British Centre for Literary Translation in August 2012, and he was to come to Scotland afterward to visit us at the University of St. Andrews where my husband is currently based. I was delighted to think that he would be sharing his talent, wisdom, and experience with students on our side of the Atlantic and had hopes of discussing with him ways of spreading that knowledge more widely in the UK. Tragically, his visit had to be cancelled. Priscilla told me how bitterly disappointed he was not to be able to deliver the workshop, but, despite the sudden onslaught of the last stage of his cruel disease, with his characteristic professionalism and generosity, he spent an hour on the phone talking to his replacement and was pleased to feel that the course was in good hands. I hope that this volume will go some way toward ensuring that Mike has an enduring presence in the field of literary translation in the UK.

I had the pleasure of seeing Mike in action at a class at UCLA and so experienced at first hand something of his teaching style with his own students: warm, natural, respectful, ready to be surprised and to learn something new himself just as he was in every aspect of his life. His students were indeed fortunate to have had such a teacher. On that occasion, I also witnessed for myself his absolute dedication to learning languages: at some risk, one would have thought—even though there was not too much traffic on his way to work, there were lamp-posts and trees—he would walk to the campus completely absorbed in a book in the most recent language to require his attention.

As everyone who knew him knows, Mike's intellect and linguistic talents were prodigious, but it was wonderful to observe also his delight in so many different aspects of the world: singing madrigals with his Priscilla, working in their pretty garden, playing with our young daughter and a little dog on our visit to UCLA in 1987. We were lucky enough that autumn to spend a memorable weekend with Mike and Priscilla in Yosemite, reveling in the inspiring surroundings, walking, sitting by waterfalls, talking. Much later, Mike and Priscilla visited us in Oxfordshire. We all shared a passionate concern with the environment and I particularly enjoyed Mike's account of himself scouring the UCLA campus with bin bags to pick up countless discarded plastic bottles from the ground and trash cans. Typically, he had also found a way of passing them on to penniless refugees who could make some small income from them. On that occasion, as we drove to Bristol to share the autumn colors at the wonderful Westonbirt arboretum, Mike asked me to stop the car as we passed through a small Cotswold village. He had spotted windfall apples on the ground and wanted to take one to eat. His delight in that small treasure, an archetypal symbol of life, innocence and renewal, struck me then as encapsulating Mike's complete and irreplaceable presence in the world.

TWO ESSAYS AND A POEM FOR MICHAEL HEIM

ANDREI CODRESCU

The two essays were broadcast on NPR's news show,
All Things Considered. The eulogy for Michael Heim
aired two days after his passing. The other was one of
many essays on the difficulties and wonders of trans-
lation broadcast over the years on NPR. I dedicate it
retrospectively to Michael, whose work inspired me
even when I wasn't mentioning his name. The third
piece is a poem written for a fellow Romanian writer,
Călin Andrei-Mihăilescu, where Michael's Hrabal and
Kundera in English are mentioned, and translation is,
again, the mystery considered.

•

IN PRAISE OF MICHAEL HENRY HEIM

It is impossible to imagine intelligent American life from the twentieth century's spectacular end until now without Michael Henry
Heim's translations from the Russian, Czech, Croatian, German, and

Hungarian. A voracious polyglot who could have written remarkable works of original fiction, Heim decided to apply his linguistic brilliance to the writings of Chekhov, Kundera, Kiš, Havel, and many others. When I look at my shelves I see not just the luminaries above, but Aksyonov, Čapek, Esterházy, Brecht, Ugrešić, and best of all, my favorite novelist, the Czech Bohumil Hrabal. All of these read, re-read, and heavily annotated books are markers and cornerstones of my education, thinking, life, and work, and I am very grateful to their translator.

Michael Henry Heim died at the age of 69. I only met him once, a few months before his premature death. He had just finished translating Max Blecher, a genius Romanian writer from the first half of the twentieth century. Blecher died at the age of 29, after a long battle with a disease that didn't prevent him from writing two astonishing novels, poetry, short stories, and essays. Max Blecher's book is a rich, sensual feast lit brightly by the knowledge of his impending demise: his character observes the minutiae of the world with a concentration and beauty of expression that keeps them alive. His translator into English, Michael Henry Heim, who also knew that he wouldn't be around much longer, allowed his own best sense of the world to shine through Blecher's prose.

Translation might seem a simple operation to some journeymen of the form, but great translators are rare. Gregory Rabassa, who brought Gabriel García-Márquez's *One Hundred Years of Solitude* into English, Suzanne Jill Levine, who translated Cabrera Infante, the Cuban James Joyce, and Barbara Wright, the translator of Raymond Queneau, are a constellation of their own. Michael Henry Heim was one of them. Their English renditions are now a permanent feature of how we conceive our creative, philosophical, and ethical landscape. Personally, these translators made my own work acceptable because they translated some of the world I come from. When I read these books, I forget that they are translations, and that's the only way genuine culture travels. Even the King James Bible is a translation, after all.

·

THE HOTTEST MARKET

for Michael Heim,
retrospectively

Translation is the emerging market of our century. The last job that only humans can accomplish is that of translation. Machines cannot translate no matter how smart we make them. The slightest nuance of a nuance, and the machine mistranslates.

That said, even humans do not translate very well. Millions of people have fallen into the gaps between words and were never seen again. In my business, poetry, which is a small preserve in the vast domain of language use, there is a high rate of casualties. Every year our academies graduate thousands of fresh faces ready to take on Baudelaire, Rilke, Pasternak, and Arghezi. Two years after graduation, you can walk through the semantic fields and count the bodies. Even the so-called "successful" translations have to be retranslated every five years in order to capture in new language what wasn't understood in the first place. Poetry is notoriously untranslatable, but other linguistic communications are no exception. Neither businesses nor the UN are exempt from the fallibility of translation.

Why are languages so refractory to having their meanings carried from one set of sounds to another? The answer may startle you: languages are different precisely because they do not wish to be translated! Poetry, which is the delicate music of the tiniest differences,

sets itself up a priori in a singular place, but all language is the story
of differences. The people of the valley spoke differently from the
people of the mountain because 1) the valley shaped them physi-
cally and spoke through them, and 2) they did not wish the people
of the mountain to understand them. The physical being of which
they were part delighted in becoming conscious of difference. The
defense of that delight required protection from other topographies.
We have a tiny switch in the language-brain that mandates the rapid
evolution of communication in response to every outside stimulus. If
the outside is changed by even one rock, language undergoes a shift.

When we moved out of the country into the city, we started to
translate each other. Mass media, the Esperanto of our age, is automatically translating every language, to produce a common virtual
landscape. It would seem then that translators are not needed in
the age of mass media. In fact, mass media dies if its language is
not constantly fed linguistic differences to smash and homogenize.
In the twenty-first century, the urban vulgate is where the quick-
est adaptations take place, which is why they are the media's most
sought-after delicacies.

Outside the media, the need for translation is greater than ever.
For business to go forward, differences must be understood. The
flattening Esperanto of media does not suffice. The transfer of
money and the transformation and circulation of goods are as delicate as poetry. The media itself, which is just another business, needs
a pre-translation before it can create the illusion of universality.

·

TRANSLATION

for Călin-Andrei Mihăilescu
(with an homage to Michael Heim's Hrabal and Kundera)

Exile is the most radical form of translation
writes Călin-Andrei Mihăilescu in *Happy New Fear*
an English-titled book in Romanian
that will never be translated into English
excepting the above line because Călin
writes in rhapsodic idiomatic punning lingo
in a Romanian resembling a wolf with seven teats
from which hang the other seven languages he is
Romulus and Remus-type pups ready to build cities
I mean essays about time-travel in the tunnel
between languages that I have traveled myself
a few times but didn't really frequent like Călin
who has a sleeping bag there and knows all the bums
some of whom are fashion models he writes odes to
many of them Czech who have read Hrabal and Kundera
and can sleep anywhere if the stories are funny
and so yes translation is just how one lives with oneself
from minute to minute from home to street from street
to office from office to the bar and to bed and in dreams
and each moment has its own language that puts it in the next
moment in another language made complicated by style
which is the design of alienation residing in orthography
or hesitant speech while translating oneself or others
thus to write on translation is to translate and to write
in language that cannot be translated is to be totally great
a state only Czech girls in sleeping bags can and do love

REMEMBERING
MICHAEL HENRY HEIM

ROSANNA WARREN

On first meeting Michael and Priscilla Heim in Cambridge, Massachusetts, in 2002, I felt I was encountering characters out of Turgenev. I say "Michael and Priscilla" because they seemed so deeply to partake in one another's lives, being, and imagination. Michael loomed: a tall, lanky, deep-browed man with dark hair and a long face made longer by bushy nineteenth-century sideburns. He had, blessedly, no small talk. In intensity and earnestness, he seemed a member of the pre-Revolutionary Russian liberal intelligentsia, as if he had just stepped out of a salon discussion of educating the peasantry, extending suffrage, and the relevance (or irrelevance) of Balzac. Priscilla, too, seemed to emerge from that world: tall, slender, wearing garments I remember as dark in hue and flowing. She seemed to embody gracious intelligence. I fell in love with them both.

It hardly needs to be repeated that Michael was a phenomenal linguist and—what is not the same thing—a phenomenally artful translator from a dizzying number of languages. But there is something even more rare in Michael. It was—is—his generosity. He was the least self-centered person I have ever met. His attention shone directly upon each object as if his ego had an eerie transparency.

Maybe it was this quality, combined with fierce intellect, that allowed him to absorb so many languages and to impersonate and inhabit so many different literary styles. His generosity also took practical and social forms: he was deeply attentive to his students, and even to other people's students. I saw this during the two presentations he gave at the Translation Seminars I ran at Boston University. He listened respectfully and carefully to the students' questions, and corresponded with several of these young enthusiasts afterward.

He was intellectually generous, happy to consider multiple points of view on the vexed and vexing questions of how literary translation should be conducted. He would argue the merits (and weaknesses) of several positions, and was flexibly willing to suppose that some tasks might call for one approach, while others would benefit from a different conception entirely. He recounted mistakes he had made as a translator, and stages of his groping for solutions in the texts of different authors and in different genres. From this radical humility, the students in the seminar learned one of the most important lessons of the semester, and, who knows, perhaps of all their years in school.

Some years ago when I was visiting Los Angeles to give a poetry reading, Michael and Priscilla invited me to lunch. As soon as I crossed their threshold I had entered an enchanted, apparently timeless realm. The wide living room was truly a "living" room; it was alive with the souls of the books on the large bookcases, with the piano (which was clearly not an ornamental piece of furniture, but an active shaper of daily life), and with the light flowing in through the large windows from the back garden. And what a garden! It bedazzled this New Englander: lemon and lime trees, boughs heavy with their brilliant fruit. A dense wall of green. And a vegetable patch, out of which had come the sorrel that my hosts had metamorphosed into the subtle soup they served that day, my favorite soup, and one which I rarely get to taste or make (not having my own sorrel patch). The Heim sorrel soup was perfection: silky, lightly creamy, with a hint of sweetness playing against a fundamental bitterness. I will never forget the long wooden table, the bowl of lemons forming a Zurbaran still life, the basket of warm, crusty bread that seemed to smell of the goodness of life on earth, the insinuating taste of sorrel.

When Michael visited Boston a few years later to give a translation seminar, he brought a gift of lemons from their trees. In 2006, he and I had a chance to talk for days on end when we were neighbors in Berlin, he at the Wissenschaftskolleg and I at the American Academy. After hours of writing, we would meet for tea in the obscure, high-minded kitchen of the Wissenschaftskolleg, or in my studio at the Academy, and we would chew over the day's labors, style, ethics, art, and literary gossip. Michael lived literature; he lived it wholly, passionately, and as sensuously as if words had the consistency of lemons, sorrel, and bread.

I saw him last in the spring of 2012 when he and Priscilla visited Boston again and he gave another talk for the Translation Seminar. He was already being treated for cancer, but nothing stopped the flow of his lucidity or his joie de vivre. He was learning Chinese! And working with a Chinese post-doctoral student to translate some of my poems into Chinese. His two-hour presentation in the seminar illuminated great chambers of the art of translation, spaces and dimensions the students had not imagined before and into which they were glad to be welcomed.

I cannot think of Michael Henry Heim in the past tense. The many authors he has translated, from many languages, hold their place in the English language, and his lesson of disinterested devotion will persist as long as there are souls to receive, practice, and transmit it.

Michael and Priscilla Heim.

IMPACT

NEW FRONTIERS FOR TRANSLATION IN THE TWENTY-FIRST CENTURY: THE GLOBE, THE MARKET, THE FIELD

In Honor of the Life and Work of Michael Henry Heim[1]

RUSSELL SCOTT VALENTINO

I would like to thank Nancy Condee, Caryl Emerson, and Sibelan Forrester for asking me to step in for Michael Heim, who was scheduled to give this talk. I wish that he were giving it instead of me.

Let me start by zeroing in a little bit on the last words of the title of this presentation: the field. What is the field of translation? How shall we define it in order to say what its prospects, its new frontiers, might be for the future?

I want to parse this question of the field into two segments that are usually conflated. But I'd like to separate them in order to give substance to each within the institutional contexts that they have come increasingly to work within today—the scholarly side of translation and the writerly or creative side. And I should also say up front that the example of Michael Heim's work is really foremost in my mind as I sketch these two domains. They did not exist when

1   This presentation was given as the keynote address at the 2013 Conference of the American Association of Teachers of Slavic and East European Languages.

Michael started out some forty years ago, and his work was fundamental in shaping the contours of the field as it would eventually develop.

There is today, on one hand, the field of translation studies, which encompasses a vast and growing array of books and book series, encyclopedias, readers, dictionaries, journals, and a seemingly endless supply of new conferences around the world (as anyone on Edwin Gentzler's mailing list can attest): translation and the city, translating race, translating oral narrative, translation and the cinema, the translation of Haruki Murakami, or pick your author, period, region, country, and so on.

On the other hand, there is translation, the practice of it, and particularly the translation of fiction, poetry, and creative nonfiction. This practice is often opposed by those who engage in it to the study of and commentary upon translation, which is the work of translation studies scholars. This is a lot like the distinction routinely made in higher education between the MFA world and the PhD world, that is, the world of makers and the world of critics and historians. While it is very nice to find an especially informed and articulate choreographer, or sculptor, or filmmaker, these people are not generally expected, if they have an appointment in an MFA granting program, to write scholarly treatises about choreography, or sculpture, or filmmaking—they're expected to engage in the practice of their respective arts. They're evaluated on the basis of the films they make, the novels they write, the exhibits they create, and so on, not on the basis of the commentary or interventions they write about their own or anybody else's artistic or cultural production.

Now I imagine that there might be some resistance among the scholarly community, particularly in language and literature circles, to the idea of literary translation fitting into the MFA world, just as there has historically been some resistance to the idea of the MFA itself as a legitimate activity and terminal degree in institutions of higher education. It's a little late for that. While both Translation and Translation Studies seem to have been in a growing mode in recent years, the MFA writing world has seen a growth explosion that does not seem to be slowing down.

Over the past approximately eight to ten years, by my unofficial count, between nine and fifteen new programs in Translation and Translation Studies have emerged (it depends on how you count what constitutes "new program") in post-secondary institutions in the U.S. and Canada. That seems pretty good for a time in which the humanities have been under pressure to reduce and consolidate. But in that same eight-year period, there have been 150 new creative writing programs—new BAs, new programs in community colleges, new low residency programs, and new MFAs at research institutions. The annual conference of the Association of Writers and Writing Programs (AWP) now rivals that of the MLA in size, with more than 10,000 registered participants and a book fair that is enormous and amazingly vibrant. If you haven't had a chance to go to the AWP, I would characterize it as a younger and hipper MLA. At the AWP, most participants are young people or older people trying to appear younger than they actually are, which contrasts nicely to the MLA, where the participants tend to be older, or young people trying to appear older than they actually are.

Creative writing is a growth field, make no mistake about it, at least for the time being, and as such, it is one of the main new frontiers for translation in the twenty-first century. This is true for translation, and also for certain aspects of Translation Studies, particularly those that deal more with questions of practice and history and are textually rather than theoretically oriented. Today, the AWP is the main professional organization for translators as writers, and the AWP member programs are where translators are likely to find the most publication venues, the biggest market for their work, and, potentially, even employment options.

Translation Studies is another animal altogether. This field, or, as I'm treating it here, co-field, saw its beginnings in Europe in the 1950s-60s. By the early 1970s, a significant body of scholarship had been produced, including influential work by Eugene Nida, Katharina Reiss, Jiři Levý, and others. Translation Studies emerged in the UK during the 1970s, as scholars like Susan Bassnett began working with colleagues in Belgium and Israel. By the 1980s, the field was institutionalized in the British Comparative Literature Association, a fact heralded by the publication of Bassnett's *Translation Studies*. Thanks to the work of Bassnett and colleagues like André Lefevere, the new field took root in the United Kingdom and the United States simultaneously, though its growth in the U.S. has tended to be slower and more diffuse.

Apart from isolated programs like the research center at SUNY Binghamton, or UMass Amherst, or more recently Kent State, Translation Studies, as opposed to translator training, has not taken place in a single, central discipline at universities. It's been spread out among a variety of disciplinary locations, from Classics and History to Anthropology, English, Communication Studies, and the national language and literature programs. Most translation research, moreover, has tended to remain divorced from the training of translators, which generally takes place in creative writing programs, on one hand, and foreign language departments, on the other—and there, mainly as an extension of foreign language instruction. Recent trends and the dramatic upsurge in Translation Studies research suggest that the division between training and scholarship has weakened, and that Translation Studies, all while drawing heavily upon other humanistic disciplines, is poised to emerge as a discipline unto itself.

One of the things that makes the field of Translation Studies of particular interest today is its move away from the more static, ahistorical comparisons between foreign and translated texts (dominant in the 1950s-70s) to an awareness that concepts of equivalence vary not only historically, from period to period, but within particular periods and among different cultural constituencies, each of whom may expect a different relation between a foreign work and its translation: the cultural and historical specificity of language makes simplistic models of equivalence implausible. Nowhere is such specificity more apparent than in the realm of literary art, where the attempt to "carry over" what was created inside one literary and cultural context into another exposes the deep rifts between cultures around the world. To take one of the most dramatic examples of recent years, when Salman Rushdie's *The Satanic Verses* was translated into Arabic, it was rendered as *Al-Ayat ash-Shaytaniya*, where *shaytan* meant Satan and *ayat* meant the "verses" of the Qur'an. This was a grave cultural error, as Rushdie's book was actually named after a quite specific Islamic legend regarding verses that Muhammad initially thought had been dictated to him by God but that he later understood had come from Satan. The phrase "satanic verses" was used by British Orientalists of the nineteenth century to refer to this excised text, not to the Qur'an as a whole. The phrase was largely unknown in the Islamic world, so that translated into Arabic it sounded like a slap in the face. The terrible consequences of the episode are still palpable today.

This extreme example takes more mundane form in the case of many "minor" languages, especially those that have existed in a historically subaltern relationship with other, more prestigious languages. The kind of apparently apolitical expressionist stand assumed by a poet in English or French ("I write for myself; I am merely expressing myself") is less available to writers in minor languages, especially when a colonial past is involved. Thus a writer of Sango, or Tagalog, or Ainu, or Basque poetry who made such a claim would likely be considered simply naïve. The politics at stake are too powerful to ignore. It is possible to identify many such cases historically, in every part of the world, while governmental attempts to neutralize the enduring strength of regional language identities are an unfortunately regular occurrence.

With the gradual transformation of literature study at U.S. universities over the past two decades (toward cultural studies models), Translation Studies has become a primary disciplinary locale for the study of world literature, particularly of its creation through translated texts. In doing so, Translation Studies has taken on some of the methodological preoccupations of its former disciplinary tutors but added a refreshing variety of others as well. Scholars of translation need thorough knowledge of literary history, literary theory, and cultural history, as well as the discrete conventional systems of two or more language traditions. Given the current trend of highly technologized translation, they may need to consider how processes and politics of translation are influenced by the media that they serve (such as cinema or the various internet and software protocols). But they must also understand the institutional affiliations that make it possible for translations to appear in the world (the King James Bible at one time, for instance, *The Brothers Karamazov* at another), and that give translations validity and power, or not. They must be prepared to ask questions about the ideological assumptions behind the selection, reception, and marketing of translated works. This, moreover, inevitably leads to questions of central texts, the texts considered central, or peripheral, to a culture. What does it mean when—as in Europe for some fifteen centuries—the central text of a culture is a translation? Who constructs the image of a writer, a work, a literature, a culture? What are the means by which this work is accomplished? How has this been done historically, in different periods and places?

In working with colleagues at the Russian State Humanities University and the University of Zadar in Croatia on a recent grant proposal, I came across a perfect example of the sorts of research that Translation Studies scholars are engaged in. The grant is intended to study the reception of various works by several cultures, focusing not only on the translations themselves, but on the mechanisms by which a work gets culturally appropriated as well: how, for instance, Dante's *Inferno* became a work of English-language poetry, or how Dostoyevsky's *Notes from Underground* was associated with existentialism in books and university classes of the mid-twentieth century. We were looking for something that worked in the other direction, outward from American literature into Russian and Croatian. Thinking that it would provide a nice symmetry to try something initially inspired by Dostoyevsky's *Notes*, I suggested Ralph Ellison's *Invisible Man*, upon which it became clear that not only had the book never been translated into either Russian or Croatian, but my Russian colleagues had only the faintest familiarity with the author's name. (My Croatian colleague had read the book in graduate school—in English.) The cultural, political, and broadly institutional factors that can encourage the appropriation of some works are also influential in discouraging others, and this has an impact on the resulting image of the foreign culture in question, a major Translation Studies topic.

As a field, Translation Studies shares many developmental aspects with the only slightly older field of Film Studies, and we can see key similarities by comparing the two, particularly where they cross paths in the domain of adaptation.

In his *Concepts in Film Theory*, Dudley Andrew notes that discussions about adaptations of narrative fiction to cinema have historically tended to devolve into statements of preference such as "the book was better than the movie." This is a familiar experience for most of us. Andrew is describing what Translation Studies scholars have more recently called "equivalences and shifts," where a source is compared with a derivative new version, and individual aspects (scenes, images, characters, descriptions, and so on) are held up to each other to see where they are similar and where different.

An equivalence, in broad terms, is something relatively the same in both the source and the adaptation: the actor John Goodman has an eye patch covering one eye in the film *O Brother, Where Art Thou?*, which stands in for the single eye of the Cyclops in *The Odyssey*: equivalence achieved. This usage is analogous to the equivalence of a word in two languages.

Such equivalences often run into problems. Guy de Maupassant stops the action of his story, "A day in the country" (*Une partie de campagne*), in order to describe the wagon in which the family Dufour is riding; but stopping the film version to do the same is not really possible—as the film scholar Seymour Chatman once showed in his "What Novels Can Do that Films Can't." And so Jean Renoir, in his film adaptation of the Maupassant story, focuses on other perspectives through various camera angles, a technique that highlights the specific virtues of the medium of film: and that is a shift. This usage is analogous to the situation in translation when a word or concept or idiom is radically different in the source culture and the receiving culture, e.g., translating the Biblical notion of the Trinity into an aboriginal language.

When done well, such analyses of equivalences and shifts can be an enlightening pedagogical tool. Often, however, the search for equivalences and shifts can become mechanical and narrowly normative, ghettoizing the resulting analyses, and perhaps even the discipline to which they belong. This is an ever-present danger, it seems to me, in the relatively young discipline of Translation Studies, for the language of equivalence and shifts has long been pervasive in discussions of translation, literary history, and literary pedagogy.

In a 2002 essay entitled "Anonymous Sources," Eliot Weinberger tells the far too familiar story of a critic who dismissed the work of a certain immensely prolific translator from the German because "somewhere in the vastness of *Buddenbrooks* he had translated a 'chesterfield' as a 'greatcoat.'" Such members of what Weinberger calls the "translation police" are, he claims, often members of foreign language departments.

As a long-standing feature of discussions about translation, even among the so-called experts, this means of measurement, this framework and standard for beginning to talk, exerts a constant marginalizing pressure on the discipline of Translation Studies, which is otherwise an expansive and naturally multidisciplinary set of related, cross-pollinating fields, as many scholars have noted. But thinking in terms of equivalences and shifts limits conversation, staking out sharp, largely technical and normative boundaries. It has tended to shut down rather than open up conversations in much the same manner as conversations about whether the book or the movie was better do. The unstated contrast is of course only visible to someone who knows the source language, a member of Weinberger's translation police. Error correction, as in a certain brand of foreign language classroom, becomes the dominant mode of discourse. This is both unfortunate and wrongheaded. It relies upon undigested and unarticulated assumptions about what translation expertise entails.

Let me instead explore some of the more promising avenues of inquiry in the recent history of Translation Studies. As in the case of Film Studies before it, these can help to open the discipline up rather than shutting it down, allowing it to take greater advantage of its fundamentally multidisciplinary character.

I suspect that Weinberger is correct in naming foreign language specialists as a major source of the kind of thinking that I am calling detrimental to the incipient discipline. But it is not just specialists. We begin to form such habits of thought at the earliest stages of education in foreign language classrooms, with the use of glossaries and lexicons. These train us to think in terms of equivalences as an easy shorthand for "accuracy" and "correctness," or just plain "learning."

So in a first-year classroom, you might learn that the Russian word *vot* is equivalent to the English word "there"; that Russian *ona* is equivalent to English "she"; and that Russian *esche* is equivalent to English "still." Together then, in this particular classroom exercise, these words would "translate," i.e., establish a coherent set of meaningful equivalences, for the Russian phrase, *Vot ona esche*, as English "There she still (is)." Equivalence achieved. The added copula at the end requires a slight shift because of the lack of a need for it in Russian and the necessity of the verb in English. I suppose some rather more literarily sensitive teachers might revise the English to read a little more naturally, something on the order of, "She's still there."

What language teachers generally will not do, however, is tell their students that the entire exercise is stacked from the start; it is a kind of cheating, a mental gymnastics analogous to what Tolstoy refers to in *War and Peace* as "retroactive ordering" in thinking about historical events, when you end up with a result and then you forget all the contingencies of the past in showing how things ended up with that result.

So in this hypothetical classroom example, we may be imagining a situation, a woman on a park bench, let us say, as spied by two playing boys. *Where's Mama? Did she get up and walk away?* (One boy takes a peek) *Oh, no, it's okay. She's still there.* This situation, or something like it, corresponds to the learning of the words in that order. The words, the context of their combination and meaning both individually and together, and also the context of their translation are completely linked together. There is no reason that those particular words in that order should be translated as "She's still there" unless we imagine this particular situation, or one like it.

We could easily come up with different English words and a different corresponding phrase, using the same Russian words, if we imagined a new situation: a pesky fly, for instance, that someone takes a swat at and then thinks it has gone away, but a few minutes later, it is back, and so the same Russian phrase, *Vot ona eshche* turns out to mean "That's it again!" "She's still there" and "That's it again" are pretty different, and I have not taken a very complicated example. The same phrase has merely been imagined as two different source situations. This is of course not news to anyone likely to be hearing these comments, and I am sure this audience could easily come up with more situations and more possible translations for the very same phrase, along with a sophisticated semantic explanation for what exactly is happening. But it would be news to many elementary language learners faced with three new words to learn that the words do not mean by themselves, they only mean when imagined in a situation that defines them retroactively, backward from the situation. This is about words in context, language as a function of rhetoric, where situation and audience condition meaning from the source context to the words used.

In the same way, situation and audience condition every choice a translator might make in the context of the receiving culture, and whether we call it rhetoric, or sociology, or something else, Translation Studies scholars are aware of this, even when it's not articulated in the particular way I've just described. So when Lawrence Venuti wrote about the invisibility of the translator in the 1990s, he was engaging in an extended sociological analysis and a study of the rhetorical category of ethos, the construction of the translator's voice in the receiving culture. The fact that he found silence, or rather invisibility, among the constructs does not alter the nature of what he was doing, for silence and invisibility, in fact, constitute a claim of trustworthy authority in the construction of a translator's ethos. And when Antoine Berman focused on the foreignizing strategies of early nineteenth-century German translators, his analysis—like the strategy itself—could be squarely situated within a sociological or broadly defined rhetorical understanding of Germany and the German language of the day, involving *lexis*, or style, as conditioned by *kairos*, or timeliness.

Another direction where Weinberger might have pointed a finger is toward teachers of literature (I might as well get everybody in here)—especially in their tendency to pick at individual words in a text, worry over them, and, in translation, often dismiss them and the translator who chose them, without any serious attempt at a sociological or deeply rhetorical understanding of the choice itself, in its context, and with consideration for its ramifications for the language and culture of its day.

To take an example that this audience should be familiar with, Turgenev's 1862 novel *Ottsy i deti* was quite early on translated into English as *Fathers and Sons*, not as *Fathers and Children*, though most Russian-English language specialists today would say *Fathers and Children* is more "accurate." But let us put on our Translation Studies hats for a moment and field a hypothetical question about the accuracy of the translated title *Fathers and Sons*, in a literature class, for instance. Given my comments thus far, what would be an appropriate answer from the standpoint of the discipline of Translation Studies?

I am tempted by the old philosophy technique of noting that the question is incorrectly formed. Accuracy outside of context does not make much sense, after all. Words do not mean by themselves, only in situations with audiences, with people accepting them and making sense of them. When you ask whether one word is more accurate than another, you generally ignore all that and assume some kind of abstract correspondence is possible. It is not. But this sort of an answer is likely to seem at best inadequate, at worst confusing or dismissive, especially to students who might not have not thought much about such things.

Let me try a different tack: It depends. It depends on what you think the book is about, on what sorts of social norms condition your interpretation and understanding of the book, on what sorts of publishing and editing conventions condition the creation of the translated text, on what kinds of institutional affiliations, grants, contracts, reading practices, authorial conventions, language-learning practices, translation techniques, and printing venues are available. This, in fact, is what the only slightly older discipline of Film Studies discovered with regard to discussions of film adaptations: the films created are inordinately complex social, political, economic, linguistic, artistic, rhetorical, cultural works in their own right. They are conditioned by, reflective of, located in, and even productive for, an entire range of social phenomena that have *very little to do* with the source text. We might start with an examination of the source, but that has to lead elsewhere if we are to give the adaptation, or the translation, its due as a cultural production that means something to the people who experience it.

The most important, not to mention the most interesting, discussions, in fact, take us eventually to how the new works mean what they mean in the receiving culture. And these in turn have the greatest potential for teaching us things about ourselves and others.

Literature teachers, who are rarely thinking in these terms, like to bring up the phrase, coined by Robert Frost, "poetry is what is lost in translation." There is a similarly worried privileging of the source text implicit in this kind of statement, a fear that we might miss something, lose it, be wrong about our understanding. We need the police to come and enlighten us with the source, in this case, the source poetry. There are different kinds of police, it turns out. The sociological and rhetorical aspects of the study of translation suggest that this is an unfortunately limited way of thinking about how translations work. Luther's German Bible, or Constance Garnett's

Fathers and Sons, or Pasternak's *Hamlet* immediately became part of the unrepeatable, context-specific life of the culture in which they were situated. Putting them "back" into the source languages, bringing all their German, American, or Russo-Soviet associations with them, would be equally impossible.

In other words, from a Translation Studies standpoint, what they have gained is always enormously more interesting and important than what they might have lost. The growing body of Translation Studies scholarship that takes account of this gain and attempts to measure, understand, and contextualize it in the relationships of people to other people, the institutions of publishing and arts promotion, questions of gender, class, politics, race, age, religion, and education—that is, in the meaningful uptake and dissemination of cultural understanding—implicitly recognizes the unfortunate limitations of the "translation as inevitable loss" point of view, especially with its accompanying emphasis on abstract "accuracy." It replaces those perspectives, in turn, with an ambitiously expansive project for cultural understanding through the prism of translated works. This form of translation research is the other extremely exciting frontier for translation that I see in the next century.

Now, as I noted at the start of my talk, this is a very different institutional world from the one in which Michael Heim began as a translator more than forty years ago. Nevertheless, until relatively recently his research profile did not fit comfortably in the scholarly world. In the minds of some, it still would not. He was acutely aware of this and tirelessly insistent that the research to which he devoted himself should be counted as not merely acceptable but also legitimate. In this he was prescient, if not revolutionary.

His chosen work was markedly interdisciplinary before interdisciplinarity had become a buzzword; it tied the basic research mission of the Research I institution to outreach and public engagement before the recent administrative emphasis on the need for outreach and engagement; and it predated the MFA writing revolution that now has made the AWP such an important force in American higher education.

Where, I wonder, would Michael Heim have focused his efforts if he were starting out today? I mean this as a serious question, because while it's true that he was trained in Slavic Languages and Literatures, received a PhD in that discipline, became a tenured professor and eventually a distinguished professor at a major PhD-granting Slavic Department, this is also a person who spent most of his career creating primary texts, not commentaries or interventions or theoretical approaches, but works of English-language literature that sold in the hundreds of thousands of copies and were reviewed regularly in the *L.A. Times*, the *New York Review of Books*, and the *Times Literary Supplement*. Looked at from the standpoint of the emergent MFA writing world, his research profile fits squarely in the arts domain. If he were being hired by a language and literature department today, would he be able to follow his professional interests, the research that made his voice so distinctive and respected in the world of language and literature study?

Or would he be told to hold off on that translation stuff until he had more scholarship under his belt, wait with the Kundera and the Ugrešić and the Chekhov, the Aksyonov, the Enzensberger, the Grass, the Mann, the Hrabal, and the Hiršal, the Matvejević, the Ripellino, and Kiš, and Claus, and Konrád, and Esterházy, and Uspenskii, and Sokolov, and Roziner, and Neruda, and Crnjanski, and Chukovskii, and Tišma, and Masaryk, and Čapek . . .

I'm not going to answer that question because I think everyone in this room knows what it would likely be. It's the safest route, the most prudent. It's probably what I would tell a new assistant professor worried about getting tenure, unless the ground were prepared well, in advance, and even then it would be a gamble.

Michael thought about this, too. He was not content to leave his own success as a fluke of UCLA's particular view of his professional profile, the forward-looking, progressive thought of a number of UCLA colleagues and administrators over the years, who were willing to accept and value a dossier with translation at its heart. He was determined in advocating for the acceptance of translation as research and, with the help of MLA President Catherine Porter in 2010, he succeeded in having a set of guidelines adopted by that organization to help other institutions evaluate the work of colleagues who, like him, put translation at the center of their research. These guidelines describe a balanced translator's portfolio, with a variety of aspects that might include teaching, reviews, essays, forewords, prefaces, workshops, and so on, all of which, taken together, would demonstrate a coherent body of work revolving around translation. They are the kind of guidelines that should be consulted by tenure-and-promotion external reviewers, by department chairs and committees charged with creating or revising internal promotional guideline documents, and by tenure-track faculty and graduate students thinking about how to organize their own work for evaluation by others. They give us all a wider lens to use in looking at translation.

When I use that lens on Michael Heim's work, it becomes clear that he occupied a place at the confluence of language learning, literary history, area studies, creative writing, criticism, and arts publishing, drawing from scholarship, his own and that of his colleagues, to create contemporary international literature in English. He would never have described his work this way, of course: most often he called himself merely a translator.

This self-description, which he would announce every year at the orientation for new graduate students, contained something of a challenge. Colleagues might have just listed a variety of specialized studies they were engaged in, or a forthcoming monograph on a relatively specialized topic, and the newly arrived students might have just been expressing their own scholarly interests and aspirations, descriptive and sometimes a little self-important, and then Michael would quietly say, "My name is Michael Heim, and I'm a translator." Sometimes he would add, "and I teach Czech," issuing, in effect, a double challenge, for this was before the advent of second language acquisition as an accepted scholarly field as well.

An important effect of Michael's challenging self-description, which he did not of course only issue at departmental functions, was to insert translation, and sometimes language teaching, into the profile of the research-oriented language and literature department and the daily, professional activity of its members. He championed, in effect, these poor cousins to the scholarly when it was much more common for translators and language instructors to keep quiet about their work, and even sometimes hide it. And it is of course thanks to him and his long dedication that there are now such exciting frontiers for translation in the coming century.

MICHAEL HEIM
AND COLLEGIAL TRANSLATION

ANDRZEJ W. TYMOWSKI

Michael Heim was a voracious translator. He needed it, like the rest of us need food. Although he had many other occupations and preoccupations—teacher, scholar, grandfather, to name the most obvious—whenever other work or other joys drew him away from translating, he grew restive, nervously awaiting the moment he could sit back down at his desk with a new text to render into English. But I wish now to write about one of Michael's passions that was not-entirely-devoted-to-translation: his desire to bring the writing of translations, and the principles of translating, closer to the center of the academic world. His interest in the translation of academic texts has been recently honored by the establishment of the Michael Henry Heim Prize for translation of journal articles from East European languages into English.[1] The prize promotes the concept of "collegial translation," that is, the translation by scholars of academic work written by their colleagues.

---

1 The prize is sponsored by the quarterly journal *East European Politics & Societies and Cultures*. http://eep.sagepub.com/site/includefiles/EEPS_HeimTranslationPrize.pdf

Language Training

My acquaintance with Michael began with his service on the Committee for East European Language Training, which I organized at the American Council of Learned Societies (ACLS). The committee reviewed applications for language grants, selected award recipients, and issued advice. Applicants were graduate students who needed summer courses to acquire research languages, and directors of summer language programs. Michael was a life-long language learner himself. That, as well as his work with graduate students, gave him insight into the skills needed for language acquisition.

Michael's work with the ACLS committee complemented his own language abilities with the experience of scholars-in-training, most of whom were far less gifted than he. (Few mortals could rival Michael's tenacious study habits and powers of retention.) He wondered about the situation of scholars who used more than one language in their academic work. Should they be encouraged, or at minimum *acknowledged*, for translating scholarly texts? It irked him that the effort to translate, and the importance of good translation, was denigrated in the academy as technical, even menial, work. Graduate students were told routinely not to waste their time on "mere" translation, but to concentrate on making truly important and unique contributions in their respective disciplines.

A Multilingual Project, "Identifications"

ACLS organized a case study on scholarship in a multilingual setting by means of the Collaborative Research Network (CRN) on "Official and Vernacular Identifications and the Making of the Modern World" (2003-2006). The network, financially supported by the Ford Foundation, developed research projects on identity formation through the analytical framework of "official and vernacular identifications" to compare various approaches used in different world areas. The lingua franca of the project was English, but its membership was international. The point was to compare research practices by different linguistic communities. Project teams focused on, and members were drawn from, Russia, France and the French Atlantic world, Southeast Asia, and China.

I invited Michael to attend the final meeting of the "Identifications" network, held at Yale University's Center for International and Area Studies on October 3-5, 2003. I had directed the project and while I was more than well-satisfied with its accomplishments, I was disquieted by certain misfires in mutual understanding across cultures and languages. The centrifugal forces in such a complex, international enterprise had given all its participants many vertiginous moments. I sensed that project members, especially those whose first language was close to being their only language, tended toward positivism about translations. Whether they worked (mainly) in English, French, Russian, Chinese, or a Southeast Asian language, when confronted with a translation, they took it for reality. For them, to paraphrase Wittgenstein's *Tractatus*, the world is all that is the case, as translated.

It seemed to me that scholars should read translations *as* translations, keeping in mind that what they were reading is the product of two intellects. Moreover, the choices made by the translator of an academic text are never simply lexical—choosing the right word—but also interpretive, cognizant of the web of meanings in which the subject matter is embedded. Especially in scholarly discussion, it seems crucial to highlight the multiple nuances of key terms such as "identifications" or "vernacular." I worried that the participants in the "Identifications" network lost some nuances through a positivistic approach to the translations they used in their work.

The multicultural and multilingual "Identifications" network was an ideal crucible for pursuing these questions. It suggested that the movement from one language to another was not only from source to target and back, but, mirroring our global reality, from a multiplicity of sources to a multiplicity of targets. Whereas we might describe the conventional situation of a scholar using a research language as a pendular movement between one language and another, the world of the twenty-first century made such movement multidimensional. It could no longer be assumed that the original text was the only creative force. In the new, multipolar, global scholarship it is possible that the first use of a key concept is not necessarily its fullest expression. It should be expected that subsequent renditions would inflect the original meaning, adding creative interpretations. Of course, a new interpretation might not be accepted by all scholars in the discipline, and dialogue would ensue. A confirmation of Michael's oft-repeated dictum, "translation is a creative force."

In the course of "Identifications," I had come to understand that problems of translation (inaccuracies, incompleteness, misleading or distracting nuances) might be in reality beckoning opportunities to use translation to probe key concepts involved. What had conventionally been considered stumbling blocks in reality might be beckoning opportunities.

Two Examples of Translation Difficulties/Opportunities

The collaborative network on "Official and Vernacular Identifications in the Making of the Modern World" coordinated discussion by historians and social scientists related to group identities—how they arise, how they change, and how they resist from below the often prodigious official efforts to manipulate and restrain them. Research teams in several world areas—China, Southeast Asia, Russia, and France/the French Atlantic world—conducted basic research and produced monographic and analytical papers. Some texts were written in English by native speakers, some in English by non-native speakers, and some in other languages.

A vivid example of the sort of translation difficulty arising in such a multilingual enterprise is the pivotal term "identifications," chosen by the authors of the project's founding statement in preference to the more conventional "identity." In English, the use of "identifications" asserted that group identities are not static facts but processes, not single but multiple. They are at root acts of identifying with—or distancing oneself from—available cultural legacies and material resources, and, of course, the categories imposed by administrative, political, and religious authorities. Despite the fact that the origins of any given set of identifications may not be clearly remembered or may be, in fact, the unintended results of contingent historical events, they nevertheless sometimes "stick" so effectively that people and groups accept them as their own.

Though the CRN never formally defined how "official and vernacular identifications" should be translated, Russian scholars used a standard formula for acknowledging CRN support: "This research was part of the ACLS project on '*Ofitsial'nye i mestnye identichnosti*' ('Official and local identities')."

However, in writing their research papers Russian participants were much less consistent. For one thing, translation of "vernacular" varied from paper to paper in its use of terms that are synonymous, but whose connotations differ significantly: "*povsednevnye*" ("everyday"), "*obydennye*" ("common, usual"), or even "*bytovye*" ("pertaining to domestic life"). These are not incorrect, but none of them convey as stark a contrast to the term "official" as does "vernacular." The heavy association of "vernacular" with the Protestant Reformation, which underscores the contrast, is not meaningful in the Russian language or the Russian historical experience.

The translation difficulties involved not only linguistic choices but also conceptual ones. "*Identifikatsia*" in the singular is an ordinary Russian word, which carries a psychological connotation, e.g., "I identify myself with the Tatar community." The word does not exist in the plural in Russian, as it did not in English until recently. Hence Russian researchers declined to translate "identifications" as "*identifikatsii*," which would be the plural form. But it was important to the authors of the CRN statement to underscore the plural, processive character of identity formation, even at the risk of awkwardness. In terms of the CRN founding statement, if the awkwardness makes the reader stop to think, so much the better.

These translation difficulties may be attributed to at least two characteristics of social science texts. The first is that social science arises in, and deals with, particular societies, and hence the use of terms, and forms of words, are tied to the historical and cultural experiences, and the ordinary language, of a given society. The second is that social science, for the purpose of analysis, tends to aggrandize familiar words for use in specialized senses or simply to invent new words.

Whatever the reasons for the non-acceptability in Russian of the plural form of "identifications" or, for that matter, for its acceptability in English, significant nuance was lost by substituting "identities" for "identifications" and "everyday" for "vernacular."

Michael was delighted to learn about the "Identifications" project and intrigued when I reported to him what I saw as translation difficulties that might in fact be opportunities. At the time, I should note, it still seemed to him that a good translator could iron out any such difficulties. The problem was one for translation, though he was ready to credit that there might be something about social scientific writing, and scholarly writing more generally, that merited special attention. For him the "Identifications" project was a crucible for distilling what, if anything, was distinctive about social science translation, and what might be done to resolve problems that arose.

THE SOCIAL SCIENCE TRANSLATION PROJECT

I approached the Ford Foundation officers who had sponsored the "Identifications" network with a request for funding a project on translation issues that had emerged and that would address broader questions related to translation in a globalizing academy. The Ford Foundation generously decided to sponsor what we called "The Social Science Translation Project (SSTP)."

The project plan began with the legacy of discussion in the "Identifications" network, but its basic intellectual framework was Michael's. He asked key questions: Are there special problems in the translation of academic texts? Who should suggest solutions? How should those who commission translations—who are not, themselves, translators—judge the quality of translations?

Within the framework of this small project, it seemed reasonable to conduct a series of meetings that could produce translation guidelines. Michael and I agreed that the working languages would be the same as those of the CRN "Identifications" and that the participants would be divided into two sections: professional translators and scholars who used translations in their own writing and teaching. The group would begin by translating a set of texts drawn from social science and history, examine the results with a view to identifying problems encountered, compare those problems with translation problems in literary or professional texts (journalism, law, business), and formulate recommendations directed at academics who would wish to commission transmissions in the course of their scholarly activity (including, of course, translations of their own work).

The project could not have stayed on course as well as it did without Michael at the helm. He commanded the respect of every participant, both scholars and translators. He was the only person who knew all four languages; he had translated into English from French and Russian, and he had just begun to revive his Chinese, which he studied at university, but which had been dormant for several decades.

Both translators and social scientists exhibited a bit of curmudgeonly trade-union consciousness: "When it comes to matters lying within our area of expertise, we should make the decisions. Period." Translators were reluctant to have their work discussed critically in the SSTP seminars, especially in the presence of non-translators, even if the discussion was not about the quality of the translation as such, but its implications for scholarship. Social scientists felt they needed to annotate the translations to make sure the source texts' disciplinary nuances were retained and that meaningful interpretations conveyed.

But as the working sessions unfolded, Michael, along with other participants in the project, came to the Socratic realization that it is precisely at the point at which we feel ourselves to be experts that we discover how little we know. Social scientists are experts in social science texts, because they have studied the worldwide literature of their respective disciplines. Yet, as became apparent, they tend to read translations of texts as though they are reading originals, without examining the relation of the two and the choices made by translators. They also assume that, when colleagues hold cross-cultural conversations in a lingua franca, using a mutually agreed terminology, the two sides are talking about the same thing. At a political science conference I attended once in Washington, Americans and

Russians were discussing political power. Both sides would have easily agreed that there was a one-to-one correspondence between the Russian "vlast'" and the English "power." But after several hours of fruitless argumentation, an insightful colleague pointed out that the two sides were operating on two incompatible cultural assumptions. Americans thought of power in the behavioralist formula: "A has power over B, if A can affect B's behavior." Russians, for their part, considered power to be a fundamental force in life and history, akin to an all-embracing fate: "the tsar (or Stalin) has power because he is the top of a pyramidal order in which everyone in the society has a pre-ordained place."

In social science texts, very basic assumptions must be examined, Michael concluded, on principle, persistently. But how? The key to a systematic analysis came in a comment by Immanuel Wallerstein that "social scientists communicate by concepts." Here it needs be said that the name of the SSTP refers to social science, but the discussion ranged over other disciplines, including history, cultural studies, philosophy, and literature. In this article I use the terms "scholarship" and "social science" almost interchangeably. The notion of key concepts focused SSTP deliberations on translation problems characteristic of the social sciences and these other related disciplines.

Discussion could founder, Michael was convinced, if it were conceded at the start that some key concepts were simply untranslatable. No, the *Guidelines* declared, "Translation *is* possible."

If social science translation is possible, then who should do it? Who should judge its quality? What are the criteria of quality? These were the basic questions posed at the outset of the Social Science Translation Project, which were to stimulate production of a set of guides to most effective practice.

Another question quickly surfaced, To whom should these guidelines be addressed? Although translators were crucial to our deliberations, the recommendations would not be written for them. The

Guidelines for the Translation of Social Science Texts,[2] as they were soon called, would not be an instruction manual for translators. The group realized that, if the main questions concerned criteria of quality, the principal audience should be "commissioners," people who commission translations.

The SSTP sponsored a series of workshops for discussion of translations written by project participants. Texts were chosen from various disciplines and from journalism based on scholarly research. Based on this exercise, several criteria of quality emerged. Some are the same as would pertain to any translation: accuracy in conveying the original and fluency in the target.

Translation of any kind must overcome a variety of difficulties in selecting the best dictionary equivalents available (or, as is often necessary, going beyond the dictionary), employing them idiomatically, and situating them in the relevant cultural contexts. Moreover, the fact that terminology often needs to be created rather than translated raises the crucial issue of the degree of "ideological imperialism" implicit in the terms employed and, by extension, in the methodology they support.

Ideally, the process of translation does not move unidirectionally from one language to another; it should be instead a dialogue between cultures. In literary and journalistic translation consensus on the "right expression" for a particular meaning is established through criteria that are not just lexical, but also aesthetic and rhetorical.

Such criteria also govern social science writing and translation; research results are always more compelling when data are presented elegantly and conclusions phrased persuasively. But good social science practice requires something more: accuracy in conveying abstract concepts for defining key terms, for establishing analytical

---

2 *Guidelines for the Translation of Social Science Texts* may be read in Arabic, Chinese, English, French, Japanese, Russian, Spanish, and Vietnamese at www.acls.org/programs/sstp

generalizations, and for framing a larger public discourse. Successful translation from one natural language to another, and from "scientific language" to political and journalistic prose, depends on choosing terms that are both literally accurate and culturally astute. A famous example of a translation that is technically defensible, but nonetheless seriously misleading, is the rendering of Max Weber's "forms of *Herrschaft*" as "forms of domination," when his intention was closer to "forms of political authority" or "political rule." The fact that the social science community accepted the awkward "domination" and used it unselfconsciously, highlights the problem of academic jargon. In such cases social scientists may effectively understand each other, but no one else understands *them*.

Who, Then, Should Translate Scholarly Texts?

The *Herrschaft* example suggests that the reader of a translation of Weber should ever be aware of the gap between contemporary social science discussions (in English) and the historical, cultural, and lexical realities of the source text. The criterion of quality is not "What is the correct translation?" or "What is the most accurate and fluent translation?" but, rather, "What word best conveys the meaning and, at the same time, signals the concepts, contexts, and controversies in which the author of the original chose the term?" In addition, by choosing one word over another, the translator is taking a stand within the contemporary discipline's concepts, contexts, and controversies.

Fluency—how well a translation reads in the target language— often becomes a naturalistic criterion trumping other considerations. It seems reasonable to allow the translator a modicum of freedom (*lege*: laxity) regarding accuracy, for the purpose of making the result read more smoothly and idiomatically. With translation of key scholarly concepts, it might sometimes be best to admit some thought-provoking, unidiomatic strangeness. *Guidelines* distinguishes between "domestication" (allowing translator's license for the purpose of a seamlessly idiomatic translation) and the jumpcut of "foreignization," in which the translator chooses an unidiomatic or not entirely idiomatic expression to remind the reader that a leap has been made from one academic culture to another.

The surprising conclusion of the SSTP deliberations was that the best translators of scholarly texts are not professional translators, but scholars themselves who have taken the trouble to get training in translation (an excellent start on such training is to read the *Guidelines for Translation of Social Science Texts*). Michael did not anticipate this conclusion because it conflicts with translators' wariness when it comes to protecting their prerogatives.

For Michael, the conclusion was clear, because the goal is a fully contextualized translation of key scholarly concepts. It is far easier for a disciplinary specialist to gain training in translation skills than for a professional translator to master the disciplinary literature in a given subject.

What about self-translation? Many scholars whose first language is not English are today under pressure to publish in English. Those, whose command of English allows it, engage in what we might call self-translation. Either they write in their own language and then translate, or they *think* in their own language and write in English. Self-translation violates a bedrock principle of the *Guidelines*—one should always translate from one's weaker language into one's dominant one. What to do? *Guidelines* encourages every scholar to write in his or her own language (not necessarily the native tongue, the language spoken at home, but the language routinely used in the academic community in which the scholar works). By writing in his or her own language, a scholar may best express thoughts and concepts with accuracy and nuance.

If this injunction were to be followed, translation would become more and more necessary, as scholars would come to rely more and more heavily on colleagues to translate their work.

COLLEGIAL TRANSLATION

But who should undertake this task, which might be called "collegial translation"? Colleagues in the relevant disciplines, of course! In thinking of how to honor Michael Heim's memory, the editors of *East European Politics & Societies and Cultures*, on whose editorial board Michael served for many years, decided to establish a prize in his name for excellence in translating into English an article written in an East European language. The translation should be collegial, that is, it should be by a specialist in a relevant discipline. Consultation with the author is possible, but not necessary. Consultation with colleagues who know both languages is highly recommended.

This might turn out to be the most important legacy of Michael's work in the Social Science Translation Project. He had always been concerned with bringing the principles and practices of translation closer to the center of scholarship and PhD training. The SSTP experience gave him arguments and sharpened his suggestions as to how this might be effected.

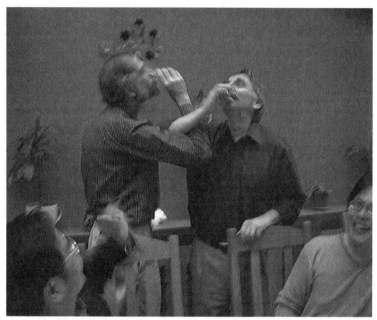

Andrzej Tymowski and Michael Heim formalize their brauderszaft *(brotherhood) at a Social Science Translation Project gathering in Moscow, July 4, 2004, while Chuanyun Bao (left) and Bin Wong (right) look on.*

MICHAEL HENRY HEIM: ON LITERARY TRANSLATION IN THE CLASSROOM

MAUREEN FREELY

We spoke only once, in August 2012. Our Skype connection was shaky, but his voice, whenever it came back to me on a surge of static, was calm and kind and almost beatific. He gave no indication of being pressed for time.

He had been teaching literary translation at UCLA for thirty years, he told me. He'd run his class as a writing workshop because in his view literary translation was a form of literary writing. Whatever else a good translation might aspire to be, it also needed to work as a literary text in English. So the emphasis in his class was on that English text. Students were free to translate into English from any language they wished. When they would read out their translations in class, the other students would put question marks in the margins next to any word, phrase, or sentence that jumped out at them. When the class opened to discussion, the student translators would then explain their choices. They didn't need to justify those choices, but if they said, "I don't know, it just sounds better," Mike would try to draw them out, encouraging them to explore their reasons.

Not once in thirty years of teaching this workshop had he heard a student making a nasty remark. They were all hugely supportive of one another. So he would let them talk, "and then I jump in, with the principles."

"Principles, not rules," he told me. Everything he did in the classroom was "based on an assumption that there are principles you can extrapolate from your work, that you can work with material in a systematic way." His overriding principle was that "languages have a genius of their own—something that makes them different from other languages." He encouraged his students to "characterize their nature" and to see all other languages in terms of genius, too. The genius of English, for example, was its rich vocabulary. "You need to keep that in mind. If you don't take advantage of it, you are losing a resource."

He elaborated his other principles as he talked me through two student translations, drawing from the examples he found on the page. Pay attention to rhythm, he said. Think about register—is it appropriate? Is it consistent? Modal auxiliary words (should, might, may, etc.) were important in relaying nuance, so it was important to get them right. Pay close attention to tense, he said. Different languages used them in different ways. Then there was punctuation, which offered different challenges for translators, because it was so important to keep the flow. "We need to make sure that our punctuation is creative, but based on certain rules. Punctuate long sentences extremely carefully. No colons unless it's very long and complicated. Use the punctuation of the target language but at the same time, stretch its rules." When his students drew back from that challenge, he would try to push them forward. "I tell them they can do it. If they want to, they can."

Concision was another thing to keep in mind. "You're translating from a language with a certain genius and sometimes that does take more words. So balance it with concision." And not to forget logic. "Always make sure that what you're saying makes sense in English." There were also what he called "first and second tier choices." It was important to use the word that reflected how English-speakers spoke, and not the word that seems at first to be its obvious counterpart. For example, German speakers use the word *auch* a great deal more than we in English use the word *also*. If you translate every *auch* as *also*, the text might be correctly translated, but it will also sound German.

Always allow space for the imagination, he said. "For the idea that comes from oneself, as the Germans say. If a student has done something really good, point it out. Tell them it's a beautiful solution."

Above all, they should understand what an important service they were providing. "I believe in translation." It is thanks to the work done by translators that we have access to literatures from across the world. Without translators, even those of us with four or five languages would be shut off from whole continents of great literature. "When I think of all the authors I would never have read . . . ," Mike said, his voice trailing off. And then it came back again: "It's literature that's my passion."

We ended our conversation with promises to stay in touch. The residential course that he had designed for the Arvon Foundation (and that I would now be teaching in his place) was the first of its kind in the United Kingdom. Mike's doctors had decided, very close to the date, that he was not strong enough to fly, but he was still hoping to speak to us by Skype if we managed to get a strong enough signal at the old manor in Yorkshire where we would be based. And then, after the course was over, we would speak again.

I promised to keep him posted.

I remember something opening up in my mind as I rose from my chair. I went into the kitchen, where Frank, my husband, was making dinner, slightly later than usual to allow time for the call from

Los Angeles. "That was amazing," I said. He carried on chopping vegetables. "I feel like I've been handed the crown jewels." He looked up at me with affectionate exasperation. A look I knew well. I tried to explain what I meant. He asked me if I could put the butter back into the refrigerator. "I'm glad I'm doing this," I said. To which he said, "I'm glad you're glad." I remember this very clearly because, as I set the table that evening, I had such a strong sense that this was the beginning of something. And yet in a matter of weeks both my husband and Michael Henry Heim would be dead.

In the end it was not possible to connect Los Angeles with North Yorkshire. But I did send Mike a long and detailed email the day after I got home. And during the weeks that followed, there were a few bright days when I was able to sit down with Frank at breakfast or before supper and talk about the new ideas now swirling in my mind. I could never quite find the words to do them justice, but (as I remember mentioning to Frank) that alone told me I was on to something. I always felt like that in the early stages of a novel.

More than a year has passed since then, and I still feel the loss of the conversations that were not to be. But here I am, holding the crown jewels. So I'll try to use this opportunity to describe them.

Let me begin with the obvious and inevitable: literature is my passion, too. I came into translation very late in the day, after publishing six novels and working for many years as a columnist and literary journalist. I was born in New Jersey, and I returned to America for college, but I spent most of the years in between in Turkey, and I have spent most of my adult life in England (though I have also lived in Texas, California, Connecticut, Florida, Greece, and Spain). With a background like that, it is perhaps not surprising that I have always regarded the very idea of a national literature as a sort of straightjacket, restricting the imagination and occluding the hybrid influences that make us who we are. Steeped as I am in the literatures of English, I would be nothing and nowhere without the many other literatures of the world. But a work of literature that is translated just for surface meaning is not literature.

Each language pair brings its own set of problems—artistic, ethical, and political. Anyone taking works from non-Western languages into English will, at some point, be made to feel the weight of history, and in the menacing shadows they will see their future critics, who, because they rarely agree with one another, representing as they do so many schools of thought, will rarely be in a position to offer blanket approval. It is, for example, impossible for me to translate from Turkish into English without someone somewhere (actually, quite a few someones) defining me as an Orientalist. I am, after all, taking a language previously marked as marginal and trying to take it into the language that rules the world. If I am also trying to make it work in that language, those concerned more with questions of politics than of literature cannot fail to see me as pandering to the dominant culture. If, here and there, I opt against domestication, choosing instead to bring a Turkish word into the English text, I am, some say, exoticizing it. If I change a sentence's grammatical structure, or even just its emphasis, I run the risk of upsetting people who correctly identify the grammatical structure of Turkish as being its greatest beauty. In the eighty or so years since the founders of the Republic decided to subject the language to some of the most severe and sweeping linguistic reforms to be seen in modern times, the grammatical structure was the only thing they didn't touch. How galling, then, to have a translator swan in to reassemble it for foreign consumption.

If I had foreseen these controversies at the outset, I might have swanned off into another, safer art. What drew me into translation was the chance it offered me to take a novel I loved to English-speaking audiences. I wanted to open the door for them, and take them into a world they hardly knew existed. It was as simple as that. Each sentence, paragraph, and chapter threw up new ghosts and dilemmas, but no matter what they were, I knew where I wanted to go, and I did whatever I had to do to get there. So I drew from everything I knew from a childhood of listening to a language I was never formally taught and a lifetime of writing novels. I worked instinctively, naïvely, and without reflection—in much the same way as I might write the first draft of a novel. A sentence or a turn of phrase either worked or it didn't. The problems began when I put the draft to one side to reflect on what I'd done.

This sort of reflection comes easily to me when I am redrafting my own novels. In fact, there would have been no possibility of redrafting without stepping outside the novel to survey it in a colder, clearer light at the end of each day—and letting a finished draft go cold before returning to look at it from the outside and in the round. At the end of each draft, I will go back to the drawing board to ask myself what it is I am trying to say, and where I am trying to go, and what it is about that draft's structure or language or voice that is blocking the way. What I mean to say is that reflecting on practice has always been part of my practice as a novelist.

But when it came time for me to attempt the same as a translator—to understand why I had made the choices I had made while translating (or analyze my practice, as my colleagues at the University of Warwick would prefer me to say), I found myself in a wilderness of competing discourses. And as intriguing as they mostly were, none gave me the language I needed to describe what I'd been trying to do, or what, in my view, literary translation should aspire to. My first inkling that such a language might exist came during that short conversation with Michael Henry Heim, two days before I met the students he had hoped to teach.

My co-tutor was the poet and translator, Sasha Dugdale, and because neither she nor I felt confident that we could deliver the Michael Henry Heim method at the Michael Henry Heim level without his help, we restructured the course so that we could spend

half of each day considering the larger questions of literary translation. Some of these morning-long conversations derived from the
principles Mike had passed on to us; some were our own first experi-
ments with the practice from which these principles were drawn.
In the afternoons, we ran two workshops in parallel. Mine was for
the fiction writers. Sasha's was for the poets, and there were a few
students who went back and forth between the two.

In the long email I wrote to MHH the day after I got home, I
described the students: in our previous correspondence, he had been
very curious about them, having been involved in their selection.
They ranged, I reported,

> from twenty-three-ish to sixty-ish and (like the students
> I've met at other Arvon courses) they were well-read, well-
> traveled, almost painfully well-mannered, and very good
> at talking across the generations. One is a published poet,
> another an about-to-be published novelist. We had quite a
> few commercial translators in search of more meaningful
> work and several young ones just emerging from translation
> studies. The Japanese student is a professor of English at a
> university in Tokyo in her real life. Her (English) language
> skills were limited: although every sentence she wrote was
> correct, she had a harder time with redrafting. But she was a
> very, very acute listener, so in her quiet way she was perhaps
> taking in even more than the others.
>
> I don't think you will be surprised to hear what a sur-
> prise—what a revelation—it was to discover how much we
> were able to notice (and discuss, and reconsider) just by
> marking the words and sentences that jumped out at us.
> On the first day I had privileged knowledge and the upper
> hand, as I knew to look out for rhythm and register, tenses
> and commas, first and second tier choices, and logic. But

by the second day the students had acquired sharper vision, and so from then on our conversations were animated and engrossing. Sometimes I felt like we were archaeologists taking the measure of a new excavation. And every time we turned over a pebble, we discovered more.

A four-day course does not really give students a chance to turn new ideas into second nature, but at Arvon you are removed from the everyday world, and meeting day and night. And there is something to be said for this sort of intensity. Whatever we did, we were always trying to get the students to understand literary translation as literary writing. Following that plan, we used our general discussions to open out and clarify points that had come up during our workshop discussions. So, for example, I took them through a number of short exercises to illustrate what I meant (as a novelist) by voice, and then I showed them how these came into play in passages I myself had translated. We were able to feed all this back into our workshops. One of our best workshop discussions was about the piece you and I discussed during our Skype tutorial. This was the German text about the disaffected music teacher who was twisting his fork around the plate that we did not yet know to be a plate of spaghetti. Here I had the advantage of remembering what you had said about the text. And Jen gave us another opening by saying that what she loved about the original text was its freshness and spontaneity. None of that was in her translation—she was the first to admit this. So what we did was to look for ways to make each sentence clearer and more immediate, so that they caught the unhappy eater's responses, and in the right sequence. Little by little the spirited music of the original began to emerge, and all this in sentences that did not alter the meaning in the slightest.

The flatness of the first draft had come from the emotional distance she had added by falling into a tone that reported rather than evoked. Jen could see this, but because I could see that others in the room did not quite understand what I meant when I spoke about shifts in perspective, I took them through a short writing exercise on perspective the next morning, and then they did get it. And of course this fed into our discussions of other texts that afternoon.

There was another strand of morning discussions and exercises in which Sasha tutored us in poetry-as-music and translation-as-sound. I'm sure she'll tell you about these in more detail. For now I'll just say that I learned as much from her as the students did.

But none of this would have been possible without your ideas, your practice, and your generosity.

For so many years now, I have been telling people that translation is not just a question of technique—that there is more to it than traveling between two languages, a literary discipline that both feeds and is fed by other forms of literary writing. I would spout out these generalities and then my voice would trail off, because I didn't know how to prove my point, or even illustrate it. My more technically minded friends would give me that glazed and understanding smile and turn away. But now you've given us a way to rescue lit trans from the theorists and the technicians. We can begin to draw our principles from our practice, and if we ask ourselves larger questions, too, it will be by drawing from the same pool . . .

I think I'll stop there! One other thing that Arvon courses have if they work well—everyone leaves on a high. That's why I wanted to write to you right away, before the gray everyday reasserts itself. If you have time for another Skype conversation before the 12th of September, that would be wonderful.

I had no idea that he was already in his last decline, with only weeks to live.

But he left us the crown jewels. And they can, I'm discovering, be translated in so many different ways. I imagine that there are already many places in the U.S. where students have gone on to become working translators and who teach by the principles that are now second nature. Here on the other side of the Atlantic it is another story. Or rather, it was. Over the past year we have been discussing his ideas intensely, both in our very active translating networks and in the universities like my own, where we are setting out to teach literary translation in our writing program, while also looking for ways in which poets, novelists, and dramatists can engage in useful conversation with the scholars who study us. The barriers between us are daunting and deep, but we are translators after all, with Michael's principles to guide us.

TRANSLATION AND ALL THAT PALAVER: MICHAEL HENRY HEIM, MILAN KUNDERA, AND BOHUMIL HRABAL

MICHELLE WOODS

If books get to have a Benjaminian afterlife in translation, then translators get to have an afterlife too. Michael Henry Heim lives on in many of our shelves and in two of my favorite novels, Milan Kundera's *The Book of Laughter and Forgetting* (*Kniha smíchu a zapomnění*) and Bohumil Hrabal's *Too Loud a Solitude* (*Příliš hlučná samota*). Both novels are about rewriting: how history is rewritten and how we rewrite our own lives, how things, lives and memories are deliberately forgotten, airbrushed, written out. Both novelists are and were inveterate rewriters; both novels exist in different "original" versions, and both novelists used rewriting (of their work and of their lives) as a means to navigate communism and its aftermath. You might have a hard time finding Heim's translation of *The Book of Laughter and Forgetting*, too: it has been rewritten and retranslated, now sold in a definitive edition, translated from the French by the late Aaron Asher. This new translation, instigated and heralded by the author, aims in a certain way to effectively rewrite the previous translation out of history. A cursory reading of both novels, though, might lead a reader to suspect that however hard we try to forget—and however officially—the past comes back, something rendered not only thematically but also stylistically in both novels, through their use of language and repeated motifs, their subverting voices. And that is where the trouble begins.

In 1972, a young American academic published a translation of a passage from a novel in a small folklore journal. The passage, he argued, showed that the "place of folklore in contemporary society is a pivotal element in one of the most important recent Czech novels, Milan Kundera's *The Joke*."[1] The passage in question, however, had been omitted from the English translation of the novel as the publisher felt it was too "abstruse for the English reader." In an exchange included in the article alongside the translation, Kundera accused his English publishers of censoring the material "in good faith that this would improve the sales . . . The mentality of a London bookseller and that of a Moscow official responsible for art seem to have a mysterious kinship." The English translator and publisher felt that the material did not add anything to the story, which was read as a topical, political narrative about Czech disillusionment with communism. But, in fact, the passage was central to Kundera's nascent thinking about novelistic style: in it a character, Jaroslav, ruminates on the idea of polyphony as a musical form and, in doing so, reflects and refracts the polyphonic style of *The Joke*, constructed as it is around multiple voices, and multiple viewpoints. Kundera felt "powerless," stuck as he was in a post-1968 Prague of "house searches and arrests," but he "had no idea that a young American professor of literature, indignant at the mutilation of *The Joke*, had translated

---

1   Michael Heim, "Moravian Folk Music: A Czechoslovak Novelist's View." *Journal of the Folklore Institute*, 9.1: 45-53.

the most important of the omitted passages and published them in
an American journal."² That young professor was Michael Henry
Heim.

Heim's and Kundera's translation relationship would prove tumul-
tuous. Heim translated three of Kundera's novels: *The Joke, The Book
of Laughter and Forgetting*, and *The Unbearable Lightness of Being*, as
well as his play, *Jacques and His Master*. When Heim's retranslation
of *The Joke* was first published, Kundera wrote in the preface to it,
that he "had done the first valid and authentic version of a book
that tells of rape and has itself so often been violated." Less than a
decade later, Kundera published his own English translation of the
novel, now claiming that he had "barely read" Heim's translation
because he had "a priori confidence in a translator whom I knew as
a defender of my novel."³ Having finally read it, he also now claimed
that it was a "*translation-adaptation*," adapted for "the taste of the
time and of the country for which it is intended" and "to the taste,
in the final analysis, of the translator"; it was "unacceptable to me."
By this time, Heim's translation of *The Unbearable Lightness of Being*
had proven a huge best-seller and even though Kundera insisted on
a retranslation of both *The Joke* and *The Book of Laughter and Forgetting* (along with his other novels and stories written in Czech), *The
Unbearable Lightness of Being* was not re-translated. Kundera's public
denunciation of Heim concealed a much more complex history that
had little to do with Heim's actual ability and work as a translator,
but it is a history that is revelatory about the translation process, a
history tied to market censorship and rewriting.

In June 1979, the French publisher Gallimard sent Nancy Nichols, Kundera's editor at Knopf, Michael Henry Heim's business card:

---

2 Milan Kundera, *The Joke*. Trans. by Michael Henry Heim (London: Penguin,
1984) ix-x.

3 Milan Kundera, *The Joke*. (New York: Harper Perennial, 1993) ix-x.

"Voilà," the Gallimard editor wrote, "the name and address of the genius fallen from the sky. Michael Heim." The editor explained that Heim had contacted Kundera because he wanted to translate an article that had appeared in *Le Monde* and that "Milan admired his Czech, I admired his French; how he writes in English," she added, "is for you to say." Gallimard knew that Nichols was looking for a new translator because of her animosity to Peter Kussi, who had translated *Life is Elsewhere* and *The Farewell Party* and had been asked to translate *The Book of Laughter and Forgetting*. Her problems with Kussi, however, were largely based on commercial difficulties. Kundera was selling well in France but that success had not been replicated in the U.S., and Kussi had kept, quite fairly and politely, demanding more time and more money for his translations. That May he had remonstrated against the contract offered for *The Book of Laughter and Forgetting*, pointing out that the rate per thousand words ($20), "was becoming obsolete when I started in this business fifteen years ago." At the same time, Nichols was under pressure from Kundera's UK publisher, John Murray, who loved the novel, but insisted that any translation "must be right for the UK market." They wanted control over the translation and were demanding, in effect, a British English translation. Their insistence that Kussi showed an "insensitive use of English" was actually located in their resistance to an American English translation and to Kundera's linguistic aesthetics, including longer sentences and his use of repetition. By July of that year, they had read and rejected Heim's translation as well, arguing in a letter to Nichols that it was not "a successful piece of writing in *English*" because the "structure of the sentences, the very order of the words, is still dictated by the original." "While this may work in French," they added sniffily, "in English it results in stilted writing that immediately suggests that it is a translation."

Exasperated, Nichols wrote to Gallimard that "we don't publish [Kundera] for the money but rather for the prestige" and yet, she added, "we keep hoping Kundera may break through here as you have broken him through in France," i.e., that he would become a best-selling success. The idea that Kundera had to be "broken through" of course was related to the question of fluency in the target language. Nichols persistently demanded more fluency from Kundera's transla-tors; she wanted a fluent form of English style that would appeal to American readers and thereby make the books commercially viable. She consistently shortened sentences and added punctuation once the translations had been completed. "P.S.," Kundera had written to her (pointedly, this time in English rather than French), "While read-ing Mr. Kussi's translation please, do not change my long sentences. Do not make them short! I do not like this type of syntax and the American *Life is Elsewhere* suffers from this a bit." Kundera had writ-ten to Kussi explaining his aesthetics and the importance of syntax and punctuation for both "rhythm and meaning," warning him that "you have a tendency toward shorter syntax and simpler punctuation than I." Yet Kundera clearly understood that there was additional editorial pressure: "From what I gathered from the manuscript, Miss Editor consolidates that tendency." He noted that the editorial pen-cil had removed "almost all of the semi-colons." "Maybe it is some typical American translation practice not to respect syntax," he wrote three years later, "but it's not good practice. Imagine if we translated Hemingway into long sentences and Faulkner into short sentences!"

Heim, then, was stepping into the waters between Scylla and Charybdis, facing the demands of an editor who wanted a more fluent, domesticated and commercial Kundera, and Kundera him-self, who was becoming increasingly demanding that his translators adhere to the stylistics and aesthetics of the text. At the end of June 1979, Heim sent Nichols his translation of the "Kundera manuscript" (a section of *The Book of Laughter and Forgetting*) as well as his folk-lore translation; two weeks later Kundera wrote to her that now she had "a nice opportunity to compare [the two translators' work] and decide." He defended Kussi and his work, though at the same time leaving the decision up to her; Nichols sent the Heim translation to Kundera with her comments and he replied with a few notes, writing that in "two or three passages, I have the impression that Heim does not always understand Czech idiom. If you choose him, it is absolutely necessary that I reread and inspect all." Nichols offered Heim a better contract than had been offered to Kussi a few months earlier: $27.50 per 1,000 words and a $1,000 advance (compared to $20 and $514 respectively for Kussi).

After "waiting with impatience for the final result of the work of M. Heim," Kundera wrote in early 1980: "I received it, I read it, I can announce that Michael is an archangel. The translation is magnificent! I read it very attentively and although I found several misunderstandings (which is normal), I was really very happy." He noted that he was "sending a *very, very long letter* with plenty of comments and reflections (which does not at all change the *exceptional* quality of his work) to M. Heim" in Czech, thus not to her (which allowed him to be frank about the aesthetics of the novel) and, with this in mind, he added that "Michael often shortens my sentences . . . but in the third chapter, 'The Angels,' it is necessary to keep the very long sentences which embrace heterogeneous enunciations like in a litany." It was a warning to Nichols not to edit the punctuation once the novel had been translated, a practice Kundera clearly equated with aesthetic and commercial censorship.

The pressures and expectations on Heim, from both publisher and author, were immense. Kundera repeated his insistence that Heim was "an archangel"—with some humor in that it referenced "The Angels" section of the novel, in which Michelle and Gabrielle transform themselves into humorless, unironic angels, flying up beyond laughter. However, a heavenly kind of hyperbole began to be appended to Heim: Nichols's copy editor wrote to her to say that "your celestial is very fluent," and Gallimard referred to him in another letter as "the genius fallen from the sky." Heim, a clearly talented translator, seemed to satisfy both Kundera's stringent and Nichols's commercial demands, but he was also being put under unattainable expectations of translatorial divinity.

Nevertheless, Heim's translation of *The Book of Laughter and Forgetting* proved to be the breakthrough book for Kundera in America. Nichols sold the book to Penguin for the relatively substantial amount of $5,000; Philip Roth, who was a champion of Kundera's ("I introduce Czechs of an erotic bent" as he wrote to Nichols), was editing the "Other Europe" imprint ("as they condescendingly call it" Nichols added) there. It was twice as much as Knopf had received from Penguin for *Laughable Loves* and *Life Is Elsewhere*. Once it was published, the novel garnered "rave reviews": it was described as "an absolutely dazzling entertainment";[4] "a beautifully crafted sonata";[5] "brilliant and original, written with a purity and wit that invite us directly in;"[6] "Dust off the glowing adjectives," John Leonard wrote in the *New York Times*, "because they apply."[7] Charles Michener, in his *Newsweek* article, noted that in Kundera's previous books, "English did not speak with the stunning lyrical precision of this one" and is one of the few reviewers to mention Heim and to suggest that, perhaps "the invisible translator [who] is Michael Henry Heim" might have something to do with it. In general, the reviews completely effaced that "invisible translator" and the fact that the book was translated at all.

---

4   Charels Michener, "Laughter goes into exile: *The Book of Laughter and Forgetting*." *Newsweek*, November 24, 1980.

5   Bart Testa, "Eastern European authors who prefer not to be read as writers of resistance. Novels of Ideas: *The Book of Laughter and Forgetting*." *The Globe and Mail*, September 19, 1981.

6   John Updike, "The Most Original Book of the Season." *The New York Times Book Review*, November 7, 1980.

7   John Leonard, "Books of the Times: Traps are Varied: Music out of History." *The New York Times*, August 15, 1980.

When Nichols sent Kundera the review clippings, he wrote back:

> I think, Nancy, that with this press you can sell the book
> this time, even if the marketing department is not convinced
> that the book will sell, because it is difficult etc. In France,
> *The Book of Laughter and Forgetting* has already sold 80,000
> copies which does not, of course, make it a best-seller (it is
> not my ambition to write best-sellers), but makes it, all the
> same, a bit more than a "modest success."

Despite Kundera's worries about the editorial commercialization
of his books, he was still very aware of the question of commercial
viability and, also, he still had some complaints about the edition: he
wrote he did not want "A Novel by" to be on the cover page to avoid
"the slightly delicate question of genre. The genre of this book is
'book' . . . I deliberately left the genre ambiguous"; and he questioned
some of the punctuation (specifically, a quotation from Ionesco's
Rhinoceros which used ellipses to indicate "eliminated passages"—"it
is too pedantic and too heavy" he wrote and, besides, Ionesco himself had read Kundera's novel and "was not at all unhappy about the
method of citation"). He suggested Nichols change these elements
when the book was reprinted (Kundera clearly certain of its success)
and urged her to use the French edition for comparison because it
was an "authorized and exact" edition. Kundera did not explicitly
explain that he had, in fact, rewritten sections of the novel when
checking the French translation, which was why the French and not
the original Czech was the "exact" version—something that would
become important when Kundera authorized a new translation of the
book by Aaron Asher.

The critical breakthrough success of *The Book of Laughter and
Forgetting* was a poisoned chalice for Nichols; almost immediately
she began to hear rumors that certain "paperback publishers [were]

trying to abduct Milan" from her. She offered him a new translation of *The Joke* "retranslated by the translator you would choose (as you know my vote goes to Michael Heim)" and a book of non-fiction based on Kundera's lectures. *The Book of Laughter and Forgetting* "has finally established you in the place you belong," she wrote, "in the forefront of American literary consciousness." In June, a month later, she wrote that she had heard that Aaron Asher had made a similar offer; Knopf could match any money he offered, she wrote, as they have "lots and now that *The Book of Laughter and Forgetting* has established you it is available as it wouldn't have been before." She asked Kundera: ". . . tell me what a publisher could do to please you . . . I'll come post haste to Paris to woo you." Asher, at Harper & Row, had offered to republish *The Joke* in a new translation, along with Kundera's next novel, both of which would be translated by Heim. Kundera chose Asher.

In 1982, when *The Joke* was re-published by Harper & Row, Charles Michener wrote that Heim, who had made a "brilliant translation" of *The Book of Laughter and Forgetting*, had "translated this fully restored edition of *The Joke*,"[8] noting that it had previously been "mutilated" by its English publishers. Harper & Row paid a $125,000 advance for Kundera's new novel, *The Unbearable Lightness of Being*, also translated by Heim, and it became a runaway international best-seller.[9] Kundera now had control over his texts, because he was a money-making author; between 1985 and 1987 he revised all the French translations of his novels (textually revising them as he did so) and he then turned to the English translations. In 1992, he republished *The Joke*, this time ostensibly in his own translation,

---

8   Charles Michener, "A Landmark Restored: *The Joke*." *Newsweek*, November 8, 1982.

9   Edwin McDowell, "Harper's Wins Rights to Reprint *The Lover*." *The New York Times*, August 15, 1985.

and in 1996, *The Book of Laughter and Forgetting* was re-published, translated from the French by Kundera's editor at Harper Perennial, Aaron Asher. "I had the pleasure," Kundera wrote in an "Author's Note," "of seeing my text emerge in his translation as from a miraculous bath. At last I recognized my book."[10] Heim is not mentioned; just like the opening anecdote of the novel in which Clementis is airbrushed out of the photograph, leaving only a trace—his hat— which he had placed on Klement Gottwald's head, Heim's name is effectively airbrushed out of the history of the translation of the novel.

Still, it was better than Kundera's public rejection of Heim's 1982 translation of *The Joke* in his "Author's Note" to the 1992 edition: "Heim is probably one of the few translators whose reputation could have survived it," Caleb Crain notes.[11] Kundera questioned the accuracy of the translation, especially with regard to syntax, and called it a *"translation-adaptation* (adaptation to the taste and the time and of the country for which it is intended, to the taste, in the final analysis, of the translator)."[12] Kundera has been, quite fairly, challenged about such a public denunciation, but the problem lies in the disingenuousness of the target of the arguments: what irked Kundera were not translatorial issues but editorial ones, especially syntax length, punctuation, typography, and the inclusion of synonyms rather than letting an intended repetition of terms stand. Kundera is most clear about these issues in an essay about another writer, Franz Kafka, called "A Sentence," in which he analyzes three French

---

10 Milan Kundera, *The Book of Laughter and Forgetting.* Trans. by Aaron Asher (New York: Harper Perennial, 1996) 1.

11 Caleb Crain, "Infidelity. Milan Kundera Is on the Outs with His Translators. But Who's Betraying Whom?" *Quick Studies: The Best of Lingua Franca*, ed. Alexander Star (New York: Farrar, Stras and Giroux, 2002) 484-500.

12 Milan Kundera, *The Joke.* (New York: Harper Perennial, 1993) ix-x.

translations of one sentence from *The Castle* and blames the translators, who "sodonymize us" by changing the text into a "good style"
for the domestic market.[13] Yet from his own experience, he was well
aware that these changes were often, if not exclusively, made at the
editorial level.

In a letter to Nichols, Gallimard spoke condescendingly of Kundera's "Slavic paranoia," but his tight control of his these elements of
his novels does seem to be rooted in his early experiences with censorship—*The Joke* spent two years at the Czech censor's office, with
Kundera arguing that he would prefer to not publish the novel rather
than have one word changed; the Czech censors gave up and published the novel. The idea, then, that publishers in the West would
flagrantly change the text for (ultimately) commercial ends outraged
him. Kundera realized, too, that he was in another power structure
in the West as an unknown East European author, that he would
have to negotiate with a publisher's demands and wishes, until he
became, of course, a bestselling author. It is, thus, essential to regard
his run-ins with these structures in order to understand his seeming
animosity to translators: in essence, they became the scapegoats of
commercial practices. The fraught Kundera-Heim relationship is, in
fact, a stepchild of the fraught Kundera-Heim-Knopf-Gallimard-
Harper & Row-John Murray-Faber relationship.

Heim provided excellent and breakthrough translations of Kundera's novels; at the same time, Kundera had a point about his
semantic and syntactical style being continuously undermined but
not, necessarily, by Heim. As we have seen, Kundera was fairly certain that punctuation changes (and, thus, the breath and tone of his
language) were being effected mainly by his editor rather than his
translators *after* the translations had been made. Heim's sensitivity to

---

13 Milan Kundera, *Testaments Betrayed*, trans. by Linda Asher (London: Faber
and Faber, 1996) 109-111.

what Kundera was trying to achieve with his personal style is clear
in a well-known example that Kundera would go on to rewrite, an
example that revolves around untranslatability:

> *Lítost* is a Czech word with no exact translation into any
> other language. It designates a feeling as infinite as an open
> accordion, a feeling that is the synthesis of many others:
> grief, sympathy, remorse and an indefinable longing. The
> first syllable, which is long and stressed, sounds like the
> wail of an abandoned dog.
>
> Under certain circumstances, however, it can have a very
> narrow meaning, a meaning as definite, precise, and sharp
> as a well-honed cutting edge. I have never found an equiva-
> lent in other languages for this sense of the word either,
> though I do not see how anyone can understand the human
> soul without it.[14]

> *Lítost je české slovo nepřeložitelné do jiných jazyků. Označuje
> pocit nesmírný jak roztažená harmonica, pocit, který je syntézou
> mnoha jiných pocitů: smutku, soucitu, sebevýčitek i stesku. První
> slabika toho slova, pronesená s přízvukem a dlouze, zní jako
> nářek opuštěného psa.*
>
> *Za jistých okolností má však lítost význam naopak velmi
> zúžený, zvláštní, přesný a jemný jak ostří nože. Hledám
> pro něho rovněž marně obdobu v jazycích, i když si neumím
> představit, jak bez něho může vůbec někdo rozumět lidské
> duši.*[15]

---

14 Milan Kundera, *The Book of Laughter and Forgetting*, trans. by Michael Henry
Heim (Harmondsworth: Penguin, 1988) 121.
15 Milan Kundera, *Kniha smíchu a zapomnění* (Toronto: Sixty-Eight Publishers,
1981) 130.

ment the notion of repetition, slightly diluted in the first paragraph (in which *pocit* ["feeling"] is repeated three times in Czech, and only twice in English). Heim's is an elegant engagement with the aesthetic intention.

When he revised the French translation of *The Book of Laughter and Forgetting*, Kundera rewrote and condensed the paragraphs, a decision followed in Aaron Asher's retranslation of the novel:

> *Lítost* is an untranslatable Czech word. Its first syllable, which is long and stressed, sounds like the wail of an abandoned dog. As for the meaning of this word, I have looked in vain in other languages for an equivalent, though I find it difficult to imagine how anyone can understand the human soul without it.[16]

It is, of course, a far more direct formulation, conveying what Kundera wants to express, and it is likely that, in rereading the section, Kundera found it too lyrical, yearning and emotional; these adjective-filled sentences that spoke to his keen sense of exile when writing the book, changed in retrospect by an author more fully at home in his adopted culture and language.

Contemporary reviewers, and publishers, blinded by the apparently heady mix of politics, erotics, and philosophy, seemed impervious to the centrality of lexical and semantic style to the meaning of the novels (something Kundera became more conscious of when revising the French translations). The unobtrusive beauty of his prose has been effaced generally in English-language criticism, what Caleb Crain calls the "careful middle path" of his prose, a language "somewhat like a medical manual for home use."[17] But Kundera is

---

16 Milan Kundera, *The Book of Laughter and Forgetting*, trans. by Aaron Asher (New York: Harper Perennial, 1996) 166.

17 Crain, 488.

attuned to everyday euphony, and call and response that does not necessarily translate (as he works with the assonance, for instance, of similar Czech verbal and adjectival endings), that carefully inscribes rhythms and counterpoints. Writing about Kafka, Kundera underlines the danger of not recognizing style in writers whose style is not flagrantly transgressive, but "subtle, barely visible, hidden, discreet."[18] Heim, as a close reader of Kundera's prose (and in epistolary dialogue with Kundera) clearly recognized Kundera's aesthetic intent but had to negotiate the demands of his editors and the expected publishing and commercial norms of the late 1970s and 1980s. The problem with Kundera's maligning of Heim is that it was not about Heim at all, but about the cultural and commercial refiguring of his novels: it is at once important and possible to recognize Heim's excellent work on the translations and, at the same time, to take Kundera's criticisms about his texts seriously in order to question our own expectations as readers and consumers of translations.

When it comes to style and linguistic invention, Bohumil Hrabal is as flagrant as it gets: Heim translated three of his books: *Too Loud a Solitude* (1990), *Dancing Lessons for the Advanced in Age* (1995), and *The Death of Mr. Baltisberger*, the former two for Harcourt, the latter for Doubleday. In his texts, Hrabal moves deftly between literary and pub Czech, invents neologisms, produces expansive, breathless sentences, and revels in recursive prose, all of which structures the black comedy and gives voice to Hrabal's *pábitelé*: gossipers or palaverers, "a talker, rowdy with anecdote," palaverers recounting "anecdote without end."[19] Translating Hrabal is a tall order, requiring great inventiveness, and Heim's work is impressive, capturing the

---

18 Milan Kundera, *Testaments Betrayed*, trans. by Linda Asher (London: Faber and Faber, 1996) 109-111.

19 James Wood, "Bohumil Hrabal's Comic World." *The Irresponsible Self: On Laughter in the Novel* (New York: Picador, 2005) 153-165.

tone of Haňt'a's original voice in *Too Loud a Solitude*, and producing the first translation of—I would argue—one of the great, if underrated, novellas of the twentieth century.

Too Loud a Solitude centers on Haňt'a, a paper compacter, who saves books and wraps his compacted paper bundles in Van Gogh prints. He discovers that he is being superceded by inhuman giant shredders; the novella is a recursive monologue covering beauty, art, love, and inhumanity (modernization, the Nazis, by implication the Communist regime). The rhythm of the prose, its tos and fros, its relentlessness, echoes the rhythm of the machine Haňt'a uses and the recursive, solipsistic rhythm of the human mind and memory. There are three versions of the novella: one in demotic language, one in verse, and one (the one translated) in a slightly more literary style. Most of Hrabal's work existed in different versions, partly because of experimentation and partly out of necessity: he published different versions in samizdat than in the official Communist publishing house, Mladá fronta. The novella was regarded as a political allegory (especially as it was published in the U.S. just after the Velvet Revolution and the fall of Communism), speaking to censorship and the attempted destruction of writers and intellectuals, but it is more than this, as James Wood and Robert Porter argue: it is "a celebration of the world of ideas" in a world that may not appreciate those ideas and the humanity they confer.[20]

Apart from the lexical ingenuity of Hrabal, a tough task to translate in itself, there is also the question of his syntactical ingenuity: "Nowhere does he approach that standard terseness of modern English prose," Mary Hrabik-Samal writes. "Mr. Hrabal does not escape the tyranny of the long baroque Czech sentence." Not only does he

---

20 Robert Porter, "Bohumil Hrabal: Small People and Tall Tales." *An Introduction to Twentieth0Century Czech Fiction* (Brighton and Portland: Sussex Academic Press, 2001) 52-86.

not escape that tyranny, he tyrannizes it, stretching the possibilities of endless clauses almost to breaking point. The problem with "Czech expansiveness and its convoluted, vague sentences," Hrabik-Samal adds, is that when they are translated they can "become verbose and ponderous in English."[21] The translator, and certainly the editors, have to choose how to translate that syntactical inventiveness for a domestic audience. Heim, to his eternal credit, stretches Anglo-American norms for the time fairly far to accommodate Hrabal's general style, as we can see from the following two passages. However, I want to argue that we as readers in the Anglo-American sphere need to push ourselves to accept the strangeness and elasticity of these sentences, to fundamentally comprehend the delicacy of their construction and the importance it has for understanding the text, in a way that perhaps a readership even a generation ago might not have been prepared or willing to do. In some ways, in 2014, I hope that—with postmodernism moving into best-seller status (with writers like David Foster Wallace and Jonathan Safran Foer)—the readership for it has evolved even since 1990, when the novella was first published.

Let me give two examples of how tiny changes in punctuation slightly change and undo the real delicacy of construction and, ultimately, the meaning of the text. The first is the opening two sentences:

> *Třicet pět let pracuji ve starém papíře a to je moje love story. Třicet pět let lisuji starý papír a knihy, třicet pět let se umazávám literami, takže se podobám naučným slovníkům, kterých jsem za tu dobu vylisoval jistě třicet metráků, jsem džbán plný živé a mrtvé vody, stačí se maličko naklonit a tečou ze mne samé pěkné myšlenky, jsem proti své vůli vzdělán, a tak vlastně ani nevím,*

---

21 Mary Hrabik-Samal, "Case Study in the Problem of Czech-English Translation with a Special Reference to the Works of Bohumil Hrabal." *Varieties of Czech: Studies in Czech Sociolinguistings*, ed. Eva Eckert (Amsterdam: Rodopi, 1993).

které myšlenky jsou moje a ze mne a které jsem vyčetl, a tak za
těch třicet pět let jsem se propojil sám se sebou a světem okolo
mne, protože já, když čtu, tak vlastně nečtu, já si neberu do
zobáčku krásnou větu a cucám ji jako bonbón, jako bych popíjel
skleničku likéru tak dlouho, až ta myšlenka se ve mně rozplývá
tak jako alkohol, tak dlouho se do mne vstřebává, až je nejen v
mým mozku a srdci, ale hrká mými žilami až do kořínků cév.[22]

For thirty-five years now I've been in wastepaper, and it's
my love story. For thirty-five years I've been compacting
wastepaper and books, smearing myself with letters until
I've come to look like my encyclopedias—and a good three
tons of them I've compacted over the years. I am a jug filled
with water both magic and plain; I have only to lean over
and a stream of beautiful thoughts flows out of me. My
education has been so unwitting I can't quite tell which
of my thoughts come from me and which from my books,
but that's how I've stayed attuned to myself and the world
around me for the past thirty-five years. Because when I
read, I don't really read; I pop a beautiful sentence into my
mouth and suck it like a fruit drop, or I sip it like a liqueur
until the thought dissolves in me like alcohol, infusing brain
and heart and coursing on through the veins to the root of
each blood vessel.[23]

Heim's translation is beautiful; he captures Haňt'a's tone and the
language well, and, like Haňt'a, is attuned to the sound of that
language—for instance, in the last sentence, his awareness of the

---

22 Bohumil Hrabal, *Městečko, kde se zastavil čas / Něžný barbar / Příliš hlučná*
*samota. (*Prague: Odeon, 1992) 181.
23 Bohumil Hrabal, *Too Loud a Solitutde*, trans. by Michael Henry Heim (New
York: Harcourt, 1990) 1-2.

importance of euphony in conveying the ingestion of the "beautiful sentence" by his use of verbs: "pop," "suck," "drop," "sip." Parts of the passage are untranslatable, notably Hrabal's use of an English phrase "love story" in the first sentence, which is funny and beautiful and sad, but seems a little more prosaic actually in English (using French as a substitute, "l'histoire d'amour," for instance, would make him sound pretentious, or using Italian, slightly silly), but on the whole it's a lovely translation.

However, the editorial element—the use of punctuation—while normalizing the passage for modern Anglo-American readers, dilutes the effect, meaning, and aesthetics of the prose. The English translation is split into five sentences (two of which are further split by semi-colons), which clarifies the "beautiful thoughts," showing them clearly and rationally moving from fact to metaphor ("I am a jug"), back to fact and back to metaphor ("suck it like a fruit drop"). In Czech, all of these thoughts flow from each other: there is the terse first (and funny) sentence, mixing wastepaper and love story, followed by one long (in the printed book, nearly thirteen lines long) lovely thought that enacts the first metaphor of Haňt'a being "a jug" who "lean[s] over and a stream of beautiful thoughts flows out of me," and these thoughts flow out through the commas and clauses until the "thought dissolves in me like alcohol" flowing through his body. What is so beautiful about this is the rhythm in the repetition of terms: his seniority in the job, "thirty-five," his "thoughts," the repetition of conjunctions, "and so," "because," "which" and sonorous, rhythmic clusters of terms—"*plný živé a mrtvé vody*" "*které myšlenky jsou moje a ze mne a které jsem vyčetl*," "*když čtu, tak vlastně nečtu*," "*v mým mozku a srdci*." These are the bass rhythm of the passage, and the form—the endless commas, the flowing of thought—its melody. We see the man and the machine (and the kinetic connection of the two) come alive in the language.

The second example comes later on in the novella. A gypsy girl who had followed Haňťa home and lived with him, disappears. He finds out that she was killed in a concentration camp and in an almost page-long sentence, describes his joy in destroying all the left-over Nazi propaganda after the war. It is an incredibly beautiful, moving, and devastating sentence, all the while conveyed in the motions of destruction: Haňťa destroying the material just as human lives were destroyed, and at the same time ending up with the image of Ilonka, the gypsy girl, in the motions of her day-to-day existence, conveyed with a sense of the sacred nature of her quotidian movement. The movement of the passage—from photographs of the cheering multitude, to photographs of Hitler, to the individual gypsy girl—encapsulates the sense of the danger of crowds, of the loss of individuality, conditions ripe for tyranny and genocide; the only thing that can stop such madness is the re-focusing on the human, the individual, kept alive in Haňťa's memory, as he destroys and outlives the remnants of the thousand-year Reich:

> *Když skončila válka, ještě v padesátých letech jsem míval plný sklep nacistické literatury, s ohromnou chutí ve světle líbezné sonáty mé malé cikánky jsem presoval metráky těch brožur a knížek na to samé téma, lisoval jsem statisíce stránek s fotografiemi jásajících mužů a žen a dětí, jásajících starců, jásajících dělníků, jásajících sedláků, jásajících esesáků, jásajících příslušníků armády, do koryta mého hydraulického lisu jsem s chutí házel Hitlera a jeho svitu, vstupující do osvobozeného Danzigu, Hiltera vstupujícího do osvobozené Varšavy, Hiltera vstupujícího do osvobozené Prahy, Hiltera vstupujícího do osvobozené Vídně, Hiltera vstupujícího do osvobozené Paříže, Hitlera v jeho soukromém bytě, Hitlera na žňových slavnostech, Hitlera s jeho věrným vlčákem, Hitlera u jeho frontových*

vojáků, Hitlera skloněného nad vojenskými mapami, a čím víc
jsem presoval Hitlera a jásající ženy a muže a děti, tím víc jsem
myslel na svoji cikánku, která nikdy nejásala, která nechtěla
nic jiného než přikládat do kamen a vařit bramborový guláš s
koňským salámem a chodit do velikého džbánu pro pivo, nechtěla
víc než lámat chleba jako svatou hostii a pak se dívat otevřenými
dvířky do kamen na plameny a zář, na melodický hukot ohně,
zpěv ohně, který znala od svého dětství a který byl sakrálně spjat
s jejím kmenem, ohně, jehož světlo nechává pod sebou všechen
žal a vyluzuje na tváři melancholický úsměv, který byl odrazem
cikánčiny představy o dokonalém štěstí . . .[24]

Well into the fifties my cellar was piled high with Nazi
literature, and there was nothing I enjoyed more than
compacting tons of pages with pictures of cheering men,
women and children, cheering graybeards, cheering workers, cheering peasants, cheering SS men, cheering soldiers.
I got a specially big kick out of loading my drum with
Hitler and his entourage entering liberated Danzig, Hitler
entering liberated Warsaw, Hitler entering liberated Prague,
Hitler entering liberated Vienna, Hitler entering liberated
Paris, Hitler at home, Hitler at harvest festivals, Hitler
with his faithful sheepdog, Hitler visiting troops at the
front, Hitler inspecting the Atlantic wall, Hitler en route
to the conquered towns of East and West, Hitler leaning
over military maps. And the more I compacted the cheering men, women, and children, the more I thought of my
Gypsy girl, who had never cheered, who had wanted nothing more than to feed the fire, make her potato goulash,

24 Bohumil Hrabal, *Městečko, kde se zastavil čas / Něžný barbar / Příliš hlučná*
samota. (Prague: Odeon, 1992) 219.

and fill my large pitcher with beer, nothing more than to break her bread like the wafer at Communion and look into the stove door, transfixed by the flames and heat and noise of the fire, the song of the fire, which she had known since childhood and which held sacred ties to her people. It left all the pain behind and coaxed a melancholy smile to her face, a reflection of pure happiness.[25]

Heim, I suspect, is working from a different manuscript than the Czech edition (as he includes and excludes some material, at the beginning of the passage "After the war," and the inclusion of a couple of extra clauses: "Hitler inspecting the Atlantic wall, Hitler en route to the conquered towns of East and West"). But he does a really admirable job here in keeping the rhythm and repetitions of Hrabal's prose, which reflect, with absurd humor, the rhythm of the destruction Haňt'a and the world has undertaken. That the sentence is split into four sentences rather than the page-long sentence in Czech may seem irrelevant, too much of a quibble (and I think Heim understood and defended the length of what he could do, given publishing norms), but it should be pointed out because even such a tiny change alters the impact of the passage.

In the English translation, Haňt'a becomes more declamatory and decisive; after destroying the "pictures of cheering men, women and children, cheering graybeards, cheering workers, cheering peasants, cheering SS men, cheering soldiers," he stops, as indicated by the period, and then declares, "I got a specially big kick out of loading my drum with Hitler." Once he dispenses with the pictures of Hitler ("Hitler en route to the conquered towns of East and West, Hitler leaning over military maps"), he stops again and rationally decides:

---

25 Bohumil Hrabal, *Too Loud a Solitutde*, trans. by Michael Henry Heim (New York: Harcourt, 1990) 1-2.

"And the more I compacted the cheering men, women, and children, the more I thought of my Gypsy girl." Finally, he remembers her by the fire and pauses again, clearly telling us in a separate sentence what that fire represented: "It left all the pain behind and coaxed a melancholy smile to her face, a reflection of pure happiness." We can see the decisive and rational movement of his thoughts. Yet to some extent it alters his character and the very delicately balanced rhythm of the prose.

On the one hand, the rhythm is not subtle, with its pounding repetition of "cheering" and "Hitler" and "fire" that conveys the rhythm of the compacter and of Haňťa's anger and sadness and the bombast—associated with the propaganda he is destroying—that articulates the stirring up of the crowds and their complicity in the making of the dictator. In the Czech text Haňťa moves seamlessly between destroying the "cheering crowds," and destroying "Hitler," and thinking of the gypsy girl: *"Hitlera u jeho frontových vojáků, Hitlera skloněného nad vojenskými mapami, a čím víc jsem presoval Hitlera a jásající ženy a muže a děti, tím víc jsem myslel na svoji cikánku, která nikdy nejásala . . ."* / "Hitler with his troops at the front, Hitler bent over military maps, and the more I compacted Hitler and the cheering women and men and children, the more I thought about my gypsy girl who never cheered . . ." (my translation). The delicate link between the cheering individuals—now a crowd—and the rise of Hitler is articulated in the comma between them; and the revenge that Haňťa takes is also seamlessly articulated above in the innate connection between the rhythm of his actions and his thoughts. The seamlessness of the passage is vital; it is typical of Haňťa's voice (his palavering) but also innately connects the actions of the individuals-become-crowds and brings the horror back to the individual, resurrecting the murdered girl—giving her back her humanity—in Haňťa's memory.

The passage clearly also relates to its Communist context, without saying so explicitly, and to get the novella published in Czech Hrabal played his own ambiguous game of commas and clauses: for him, his "refusal to be polite, and stop talking" was "my defence against politics, my policy in fact."[26] In his memoir *Totální strachy* (*Total Fears*), he relates his avoidance of Václav Havel and signing the dissident petition, *Několik vět* (*A Few Sentences*), so that he can publish the novella under Communism (ironically in November 1989) in a similar, and signature, style (the style that is his means of protest):

> Because I wouldn't swap that signature on "A Few Sentences" for eighty thousand copies of my *Too Loud a Solitude*, due in November, I won't swap "A Few Sentences" for the eighty thousand afterwords by Milan Jankovič . . . I mean, Dubenka, the only purpose of my being in this world has been to write this *Too Loud a Solitude*, that *Solitude* which Susan Sontag in New York said was one of the books, the twenty books that form the image of the writing of this century . . .[27]

In fact, as he writes later in the book: "Susan Sontag said, the way Mike Heim had translated my *Too Loud a Solitude*—she thanked me for it—she reckoned it would be one of the twenty books of the twentieth century. Michael Heim, a Hungarian with Gypsy blood by the way, so he's Ost-Modern too."[28] Hrabal's—and Sontag's—appreciation for Heim's work is clear, as is Hrabal's personal connection with

26 Adam Thirlwell, *The Delighted States* (New York: Farrar, Straus and Giroux, 2007).
27 Bohumil Hrabal, *Total Fears: Letters to Dubenka*, trans. by James Naughton (Prague: Twisted Spoon, 1998) 68.
28 Ibid. 78.

and respect for a fellow "Ost-Modern" (a term invented by another translator, Paul Wilson, to describe postmodern Czech texts). Heim's translations of Hrabal's work established him, at least among writers and critics, in the Anglo-American world and did well, demonstrating a nuanced understanding of Hrabal's particular lexicon and style. The limitations lay in the expected norms of Anglo-American culture, in the expectation, perhaps, that readers anticipating a book about politics and dissidence might not have the patience for Hrabal's "policy," for his endlessly digressive refusal to stop talking.

Heim's contribution to the translation of modern Czech literature is central; he was a pioneer translator for, then, relatively unknown writers from what was perceived as a marginal culture. The high regard with which Kundera's and Hrabal's work is held underscores that Heim's work should be celebrated and remembered with an additional acknowledgment of the strictures pioneer translators had to (and often still have to) function within: resistance in the target culture to new voices; hegemonic assumptions toward other cultures, especially within the Anglo-American sphere; an insistence (among mainstream publishers) with new foreign-language writers that they somehow fit into normative domestic and commercial aesthetics; and a dismissive attitude toward translators, who were supposed to be neither seen nor heard. Heim's translations of Kundera and Hrabal articulate the tightrope walk between the authors' aesthetic styles and the style and power over the text insisted upon by the Anglo-American publishers. That Kundera's and Hrabal's voices came through so strongly (and successfully, in commercial and critical terms) in these pioneer translations shows that another voice—Heim's—delineated a path that allowed them passage.

O PIONEER!
MICHAEL HENRY HEIM AND THE POLITICS OF
CZECH LITERATURE IN ENGLISH TRANSLATION

ALEX ZUCKER

I.

Czech literature has long dwelled in the shadow of not only of its big brother, Russian, but also its linguistically friendlier European cousins. Without skilled, committed, and persevering translators, it doesn't stand a chance. Fortunately, it had Michael Henry Heim.

Of the dozen tongues Heim mastered well enough to translate, Czech is the one he's most strongly identified with. Ten of the more than thirty book-length works he brought into English during his lifetime were written by Czechs (four by Milan Kundera, three by Bohumil Hrabal, plus one each by Jan Neruda, Karel Čapek, and Josef Hiršal), and most of his renown as a translator, to this day, rests on three of them: *The Unbearable Lightness of Being* (Kundera), *The Book of Laughter and Forgetting* (Kundera), and *Too Loud a Solitude* (Hrabal).

Even a translator as great as Heim, though, works under constraints, including international politics and publishers' preferences. In writing this essay I tried to gauge Heim's impact on Czech literature in English, and discovered it wasn't so simple, in some interesting ways. His impact on me, on the other hand, is pretty clear.

II.

Until I read *The Unbearable Lightness of Being*—Heim's 1984 translation of *Nesnesitelná lehkost bytí*, loaned to me in 1985 or '86 by a college girlfriend who'd been assigned it for a poli-sci course—my only consciousness of Kundera's native country derived from the fact that every vulcanized rubber disk I dribbled, poke-checked, or slapshot during my eight years playing hockey as a kid growing up in Michigan was, according to the stamp on the side, MADE IN CZECHOSLOVAKIA. That and the "Wild and Crazy Guy" skits by Steve Martin and Dan Aykroyd on *Saturday Night Live*.[1] In other words, zilch. We didn't learn about Eastern Europe in school. Actually, we didn't learn much about Western Europe either, but at least I'd heard of the countries.[2]

Kundera's depiction of Czechoslovakia sparked my curiosity enough that in summer of '86, after I had graduated, I bought a copy of *The Book of Laughter and Forgetting*, Kundera's third novel and

---

1   And also Kafka. But Kafka isn't really Czechoslovakia. In fact I'd argue he isn't really even Prague. He's just Kafka.

2   Most of what I knew about Europe before I went to college had come from my mother's parents, who were French and Jewish and emigrated to New York, by way of Portugal and England, when Nazi Germany invaded France in 1940. My father's parents were also European Jews (from towns now belonging to Austria and Poland) and also settled in New York, but came before World War II and died before I had a chance to talk with them about their pasts.

another Heim translation (1980, from *Kniha smíchu a zapomnění*), which made an even bigger impression on me. What attracted me to Kundera's writing wasn't the sex so many reviewers go on and on about, or the political implications, or the philosophical asides, but the fragmented structure of the narrative, the black humor, and the fact that it portrayed a Europe I never knew existed before.

> The mechanic leaned down over the engine and said, "Right in the middle of Prague, Wenceslaus Square, there's this guy throwing up. And this other guy comes along, takes a look at him, shakes his head, and says, 'I know just what you mean.'"[3]

This wasn't the Europe I met for the first time in summer of '85, between my junior and senior years of college: England, France, Italy, Germany, Switzerland, a Europe of churches and art and cross-continental trains and river-split metropolises and—this much was the same—history, relentlessly, in every nook and cranny, especially "the war." Wherever I went I met older people, mostly men, who insisted on telling me what had happened during World War II, right there, on that very spot. Yet these West European stories of death and suffering and hunger were all set in the past, while the stories of death and suffering and hunger (or, at least, privation) were still in the present for East Europeans. I needed to know more.

So, one Heim translation of a Kundera novel led to another, which led to a one-week visit to Brno (Kundera's hometown) and Prague in spring '87 (with the girlfriend who had loaned me *Unbearable Lightness*), which led to a month-long stay in Czechoslovakia in summer '87 (including two weeks in an international youth labor

---

3   p. 7 (Part One: Lost Letters), *The Book of Laughter and Forgetting*

camp, promoting understanding across the Iron Curtain), which led
to a burst of reading on Czechoslovak history in fall '87, which led
to an application in winter '87/'88 to study international affairs at
Columbia (the only university in the country that had both a master's program in international affairs and somebody teaching Czech),
which led to my first class in Czech, in spring '88, with Karen von
Kuneš at Harvard University's Extension School, in Cambridge, and
in fall '88 I entered the School of International and Public Affairs, in
New York, where for the next two years I studied Czech with Peter
Kussi, who had previously translated two of Kundera's novels (*Life
Is Elsewhere* [*Život je jinde*], 1974; and *The Farewell Party* [*Valčík na
rozloučenou*], 1976). When I took my first course with him, he was
at work on a third (*Immortality* [*Nesmrtelnost*], 1991). In our first
class he gave us a Miroslav Holub poem to read, in both the Czech
original and the English translation. By the time I'd spent two years
studying Czech with Kussi, I had caught the translation bug.

III.

The dominant image of not only Czech but *all* of East European
literature in the '70s and '80s, for most English speakers, came from
Penguin's "Writers from the Other Europe" series, edited by Philip
Roth from 1974 to 1989. Seventeen books by eleven authors from
three countries. Geography aside, what did they have in common?
They were male, heterosexual, intellectual, and most were critical of
communism as well. (Although the Polish authors confront Nazism
rather than communism, from a marketing standpoint the principle
of writer-against-oppressive-ideology is essentially the same.)

In short, the large success and high visibility of Czech literature
in the 1970s and '80s relative to the small population of the Czech

lands[4] was due as much to the ideological perception of Czech writers as dissidents championing Western values of freedom and democracy in the face of an oppressive regime as it was to the quality of the literature itself.

Certainly the Czech authors Heim is best known for translating, Kundera and Hrabal, fit this paradigm, each in his own way. Kundera, along with many other young Czech intellectuals, joined the Communist Party after World War II. He was then expelled, allowed to rejoin, and expelled yet again. In the wake of the 1968 Soviet invasion, he was branded a counterrevolutionary. He lost his position teaching literature at Prague's FAMU film academy and his books were banned. In 1975, he left the country and took up residence in France. Hrabal, on the other hand, was never a Party member, and never held a position that could be called intellectual, moving instead through a series of odd jobs, which not only afforded him more freedom (and time to drink) but also brought him into contact with a wider range of people than he would have encountered otherwise, and provided more colorful material than a teaching or desk job would have. To most of his English-speaking audience, though, he was viewed (marketed?) as a resister, defending Western cultural values against the Communist barbarians.[5]

---

4 The term for the three historical regions of Bohemia, Moravia, and Czech Silesia (Čechy, Morava, Slezsko), which today comprise the Czech Republic. In the '70s and '80s, as today, their population was about 10 million. Slovakia had another 5 million people or so, giving Czechoslovakia as a whole a population of roughly 15 million.

5 This is of course a reductive view—as Jonathan Bolton, a professor of Slavic languages and literatures at Harvard, has pointed out (http://zpravy.idnes.cz/o-uskalich-prekladu-i-kauze-kundera-s-bohemistou-z-harvardu-p4o-/kavarna. aspx?c=A090918_165220_kavarna_bos)—based solely on the two authors' works published in English, which in Hrabal's case amounts to but a tiny slice of his oeuvre and in Kundera's case, as Jan Čulík notes (http://www2.arts.gla.ac.uk/Slavonic/Kundera.htm), ignores his writing of the '50s and early '60s, especially his poetry and nonfiction, which were heavily laced with Marxist dogma.

The political slant of Czech literature translated into English prior to '89 has been noted before, but to be honest, I find the overwhelming maleness even more striking. Heim is in good company in this regard: It turns out none of the best-known translators of Czech into English during my life—Heim, Kussi, or Paul Wilson—has translated a book-length work of literature by a Czech woman.[6]

As you might guess, there's a long history to this: A bibliography of Czech literature published in English in 1980 cites roughly one hundred and seventy works by men versus seven by women.[7] Nor is it simply a question of the translator's gender. A survey of works published by female translators of Czech reveals the same overwhelming bias in favor of male authors (generally with smaller, less prestigious publishing houses, as well as to lesser acclaim and almost certainly with lower sales).[8]

I want to be clear that I'm not pointing the finger at Heim (or

6 Meanwhile a survey of anthologies of Czech literature in translation from the same decades as "Writers from the Other Europe" reveals the names of a dozen women who were repeatedly anthologized and therefore presumably worthy of translation: Eva Kantůrková, Eda Kriseová, Daniela Fischerová, Zuzana Brabcová, Tereza Boučková, Daniela Hodrová, Alexandra Berková, Lenka Procházková, Věra Linhartová, Sylvie Richter(ová), Zdena Salivarová, and Iva Pekárková. Only five of the twelve have had full-length works translated into English: Kantůrková, Fischerová, Hodrová, Salivarová, and Pekárková. Only one, Pekárková, was published by a house as prestigious as those of Kundera or Hrabal.

7 George J. Kovtun, *Czech and Slovak Literature in English: A Bibliography*, Second Edition (Washington: Library of Congress, 1980). http://lcweb2.loc.gov/service/gdc/scd0001/2007/20070628001cz/20070628001cz.pdf

8 Marie Winn (Jiří Weil, Salivarová, three Havel plays), Norma Comrada (Karel Čapek), Vera Blackwell (first English translator of Havel's plays), Iris Unwin (Ladislav Fuks: *Mr. Theodore Mundstock*; Lustig: *Diamonds in the Night*; Olbracht, Grosman), Marketa Goetz-Stankiewicz (one Klíma play; otherwise mainly editor of Havel and other drama), Edith Pargeter (Neruda: *Tales of the Little Quarter*; Němcová: *The Grandmother*; Mácha: *Máj*; Hrabal: *Closely Observed/Watched Trains*, Vančura: *The End of the Old Times*; Josef Bor: *The Terezín Requiem*; Klíma: *The Jury* and *A Ship Named Hope*), Suzanne Rappaport (Kundera: *Laughable Loves*), Jeanne Němcová (Škvorecký, Lustig), Káča Poláčková Henley (Škvorecký, Vaculík).

any other translator). Among other things, I have no way to know whether he proposed projects by female writers that were rejected. And as Michelle Woods makes abundantly clear in *Translating Milan Kundera*, editors and publishers have historically been the ones wielding the power to decide who and what is published.[9] What I would conclude, though, is that while Heim, through the excellence of his translations, certainly raised the profile of Czech literature in English, he didn't alter the prevailing image of it. It took history to do that.

IV.

While Czech authors wrote and published, when they managed to do so at all, under restrictive conditions in the Communist system, their translators, too, had a hard time finding out what they were writing and getting hold of it. Many of the Czech novels translated into English during the '70s and '80s weren't published in Czechoslovakia itself but in exile publishing houses such as 68 Publishers, founded and run by Zdena Salivarová and Josef Škvorecký in their adopted home of Toronto from 1971 to 1994.[10]

---

9 Woods also argues in this volume that editors and publishers had more power then than now in determining the style of an author in translation. I can attest from personal experience that all of the issues she notes in the final paragraph of her essay ("resistance in the target culture to new voices; hegemonic assumptions toward other cultures, especially within the Anglo-American sphere; an insistence [among mainstream publishers] with new foreign-language writers that they somehow fit into normative domestic and commercial aesthetics; and a dismissive attitude to translators, who were supposed to be neither seen nor heard"), with the exception perhaps of the last one, which has improved in recent years, remain pertinent today.

10 Petr Koura and Pavlína Kourová, "Sixty-Eight publishers—books of dissent," trans. Anton Baer, *Presseurop*, Dec. 27, 2011. http://www.presseurop.eu/en/content/article/1321271-sixty-eight-publishers-books-dissent

With the end of communism in 1989 came an explosion of Czech publishing that also made much more available to translators—more women, more genres, and not just new writers but old ones as well, sometimes in unabridged or uncensored editions for the first time. Whether translations have reflected that change is a separate question of course. To give a few examples: In 1990, Bára Basiková, known primarily as a rock singer, published a book that had been circulating in samizdat since 1982, *Rozhovory s útěkem* (*Conversations with an escape*), which featured a love affair between two women, including sex scenes, previously a taboo; Hrabal himself compared its style to Episode 18 of Joyce's *Ulysses*. *Paci, paci, pacičky* (*Pattycake, pattycake*) by Václav Bauman (a pseudonym for František Růžička), also originally published in samizdat in the '80s, was a comic novel about the childhood and early teens of a boy growing up under "real socialism" that in 1990 became the first openly gay novel published in post-Communist Czechoslovakia. A few women writers who began publishing only after 1989 and have met with critical success are Iva Pekárková, also an outlier in that she began writing only after leaving Czechoslovakia and all of her novels take place in foreign countries; Eva Hauserová, a biologist by training, unique in that she's one of the country's few self-declared feminists and also one of its few science fiction writers; and Daniela Hodrová, a literary scholar as well as an author, who began writing in the '70s but saved it all, eschewing even samizdat, till the '90s, when, in rapid succession, she published her first three novels, typically described as postmodern and often compared to Kundera's. Again, this is just a sampling to illustrate the increase in variety and diversity of authors published in Czech since 1989.[11]

---

11 For more on women authors, see for example Elena Sokol, "Diverse Voices: Czech Women's Writing in the Post-Communist Era," *Argument*, vol. 2, no. 1, 2012. http://argumentwp.vipserv.org/wp-content/uploads/2012/pdfv2n1/argument-3-03-Sokol.pdf

I would be lying if I said I was fully aware of this history when I myself began to translate, living in Prague in the early '90s. I only knew I didn't want to do any "old" authors—that is, authors who had been translated before—and of course I knew what I liked.[12] The point is, I had vastly more choices than Heim ever had. In general, translators from Czech to English, in choosing authors and texts, like Czech readers themselves, no longer need consider a writer's political status. By the same token, U.S. and UK publishers can no longer claim to be supporting freedom, democracy, and human rights by the act of publishing an East Bloc writer, or sell a Czech novel by telling readers it will offer them a peek behind the Iron Curtain. (One reflection of this was Northwestern University Press's decision, announced in 2011, to shut down its Writings from an Unbound Europe imprint.)

Yet, even in this new, enlarged world of Czech literature, Heim's influence continued, if in less conspicuous ways. I recently learned, thanks to Breon Mitchell, who has gathered Heim's papers in the Lilly Library at Indiana University, that Heim played a role in one of my own translations: It turns out he wrote the reader's report for *Paměť mojí babičce*, Petra Hůlová's eye-opening first novel, which I translated for Northwestern University Press as *All This Belongs to Me* (2009).

Reader's reports, for those who aren't familiar with them, are solicited by publishers who are interested in a foreign book but don't read the language, so they ask somebody, often a translator, to read the book in question and provide a summary of the plot, an idea of where the book fits in to the literature of the country it comes from, and an estimation of how likely the book is to appeal to the

---

12 My first published literary translation, if I remember correctly, was an excerpt from *Paci, paci, pacičky* in *Yazzyk* magazine (tagline: "mostly writing from Eastern Europe"), in 1993. http://www.scribd.com/doc/26366775/Yazzyk-Magazine-Issue-Two-1993-Erotica-sexuality-and-gender

publisher's audience. Though they typically run two pages or less, they can carry enormous weight, particularly when the reader is a recognized authority. Heim, of course, was one such authority, and in this way, at least in this case, he had a hand in bending the arc of Czech literature in a new direction.

All This Belongs to Me, except for being contemporary and literary, represented a break with the typical Czech novel translated into English. It is written by a woman, with all female characters, and no mention of politics or living conditions in the Czech lands—because the story takes place entirely in Mongolia, where Hůlová spent nearly a year as an undergraduate in cultural studies and Mongolian studies at Charles University. Although the novel wasn't widely reviewed in the English-language press, it did receive a write-up in the notoriously hard-to-crack *Times Literary Supplement*[13] and the annual award of the American Literary Translators Association, indicating at least some level of recognition by important arbiters of culture that it was an unusual and noteworthy book.

So, to return to the question of how greatly Heim altered the image of Czech literature in English translation, I think the answer depends not only on the works he translated himself over the years, but also on the works he championed via reader's reports. I have no idea how many such reports he wrote—we'll probably never know—but a full reckoning of his impact would have to take them into account. (Scholars, the glove has been thrown down.)

Over the years I've come to realize that being a translator carries with it a burden of responsibility. Given how little a typical literary translation pays, at a certain point I decided, for my own mental health, to view my work as a service—to the authors whose books I translate, to the readers who read and (I hope) enjoy those books,

---

13 A search of the *TLS* website suggests that, as of 2009, the only living Czech writers to have had translations of their works reviewed in the *Times Literary Supplement* were Hrabal, Kundera, Havel, Klíma, and Škvorecký.

to the Czechs whose perspective and culture I help propagate (even if that's not my main goal), and, ideally, to literature itself (whatever that means). All the evidence indicates that Michael Henry Heim felt the same.

There's no doubt English-speaking readers' (and publishers') expectations have evolved since 1990. But if Heim and his peers, the "pioneer translators" as Wood calls them, succeeded in moving Czech literature away from the margin and toward the center of contemporary culture, maybe part of my generation's responsibility is to consider who's been marginalized *within* Czech literature and to try, while meeting the same high aesthetic standards that Heim set during his career, to bring them toward the center as well.

THE UN-X-ABLE Y-NESS OF Z-ING (Q): A LIST WITH NOTES

SEAN COTTER

the unbearable lightness of being
the unbearable lite-ness of being
the unbearable blightness of being
the unbearable nice™ness of being
the unbearable "like"ness of being

Milan Kundera opposed using "the unbearable lightness of being" to title the English translation of his *Nesnesitelná lehkost bytí*, even though it is relatively close to the Czech original. "I realize that for you Americans the title will be a bit hard-going," Kundera states in Michael Heim's account,

> "so we can try something else," and he suggested one of the chapter titles: "Karenin's Smile." I protested. "We're not children," I told the editor. "If *The Unbearable Lightness of Being* is the title, so be it."

Heim's translation, like a spot of dye, dropped into the flow of culture and altered the hue of English as it diffused downstream. A meme before memes, the snowclone of Central Europe, the breadth of this title's reach lets us see something we know is true but can rarely prove: translation choices transform our language and our experience of the world.[1] The list in this essay, all actual examples, is drawn from internet and library catalog searches of article, chapter, blog, and book titles.

the unbearable lightness of meaning
the unbearable lightness of acting
the unbearable lightness of community
the unbearable lightness of exodus
the unbearable lightness of sight
the unbearable lightness of games
the unbearable lightness of the climate change industrial complex
the unbearable lightness of anthropology

Heim's gallant defense of American intellectual pride has been seconded, and thirded, and thousandthed, by writers who fit their own titles into the algebra of these abstract words. It has become an English given, a linguistic formula like Raymond Carver's "what we talk about when we talk about [x]" or R. F. C. Hull's "zen and the art of [x]." The English words that Heim poured into the original Czech have become the form where other authors cast their words.

the unbearable wine-ness of being a light
the unbearable busy-ness of being
the unbearable rambo-ness of being
the unbearable sade-ness of being
the unbearable panda-ness of being
the unbearable stuff-ness of being

---

1   I am grateful to Susan Harris for her suggestions to the manuscript and to Ellen Elias-Bursac for introducing me to the term "snowclone." For other examples, see snowclones.org.

the unbearable khaki-ness of being
the unbearable bro-ness of being
the unbearable wasp-ness of being
the unbearable clown-ness of being
the unbearable madness of being

Falling somewhere between pun and prayer, each repetition explores
a possible application of the translated title to a new topic. En masse,
they offer a visual, graphic testament to Heim's intuition of American culture and literary value. In a series, they twist and pull the
English, exposing its formal characteristics and cultural potential
through reversals, unraveling, decomposition, and play.

the unbearable wholeness of being
the unbearable sassiness of being
the unbearable loudness of being
the unbearable eroticism of being
the unbearable awkwardness of being
the unbearable sadness of being sad
the unbearable darkness of being
the unbearable randomness of being
the unbearable dourness of being
the unbearable lightness of Elizabeth Bishop
the unbearable lightness of "the 'n' word"
the unbearable lightness of new urbanism
the unbearable lightness of retirement
the unbearable lightness of incessant change
the unbearable lightness of dragons

These variations are a feature of the English translation, not the
original. Czech writers do not vamp on Kundera, a fact explained
in part by the delayed publication of the Czech version. Although

it appeared in an edition from Josef Škvorecký's 68 Publishers in Toronto in 1985, the book was not published in the Czech Republic until 2006, twenty-two years after the English translation. When Czech plays on the title do appear, therefore, they are translations of the English-language practice of riffing.

unbearable lightness
the incredible lightness of laughing
the incredible lightness of be(coming) a cyclist
the unbareable lightness of being wrong
the wearable lightness of being
the infinite lightness of being
the unbeatable lightness of being
the eternal lightness of being
the exquisite lightness of being
the divine lightness of being
the uncomfortable lightness of being
the un-bear-able lightness of being
the un-bear-able lightness of equity
the un"bear"able lightness of "bee"ing
the un-bear-able lightness of being . . . stupid
the un"bear"able lightness of being in Berlin
the un"bear"able lightness of bear
the un-burj-able lightness of being

The formula "The Unbearable Lightness of Being" (TULOB) contains three points of variation (x, y, z) with an optional finale (q). To plot it mathematically requires three axes and an additional dimension for the final fillip, so its complexity suggests three-dimensional space plus time. If we isolate one variable, "the unbearable lightness of [z]," we may use Google's Ngram reader to search its corpus of scanned books published in English in a particular year. The

TULOB variations occupy more ground than comparable phrases. In 2000, "the unbearable lightness of" accounts for 101 x 10-9 (0.00000101) percent of the text in the Ngram corpus, while "zen and the art of" produces just 8 x 10-9 % and "what we talk about when" 17 x 10-9 %. Shakespearean phrases do no better: "all that glitters" comes in at 5, "the game's the thing" at 6, and "out damned spot" at 12 x 10-9 %. We have to turn to Biblical comparisons (also, of course, translations) to find serious contenders. "In the beginning" scores 569, while variations on "thou shalt not" chalk up 1564.

the unbearable nonsense of being
the unbearable obsessiveness of being
the unbearable lightness of being polar rays
the unbearable lightness of boredom
this unbearable boredom of being
the unbearable brightness of Beane
the unbearable rightness of stealing
the unbearable lightness of tagging
the unbearable brightness of Boeing
the unbearable weirdness of being
the unbearable tightness of vision
the unbearable lateness of being

Ngrams reveal another oddity. We might expect the presence of "the unbearable lightness of" to boom with the publication of the translated novel (1984) and the popularity of the movie (1988) and to wane as years pass. The opposite, however, is the case: through 2000, the frequency of "the unbearable lightness of" is rising.[2]

2   https://books.google.com/ngrams/graph?content=unbearable+lightness+of &year_start=1800&year_end=2000&corpus=15&smoothing=5&share=&dire ct_url=t1%3B%2Cunbearable%20lightness%20of%3B%2Cc0. Accessed November 28, 2013.

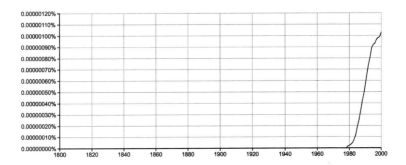

the unbearable lightness of politics

the unbearable rightness of Beijing

the unbearable rightness of indecision making

the unbearable lightness of Syria policy

the unbearable whiteness of pro-lifers and pundits

the unbearable tightness of voting

the unbearable tightness of being in a monetary union

the incredible lightness of Obama

the unbearable heaviness of the left-wing blogger

the incredible lightness of Obamalove

the unbearable heaviness of Obama's ego

the unbearable heaviness of being Newt Gingrich

the incredible lightness of being Dick Cheney

the incredible lightness of being Thomas Friedman

the incredible lightness of being Roger Federer

the unbearable lightness of being Jim Douglas

the unbearable brightness of being a Mets fan

the unbearable lightness of being Sam Querrey

the unbearable whiteness of cheerleading

the unbearable triteness of skiing

the unbearable hotness of Eli Manning

Two fields share exceptional devotion to plays on the title: sports and politics. What is their connection? Both demand important, often hurried decisions regarding complicated information, and both subject these decisions to lengthy scrutiny by Monday-morning quarterbacks and armchair generals. Commentators in both fields are motivated to find their leaders' fallibility, their lightness, particularly unbearable. Perhaps such tension generates a spiritual need.

the unbearable rightness of Bush v. Gore
the unbearable wrongness of Bush v. Gore
the unbearable rightness of Marbury v. Madison
the unbearable slightness of being Joe Klein
the unbearable whiteness of being GOP
the unbearable whiteness of being the Democrat convention
the incredible lightness of John Kerry
the incredible lightness of being in charge

These writers' appeals to TULOB offer a moment, if only in the title, to link the wound of disappointment to a greater statement about existence. By raising their topics to the level of "being," the harshly ephemeral problems of football and policy are diluted into the eternal. The opposite may be more accurate: the structure generates the titles. Would so many writers make claims about "being" if they were not provided a pattern for doing so? The algorithm of the title generates metaphysicians out of sportswriters and wonks.

the ineffable lightness of being
the unboreable lightness of being
the unknowable lightness of being
the unbearable anxiety of being Ken
the unbearable inevitability of being android
the unbearable brightness of seeing

the unbearable brightness of speaking
the unbearable being of Sasquatch
the unbearable meh-ness of being

The phrase appeals in its peculiar, modern rhetoric. In contrast to a classical formulation, which would increase the length of terms over the series (as in, "life, liberty, and the pursuit of happiness"), TULOB decreases: its main terms have three syllables, two, and two. The last word even violates the pattern of descending length. It might want to be just "be," in one syllable, if a masculine ending were not too old-fashioned for an anti-classical formula. The history of the phrase is ambivalent, evincing some regret for ending on an unaccented syllable. One-syllable substitutions are common.

the unbearable slightness of Bean
the unbearable whiteness of Dean
the unbearable brightness of bling
the unbearable sadness of zilch
the unbearable triteness of clam
the unbearable triteness of love
the unbearable heaviness of truth
the unbearable heaviness of slate
the unbearable lightness of scones

If scansion shows some strangeness in the phrase, it also reveals the translation's kinship with the English language. TULOB is built on anapests (the un béar a ble líght ness of bé ing), a pattern as common as the feminine endings in "'twas the night before Christmas."

the unbearable stiffness of being
the unbearable tallness of being
the unbearable cuteness of being

the unbearable straightness of being
the unbearable smartness of being
the unbearable lightness of painting
the unbearable numbness of being
the unbearable whiteness of being human
the unbearable "whiteness" of being Jewish
the unbearable likeness of being a tourist
the unbearable light-ness of being a spammer
the unbearable lightness of being Quaker

The story of the English title begins with prophetic unintelligibility. Heim recalls, "The editor who commissioned me to do the translation first heard the title over a bad transatlantic phone connection from Kundera in French. All he could make out was that it consisted of three abstract words." The list of permutations suggests that everyone, from Tony Judt ("The Unbearable Lightness of Politics," in *Ill Fares the Land*) to Slavoj Žižek ("The Unbearable Lightness of Being No One," in *The Parallax View*) to Portia de Rossi (*Unbearable Lightness*, her memoir), has heard the title in translation over a bad transatlantic phone connection.

the unbearable Italian-ness of being Chinese
the unbearable Eliot Ness-ness of Inspector Walpin
the unbearable chic-ness of Daphne Guinness
on the unbearable uselessness of Mother Wisdom
the unbearable rightness of catastrophizing
the incredible lightness of being "crime fighter" Alonzo Washington
the unbearable burden of being a Bulgarian voter abroad
the incredible lightness of being at an Eco-Lodge in Algonquin Park

Everyone has heard what she wanted in the three abstract words, everyone has heard Kundera's capacious algebra speaking to her ear.

And perhaps people imagine Kundera is the one calling, no matter what the topic at hand, to offer accommodation within a literary world.

the unfuckable lightness of being
the incredible lightness of boinking
the unbearable hotness of dong
the unbearable heaviness of boobs
the unbearable hotness of fucking

Most of the stems of permutation include a sexual or scatological version.

the unbearable brightness of peeing
the unbearable rightness of peeing
the unbearable tightness of peeing
the incredible lightness of peeing
the unbearable triteness of weeing
the unbearable shit-ness of being
the unbearable shite-ness of being
the unbearable whiteness of pooing
the unbearable heaviness of being divine shit

The corollary to cultural accommodation is the joyful perversion of high culture into low. The reversal is not a betrayal of the original; in fact, the title is built around opposite terms, the paradox of "unbearable lightness." That tautness gives more energy to the title than to the novel itself, which explains the paradox away. The title has more readers than the novel, and it generates more writers. As its spring uncoils, however, it produces other, less tense variations: "bearable lightness" is simply an explanation; "unbearable heaviness" is not an opposition but an exaggeration.

the bearable lightness of being a laptop
the bearable lightness of being Orthodox
the bearable lightness of being in Noosa
the Blairable lightness of being
the bearable lightness of being
the beerable lightness of being
the unbearable heaviness of luggage
the unbearable heaviness of Claudia's backpack
the unbearable heaviness of trauma
the unbearable heaviness of humankind
the unbearable heaviness of skin and bone
the unbearable heaviness of being human
the unbearable heaviness of being Muslim
the unbearable heaviness of being Czech
the unbearable heaviness of being . . . Lebanese
the unbearable heaviness of being Armenian in Turkey
the unbearable heaviness of being no one
the unbearable heaviness of being Misbah-ul-Haq
the unbearable heaviness of being . . . poor
the unbearable heaviness of being "k"
the unbearable heaviness of being a child
the unbearable heaviness of being in India
the unbearable heaviness of being in the closet
the unbearable heaviness of being in eighteenth-century studies
the unbearable heaviness of being the parent of a toddler
the unbearable heaviness of being
the unbearable heaviness of not being

"Unbearable whiteness" is one of many variations that replace a paradox with something actually intolerable.

the unbearable whiteness of being

the unbearable whiteness of being an Andrews character

the unbearable whiteness of breaking things

the unbearable whiteness of urban farming

the unbearable whiteness of eating

the unbearable whiteness of green

the unbearable whiteness of emceeing

the unbearable whiteness of Barbie

the unbearable whiteness of alternative food

the unbearable whiteness of suicide

the unbearable whiteness of Ken Burns

the unbearable whiteness of white meat

the unbearable whiteness of craft brewing

the unbearable whiteness of college

the unbearable whiteness of tving

the unbearable whiteness of Portland

the unbearable whiteness of cable

the unbearable whiteness of Brothers Tsarnaev

the unbearable whiteness of the Irish

the unbearable whiteness of Slovaks

the unbearable whiteness of Piet-ing

the unbearable whiteness of skiing

the unbearable whiteness of (my) being

the unbearable whiteness of literacy instruction

"the" unbearable "whiteness" of "science"

Only this principle of relaxation can explain the heap of "incredible lightnesses," the replacement of "unbearable" with a word that, due to overuse and imprecision, means almost nothing at all.

the incredible lightness of being

the incredible lightness of being transparent

the incredible lightness of being focused

the incredible lightness of being in Paris

the incredible lightness of being in Hollywood

the incredible lightness of being Tucker Carlson

the incredible lightness of being Tabu Ley Rochereau

the incredible lightness of part-time investing

the incredible lightness of boxes

the incredible lightness of . . . electronics

the incredible lightness of metal art

the incredible lightness of "no labels"

the incredible lightness of bees

the incredible lightness of Biden

the incredible lightness of drawing

the incredible lightness of modernity

the incredible lightness of metapages

the incredible lightness of bee-ing

the incredible lightness of Maddy

the incredible lightness of eating

the incredible lightness of seeing

the incredible lightness of busing

the incredible lightness of buy-side volume

the incredible lightness of the U.S. media

the incredible lightness of the S&P 500

the incredible lightness of Beene

the incredible lightness of soaring sculpture

the incredible lightness of flying

the incredible lightness of *Die Fledermaus*

the incredible lightness of being wrong

the incredible lightness of simplicity

the incredible lightness of learning

the incredible lightness of the Chron's pre-season Texans coverage

the incredible lightness of being a dinosaur

the incredible lightness of the universe

the incredible lightness of moving

the incredible lightness of an empty basket

the incredible lightness of beams

the incredible lightness of cycling

the incredible lightness of Beaujolais

the incredible lightness of traveling

the incredible lightheadedness of being German

the incredible lightness of the *Washington Post*

the incredible lightness of beekeeping

the incredible lightness of being a violinist

the incredible lightness of fishing

the incredible lightness of being (someone else)

the incredible lightness of being polite

the incredible lightness of bel canto

the incredible lightness of Beano

the incredible lightness of being the Grateful Dead

the incredible lightness of light

the incredible lightness of decluttering

the incredible lightness of living in an uncluttered home

the incredible lightness of the Ottawa press corps

the incredible lightness of white

the incredible lightness of being a car

One subcategory of permutation has a heartbreakingly high frequency: being as unbearably lonely. The word "loneliness" does not fit easily into the space of "lightness." It is one syllable too long. The extra syllable almost completely impedes the title, making it wallow in the moment of loneliness. Then, once we make it through the word, loneliness turns out not to be a moment, but an eternal condition.

the unbearable loneliness of being
the unbearable loneliness of being homo sapiens
the unbearable loneliness of being Bibi
the unbearable loneliness of being sick
the unbearable loneliness of being (here)
the unbearable loneliness of being the coat check girl
the unbearable loneliness of being wrong
the unbearable loneliness of cacti

TULOB strips "being" of any brave existential gesture, to reveal its redundancy: loneliness is the permanent state of being, being reduces to loneliness. Loneliness turns the title into a chiasmus. Yet this conclusion is challenged by the frequency of another variation: affixing a proper name to the end. In these versions, an actual being appears, just past "being" itself. We would find a person, if only we could make it through the preceding words.

the unbearable lightness of being Stanley Fish
the unbearable rightness of being Stephen Harper
the unbearable triteness of being Teddy Greenstein
the unbearable brightness of being Erica Angeline
the unbearable brightness of being Ken
the unbearable lightness of Ezra Klein
the unbearable slightness of being (Oprah)
the unbearable burden of being Robert
the unbearable ennui of being Sherlock Holmes
the unbearable heaviness of Nitin Gadkari
the unbearable politeness of Sheen
the unbearable brightness of Bunny
the unbearable politeness of Daniel Day-Lewis
the unbearable hotness of Andrew McCarthy
the unbearable rightness of being Nancy

the unbearable rightness of Padma
the incredible lightness of Tim Roth

The proper names compliment the variations trapped in loneliness.
One calls to the other across the chiastic miasma. The co-presence
of these two sets of variations suggests that the difference between
loneliness and the lightness of human contact is a single syllable.

the unattainable lightness of being
the unbearable triteness of *boum*
the unbeatable lightness of being Florida
the uncomfortable lightness of being unemployed
the aerodynamic lightness of being
the surprising lightness of being a hijabi
the amazing lightness of being
the healing lightness of being
the implacable lightness of being
the imaginary lightness of being pregnant
the unbreakable lightness of being
the unforgettable lightness of being
the unavoidable lightness of being an amoeba
the barely imagined lightness of being
the terrible lightness of being
the pleasurable lightness of being
the unbookable lightness of being
the unbearable weight of being
the bear-able lightness of being
the beer-able lightness of being
the unbeard-able lightness of being
the underwear-able lightness of being
the unblairable lightness of being
the unbearable burden of being mentally ill

the unbearable burden of living life in reverse

the unbelievable lightness of being club

the incredible lightness of being an openly gay artist

the unbearable brightness of being

the unbearable brightness of being the world's greatest cinema

the unbearable brightness of the uncanny

the unbearable brightness of spring

the unbearable burden of doing

the unbearable burden of forgetting

the unbearable burden of history

the unbearable burden of ID papers

the unbearable brightness of dreaming

the unbearable brightness of Beijing

the unbearable brightness of the neoconservatives

the unbearable brightness of incredible stupidity

the unbearable brightness of weaving

the unbearable rightness of being

the unbearable rightness of being certain

the unbearable rightness of being green

the unbearable rightness of being armed

the unbearable rightness of being stupid

the unbearable rightness of being wrong

the unbearable rightness of maybe being wrong

the unbearable rightness of being happy

the unbearable tightness of bad jeans

the unbearable tightness of pants

the unbearable tightness of corset

the unbearable tightness of marmalade

the hilarious lightness of being

Michael Heim is laughing: "The unbearable lightness of this and the unbearable lightness of that. I laugh when I run across newspaper headlines adopting the formulation." The history of permutations offers delight to punsters and others who enjoy the free play of language, who take pleasure in the slightness of a one-letter shift to or from lightness.

the unbearable fatness of being
the unbearable phatness of being

The game resembles other techniques of formal translation, particularly those devised by the Oulipo: homophonic translations, or substitutions of words by others with the same number of letters in another language. As Harry Mathews writes in "Translation and the Oulipo," "These strange dislocations of the original may seem cavalier, but they are useful in drawing attention precisely to elements of language that normally pass us by, concerned as we naturally are with making sense of what we read. Nominal sense becomes implicitly no more than a part of overall meaning."[3] Anyone who has read poetry in translation will not be surprised by the idea that one translates the form and the nominal sense of a text. The Oulipo translates only the form, and the Oulipo-esque permutations of TULOB translate the form of the original translation.

the bearable whiteness of being gay
the exquisite lightness of being
the incredible brace-ness of being
the incredible duck-ness of being
the incredible enough-ness of being (bumped)
the incredible lighted-ness of being in St. Paul
the incredible lightness of being (a bride!)

---

3 http://www.electronicbookreview.com/thread/electropoetics/ethno-linguist. Posted January 3, 1997, accessed November 28, 2013.

the incredible lightness of being in Australia

the incredible lightness of blogging

the incredible lightness of deepness

the incredible lightness of feeding

the incredible lightness of play

the incredible like-ness of being

the incredible Pollyanna-ness of being

the incredible tan-ness of being

the incredible white-ness of being

the new lightness of being

the unbearable brightness of busing

the unbearable brightness of golden dazzling

the unbearable brightness of neon

the unbearable brightness of wallpaper

the unbearable burden of Alice Walker

the unbearable burden of always being right

the unbearable burden of being a barnstormer

the unbearable burden of being a lawyer

the unbearable burden of being a woman

the unbearable burden of being important

the unbearable burden of being millennial

the unbearable burden of being right

the unbearable burden of crappy sequels

The most far-reaching effect of the translated title is not a widespread knowledge of Czech literature. Far from it: how many of those who play on the title could name the original author? Rather than the transmission of authorship or a certain content, the repetition of the form is itself the achievement. Rather than readers, the translation has created, in the first place, a bevy of translators working from one English version to another. Heim's translation saturates the English language with translations of translations of translations.

the unbearable burden of kindness

the unbearable burden of lightness

the unbearable burden of niceness

the unbearable burden of raising a child with Down Syndrome

the unbearable burden of reasonableness

the unbearable burden of true genius

the unbearable burden of uniqueness

the unbearable burden of walking

the unbearable heaviness of "Borges words"

the unbearable heaviness of (not) blogging

the unbearable heaviness of a new poll

the unbearable heaviness of acting

the unbearable heaviness of baking cake

the unbearable heaviness of breathing in Thailand

the unbearable heaviness of business class

the unbearable heaviness of change

the unbearable heaviness of chronic disease

the unbearable heaviness of colloids

the unbearable heaviness of cookbooks

the unbearable heaviness of debt

the unbearable heaviness of feeling

the unbearable heaviness of forgiveness

the unbearable heaviness of governing

the unbearable heaviness of government debt

the unbearable heaviness of grief

the unbearable heaviness of having

the unbearable heaviness of industry

the unbearable heaviness of java strings

the unbearable heaviness of Jewish power

the unbearable heaviness of Jewish self-hatred

the unbearable heaviness of knowing

the unbearable heaviness of philosophy

the unbearable heaviness of psychiatric drug withdrawal
the unbearable heaviness of remembering
the unbearable heaviness of soul
the unbearable heaviness of spuds
the unbearable heaviness of stuff
the unbearable heaviness of the pension protection act
the unbearable heaviness of the tripod
the unbearable heaviness of truthtelling
the unbearable heaviness of voting in Texas
the unbearable heaviness of words
the unbearable hotness of being
the unbearable hotness of chefs
the unbearable hotness of drewt90
the unbearable hotness of Elyse
the unbearable hotness of Heather
the unbearable hotness of heating
the unbearable hotness of high density storage
the unbearable hotness of LA
the unbearable hotness of Levi
the unbearable hotness of Neandertals
the unbearable hotness of Ricci
the unbearable hotness of Skarsgård
the unbearable lightness of being no one
the unbearable lightness of being portrayed
the unbearable lightness of debating
the unbearable lightness of being the proletariat
the unbearable mightiness of deflation
the unbearable politeness of being
the unbearable politeness of being at Lambeth Conference
the unbearable politeness of being Indian
the unbearable politeness of certain beings
the unbearable politeness of human beings

the unbearable politeness of media

the unbearable politeness of poetry readings

the unbearable rightness of archives

the unbearable rightness of bedside rationing

the unbearable rightness of being a Stanford fan

the unbearable rightness of being Mumbai

the unbearable rightness of contrariness

the unbearable rightness of criticism

the unbearable rightness of diversity

the unbearable rightness of editing

the unbearable rightness of fiction

the unbearable rightness of fleeing

the unbearable rightness of penny

the unbearable rightness of pushing buttons

the unbearable rightness of questioning

the unbearable rightness of seeing

the unbearable rightness of voters

the unbearable "rightness" of whiteness

the unbearable slightness of being

the unbearable slightness of being foreign

the unbearable slightness of being indie

the unbearable slightness of *Jackass*

the unbearable slightness of latter-day French cinema

the unbearable slightness of partitions

the unbearable slightness of polling

the unbearable slightness of seeing

the unbearable slightness of the architectural form

the unbearable tightness of being

the unbearable tightness of being (a superhero)

the unbearable tightness of being me

the unbearable tightness of chingy

the unbearable tightness of lending

the unbearable tightness of money

the unbearable tightness of service

the unbearable tightness of the unbearable lightness of being

the unbearable triteness of (not) being (at AWP or the Superbowl)

the unbearable triteness of being

the unbearable triteness of being (an unpaid intern)

the unbearable triteness of being a TV critic

the unbearable triteness of being fashionable

the unbearable triteness of best-selling BS

the unbearable triteness of blogging

the unbearable triteness of cheating

the unbearable triteness of Facebook

the unbearable triteness of hating

the unbearable triteness of leaving

the unbearable triteness of no bank holiday

the unbearable triteness of preening

the unbearable triteness of sucking

the unbearable triteness of vlogging

the unbearable triteness of whiteness

the unbearable agony of being

the unbearable being of light

the unbearable b-ness of software

the unbearable brightness of being right

the unbearable brown-ness of Raj Rajaratnam

the unbearable burden of intellectual indebtedness

the unbearable burden of being in the same boat

the unbearable chunkiness of being

the unbearable complexity of being me

the unbearable dullness of being successful

the unbearable embeddedness of being

the unbearable hotness of being Raghuram Rajan

the unbearable laxity of being

the unbearable lightness of being (a neutrino)

the unbearable lightness of being away

the unbearable lightness of being fake

the unbearable lightness of being intercultural

the unbearable lightness of being vegan

the unbearable liteness of being teen

the unbearable loudness of chewing

the unbearable meta of glee

the unbearable obnoxiousness of "being"

the unbearable paranoia of being South African

the unbearable pettiness of being rich

the unbearable pleasure of being a woman

the unbearable plight of wireless-less-ness

the unbearable rightness of being alive in Leitrim

the unbearable sadness of being Korean

the unbearable schizophrenia of being the PN

the unbearable shame of being an unblogger

the unbearable Sheitness of being

the unbearable lightness of regulatory costs

the unbearable sweetness of yoga

the unbearable thinness of being a model

the unbearable wholeness of beings

the unbearable wrongness of being

THE LIVES OF THE TRANSLATORS

BREON MITCHELL

(inaugural lecture delivered at UCLA on April 18, 2013,
opening the university's Michael Henry Heim Lecture Series)

My life, growing up on the plains of Kansas in the 1950s, was not quite as far removed from art, literature, and culture as you might think. It's true that it wasn't until my junior year in high school that I heard classical music performed live, and the great paintings of the world remained, in those years, mere reproductions in books. But in one important sense, I was as deeply immersed in the life of the mind as any young boy in New York, Paris, or London, for from the age of twelve my life was shaped and changed in profound ways by reading the great works of world literature.

You won't be surprised to learn that the major impact that *Crime and Punishment* and *The Brothers Karamazov* had upon me was not based on any knowledge of Russian, nor did I read *The Magic Mountain* and *The Stranger* in German or French. Dostoyevsky, Thomas Mann, and Albert Camus, among others, influenced me deeply as a teenager, as they no doubt did many of you. I owe them, and other great writers, a debt I can never fully repay.

But did I not also owe a debt to those other, somewhat shadowy figures, men and women who had opened those doors of perception?

Who were Constance Garnett, Helen Lowe-Porter, Stuart Gilbert? I still remember their names after all these years, and not only because I later grew to understand their importance to our culture. Yet few of us know anything about them. I still ask myself today: What would my life have been without them? Without the works they brought to life for me? Without their dedication, without their craft, without their art?

And so today, as we remember how Michael Henry Heim enriched our lives, and the doors *he* opened for us, I would like to say a few words about the lives of translators: not the Lives of the Artists, then, nor the Lives of the Saints, but the much more humble Lives of the Translators.

•

Roman Jakobson's concept of the bipolar structure of language, first posited in a paper he delivered at a linguistics conference at Indiana University over sixty years ago, includes the now famous distinction between metaphor, based on similarity, and metonymy, based on contiguity. This polarity seems to suggest something fundamental about the way our brains work. Jakobson used the concept broadly, to distinguish, for example, Romanticism from Realism, but he also made the same distinction between poetry and prose: "The principle of similarity underlies poetry; prose, on the contrary, is forwarded essentially by contiguity. Thus, for poetry, metaphor, and for prose, metonymy, is the line of least resistance."

This seminal concept of language may well explain why it is that so few major novelists have written poetry of high quality, and why accomplished poets are so seldom successful novelists. James Joyce, Thomas Mann, Marcel Proust, and Franz Kafka are hardly known for their verse. And it is difficult to think of a famous poet who wrote an important novel.

It seems to me that the same distinction is true for literary translation: almost without exception, the best-known literary translators specialize either in poetry or in prose. Moreover, almost all poetry is translated by men and women who write poetry of their own, and often think of themselves primarily as poets. For them, translation may seem a secondary activity, feeding their own creative impulse. Prose translators, on the other hand, are generally more . . . prosaic. They are not, with two or three notable exceptions, published novelists, nor do they think of themselves as literary authors. Today I want to discuss this latter group, and the role they have played in our cultural life.

What are their lives like, and what can we learn from them?

•

It would be gratifying to imagine the lives of the translators as exciting, perhaps even dangerous. And indeed they sometimes are: William Tyndale was strangled to death, then burnt at the stake in 1536 for translating the Bible; we are told that leaves from his manuscript bibles were used as kindling for the fire. His final words, spoken at the stake, were reported to be "Lord, open the King of England's eyes."

In those days the unlicensed possession of Scripture in English was punishable by death. And Tyndale's translation, the first English Bible to draw directly from the Hebrew and Greek sources, was also the first to take advantage of the printing press for broad dissemination. He was clearly a dangerous man. Yet only two years after Tyndale's death, Henry the VIII's eyes apparently were opened, and he authorized the Great Bible for the Church of England, a bible that was largely Tyndale's work.

In our own day, religious fanaticism has again made the act of translation more than a little risky. The Japanese translator of Salman

Rushdie's *The Satanic Verses*, Hitoshi Igarashi, was stabbed to death in his office at the University of Tsukuba in 1991, in response to the well-publicized fatwa of the Ayatollah Khomeini, while the Italian translator of the novel, Ettore Capriolo, was stabbed and seriously injured that same year in Milan.

Our colleague Peter Theroux, a prolific translator from the Arabic, who vetted the English and Arabic versions of Iraq's new constitution a few years ago, had to wear a flak jacket while serving in that role and was trained to handle automatic weapons as part of his assignment. He later served in the White House on the National Security Council for the Arabian Peninsula, and is now again translating in the Middle East.

But in general, to rephrase Henry David Thoreau, most translators lead lives of quiet inspiration. My personal acquaintance with many literary translators, and the insights I've gained from sifting through their archives, has given me a picture I believe is relatively accurate. Translators clearly love literature, and have a special penchant for close reading. They are hardworking, dedicated, generally modest, and self-effacing. They are motivated not by financial rewards (which are nearly non-existent), but by a desire to share with a wider audience their enthusiasm for literary works of international significance.

Of course both authors and translators are in love with language, but the translators' love affair is a special one. What fascinates literary translators is the complex relationship between languages, what is unique to each, and how one may be shaped into a replica of the other. Translating even a sentence from one language to another is like solving a puzzle, with all the attendant pleasures and frustrations. Most translators love taking on such challenges. Fortunately, translators are seldom troubled by writer's block, since there is always a text in front of them. But solving the puzzle is never as easy as the author of the original might imagine.

A well-written novel I read recently demonstrates how even a sensitive writer may totally misunderstand the task of the translator. In *The Imposter Bride* (2012) by Canadian novelist Nancy Richler, a young woman is being read to from a diary her mother found while fleeing through Eastern Europe during World War II. The notebook is in Yiddish, and her father Nathan is reading it aloud. It should be noted that Nathan never finished high school and has shown no particular linguistic talent of any kind in the course of the novel. We are told that he "translated slowly but easily. Fluently in fact." And the impromptu translation is fluent indeed, flowing forth "easily" in one long sentence:

> She had been my dearest friend since childhood, a friend-ship that had been heightened by longing during the ten month separation we were forced to endure every year, and deepened by the impassioned letters we wrote to each other, letters sealed with kisses and tears in which we revealed our deepest selves to one another and planned everything we would do together when the school year ended and we could finally be together again.

Not bad for a high-school dropout translating *ad hoc* for the first time. Yet when Elka, a woman of similarly limited background and education, writes a brief letter to Nathan's brother, the words don't come so easily: "Dear Sol," she begins, "I'm not sorry we have had no contact with each other since the evening we spent together a month ago." The narrator continues: "The letter had taken her three days to write. She had wrestled with every line and phrase for hours."

Why does an intelligent and talented novelist find it believable that Nathan could dash off a highly literary, complex, sight transla-tion from the Yiddish when he has shown no special aptitude at all for language, spoken or written? Elka's three-day struggle with her short letter to Sol is much more believable.

An unstated attitude toward writing itself underlies this strange contradiction: as a novelist, Richler knows the effort required for a young woman like Elka to compose a letter—after all, writing is a difficult business: it is a creative act of composition, and even a simple letter is never that easy. Whereas in Richler's eyes, Nathan is merely translating, an act that apparently strikes her as simple and straightforward, since after all, Nathan has the text right in front of him. His smooth and fluent translation reveals an underlying assumption on the part of the author: that translation is a mechanical process that anyone with a modicum of linguistic knowledge should be able to handle, since the words are already there on the page and need only be repeated in another language. This may be why so many authors who have never tried translating think of it simply as a professional craft, while those who have translated novels, such as Paul Auster and Julian Barnes, often praise it as a valuable tool for learning how to write.

It is true both writers and translators love the written word, but the translators live in a world in which the infinite possibilities of *two* languages are constantly foregrounded. The creative task for the translator is not to produce a text *ex nihilo*, but to mold language into shapes that most nearly fit the text to be translated.

Faced with any novel or short story of quality, literary translators are acutely aware that their translations, no matter how accomplished, can never fully reflect the power and creativity of the original. When they have finished a translation, they dream only of how they might have done it better. They strive at best toward Samuel Beckett's melancholy goal: "Ever tried. Ever failed. No matter. Try again. Fail again. Fail better." But unlike Beckett, no Nobel Prize awaits them.

Living with failure, even of the better sort, is a strange type of life, modest and often obscure, with little recognition, and limited financial reward, both within and outside academe. Who then are literary translators, and why do they dedicate themselves to this task?

To begin with the obvious, most of them have a day job. The number of literary translators in the United States who manage to make a living solely by translating can be counted, almost literally, on one hand. And they must work constantly, translating at least two or three long novels a year to earn their daily bread. Ralph Manheim was a case in point: When I first met him in Paris in 1982 he was translating 10-12 hours a day in a tiny garret looking out on the Luxembourg Gardens, and caring for his wife, who was too ill to leave their small apartment. Yet, he was among the best-known translators of his time, with a career stretching back over decades. Until he was finally awarded a MacArthur Foundation "genius" award in 1983, he remained a slave to the work he loved. And the financial security he finally gained remains a shining exception to this day.

•

What then, are the translator's true rewards?

First and foremost among them is the intellectual pleasure granted by an intimate knowledge of the text based on the closest possible reading. James Joyce once said he spent seventeen years writing *Finnegans Wake* and expected people to spend seventeen years reading it. Whether or not they realize it, most authors find in their translators the ideal readers they seek, ones willing to spend years at the task if necessary. The literal meaning of the text is merely the starting point. Sentence by sentence, the syntax, style, tone, and vocabulary that produce the aesthetic effect are studied and restudied in an attempt to render that same effect in another language.

The first reward of the translator, then, is that deep reading itself.

Secondly, the translation of living authors often brings a special gift: a close relationship, often friendship, with living authors whose works they admire. Most foreign authors want to be translated into English and other major languages. Their first close contact abroad is often with their translators, who, rightly or wrongly, appear as gatekeepers to world literature. In the course of consultation on the finer points of a translation, authors and translators draw closer together, and work at times almost in tandem. Samuel Beckett spent long hours with his German translator Elmar Tophoven, Nicholas de Lange works closely with Amos Oz on the English versions of Oz's novels, and I recall with special pleasure my own stay at Uwe Timm's apartment in Munich while we went through his novel *Morenga* page by page. Such examples could be multiplied at will. And the human reward of such contact for the translator is profound.

Finally, literary translators are rewarded by a sense of accomplishment: the realization that through their efforts, they have contributed to the creation of an international literary culture, that somewhere in Kansas a young boy's life may be changed by what they have done. This may be a quiet pride, but it provides a deep satisfaction.

•

Goethe's early nineteenth-century concept of *Weltliteratur* is well known: works of literary art that pass beyond the boundaries of a national literature and are universal in their appeal. But world literature exists, almost by definition, only as literature in translation. Or to put it another way, without literary translation there would be no world literature.

The whole question of how and why world literature is created and impacts our lives rests centrally on sources often slumbering in the apartments and offices of literary translators. To neglect this material is to risk losing a deeper understanding of literary history in general. Here too, the lives of the translators repay closer scrutiny.

Until recently, the papers of literary translators have rarely been preserved, and then often almost by accident. Their manuscripts have appeared sporadically, if at all, in collections of other types: those focusing on a particular well-known author or publisher, for example, as with UCLA's Hogarth Press material, which includes letters and manuscripts of Virginia Woolf's co-translations with S. S. Koteliansky of several texts by Dostoyevsky. But there has never been a systematic attempt to preserve the archives of literary translators for their own intrinsic value.

For this reason, the Lilly Library embarked in 2002 on a proactive project to find and preserve the papers of literary translators here and abroad, both for the insights they provide, and as a way to recognize and honor their role in world cultures.

Let me share with you a brief memoir recalling how one such archive came to the Lilly Library, and why it meant so much to us:

On a misty day in Manhattan, over thirty years ago, I asked Barbara Wright if she had been saving her own manuscripts and correspondence. "Who would care?" she asked, as the bus pulled up.

Years later, she recalled the falling rain, the question, her own surprise—not that someone might be interested in Raymond Queneau, Nathalie Sarraute, or Robert Pinget, among the major French authors she had translated—but that someone might be interested in her, and in the seemingly modest part she had played in literary history.

The question I originally put to Barbara, following a pleasant lunch with our editors at New Directions, arose from my delight in her quick mind, the cleverness with which she handled difficult questions of literary style, and her insights into the works of some of the leading writers of our century. Shouldn't this all be preserved somehow? What would happen to the complex record of her life as a literary translator? Was all that going to be lost? I asked as a fellow translator, fully realizing how little, in fact, most people cared about translation, how seldom they realized its possible importance in their own lives.

Years passed, but neither Barbara nor I forgot our conversation. Then, in 2002, as the new director of the Lilly Library, I finally had a chance to follow up on my question concretely. I wrote to Barbara, told her I was coming to London, and that I would like to see her. She invited me to her home in Frognal, I arrived, and she listened patiently to my ideas.

I told her of our desire to create a broad research archive of translators' papers at the Lilly Library, including correspondence with authors and publishers, drafts of translations, annotated copies of original texts, corrected galley proofs—in short anything that would shed light on both the process and context of literary translation. I told her I feared that this vital material would be lost to future generations if we didn't save it now. Her response was immediate, generous, and warm.

She had, in fact, kept almost everything over the years—all her correspondence with publishers and authors, her notebooks, her reviews and periodicals, the heavily-annotated copies of each book she had translated. The depth of her study for individual translation projects was amazing, and clearly evident in the thick and clearly-labeled files.

Barbara's letters were a constant delight, flowing easily and openly, sometimes page after page. Here's one that sheds light on her feelings at the time:

> 7 April 2002: I'm also a bit scared because I realise that it's more or less going to be like revealing my whole life to anyone who wants to poke his or her nose into it. (All

right, I could have phrased that less scornfully . . .) And that
seems to me to be against my nature. I have always refused
to be interviewed. A) Because I just don't want to be, and B)
because it would bore me—I reckon I know about myself!
One the other hand I love being the interviewer and talking to other people about themselves. Some years before I
started to translate her, some literary mag sent me to the
Institut Français here to interview Nathalie Sarraute, and
she was so lovely and simple and friendly and interesting
and prepared to talk . . . Well, she was such a professional
that whenever she gave a lecture it was just as if she was
talking to close friends. With me, on the other hand, whenever I have allowed myself to be pushed, screaming and
shouting (metaphorically) into talking in public, it has had
every chance of becoming a disaster.

Barbara's ambivalence about revealing her personal life ran like a
leitmotif through our letters, although in the end she left it up to
the Lilly Library to draw the line, passing on nearly everything she
had kept.

"Posterity! Yuk!" was Barbara's normal reaction whenever I suggested someone might eventually care about what she had written,
and in another letter she tackled the issue (new for her) of her letters
being read by strangers:

[A friend said] on a postcard (undated, as usual, but I date
them) on 9 April 2002: "Please let's throw out our letters
from now on so we can write what we like." Well me—I
have never not written what I liked, I have never thought
of anything or anyone other than my immediate correspon-
dent. Writing a letter is pretty nearly as good as being in the
company of the pal you're writing to. . . . But when I was

told that [a friend] had kept all my letters . . . Well, I kind
of woke up. And I realized that **ALL** the things one does,
spontaneously, and just because one is alive . . . .
are, in a way, there, engraved in stone.

So clearly, the thing to do is to carry on regardless (which
was a saying during the war!), but be aware that God's, or
Buddha's, Databank has got you taped, whether you like it
or not.

Barbara's papers were among the first to come to the Lilly, providing
a firm foundation for a collection that currently holds the archives of
over forty translators from around the world, including those given
to us, in a typical act of warm generosity, by Michael Henry Heim,
highlighted by his fascinating and lengthy exchange (in Czech, English, and French) with Milan Kundera on Mike's translation of *The
Joke*.

Michael with Kilhna Winton at the Lilly Library
in Bloomington, Indiana, February 2002.

The Lilly Library is one of the major rare book libraries in the world, where you can see a copy of the Gutenberg Bible, a Shakespeare first folio, and other treasures of human thought. Among the over seven million manuscripts are the papers of such authors as Nadine Gordimer, Sylvia Plath, Kurt Vonnegut, Ian Fleming, and Orson Welles. Why should we care to add to these the papers of literary translators?

Why are such archives important, and what can future generations of students and scholars learn from them? Here are four answers to that question:

1. The papers of literary translators increase our knowledge of the authors they have translated, providing us with unique insights into the author's mind and intentions, and revealing in part the creative process by which the original work came into being. Letters to and from the author generally offer the clearest evidence of this research potential. The Lilly's archives include, for example, over 300 letters between Leila Vennewitz and Nobel Prize winner Heinrich Böll, an equally extensive correspondence between Barbara Wright and Robert Pinget, and a lengthy exchange between William Weaver and Italo Calvino. In each case the letters include scores of specific questions on the original text along with the author's responses.

An except from the files of Helga Pfetsch, the German translator of Saul Bellow's *The Actual*, reveals how fascinating such exchanges can be. Helga's queries are followed by Saul Bellow's responses:

> p. 7: the appointments secretary: is she—in your imagination—a woman or a man? In German I will have to decide—there is no gender-neutral word.

> Probably, although not necessarily, a woman.

p. 20: Indiana Limestone: what does it look like? Is it something special? What is your reason for mentioning this detail? What does it say about Amy's family?

Limestone is a gray material used in building. It is mentioned because noticers do notice such facts. For Chicago builders, Indiana was a convenient source, in the nineteenth century, for building stone.

p. 55/6: One of his favorite Russians said that: Do you happen to know, who Jay's favourite Russian is and what book or story the quotation comes from? I'd love to look up the German translation of these lines, especially for "the most amazing thing in the life of the world . . ."

V.V. Rozanov is the Russian. The quotations are from a book called *Solitaria*.

P.S. I don't at all mind answering your questions. I rather enjoy doing it. Saul Bellow.

But translators' archives reveal more than occasional insights into the author's intentions—in some cases the original text itself has been altered and transformed in the process. Martin Grzimek, for example, shortened and revised his novel *Die Beschattung* while working with me on the English version, cutting ten pages from the opening sections, and insisting that these revisions be followed in the French version later published by Belfond. Uwe Johnson's *Jahrestage* (*Anniversaries*) was also considerably shortened in the translation process, with passages excised by Johnson before the text was sent to Leila Vennewitz for translation (she was, predictably if unfairly, criticized by some reviewers for these puzzling "omissions").

2. The archives also give us a clearer understanding of the way in which literary works enter a new culture, providing evidence of how and why particular works get translated, and detailing a process of selection that includes reader's reports and the enthusiasm of individual editors.

Publishers often turn to translators for reader's reports on works from abroad, and these reports are crucial to their success. Mike Heim's reports were models of the genre, providing unusually cogent and informed insights into newly offered works of international literature, often including a brief history of how each text fit into the general history of Czech, German, or Russian literature.

Mike's detailed reader's report on Milan Kundera's *The Unbearable Lightness of Being* is typical of the depth of his analysis. Here is an excerpt from that document, preserved at the Lilly Library:

> A higher metaphysical level brings together a wide range of ideas. Primary among them is Nietzsche's concept of "eternal return," which emblematically recurs at several points in the novel and represents a development of the theme of forgetting, a kind of future-oriented forgetting: we act without realizing that everything will take place over and over again (Tomas's long lost son returns as a personification of the idea). The interplay between chance and fate appears in the *"muß es sein?"* and *"es muß sein?"* motifs in Beethoven's last quartet (was Tomas pre-ordained to marry Tereza? To become a surgeon?). Parmenides's oppositions are reflected in the title (unbearable lightness), in the headings "Lightness and Weight" and "Soul and Body," in in various guises throughout the narrative . . . Startling as this material is and disparate as it may seem, it always complements and enriches the action . . .

3. On a more mundane, but often fascinating level, translators' archives reveal a great deal about the business of translation: contracts, book production, royalties, and advertising. Translators' papers are filled with royalty statements, contracts, and queries about payment. Although this material reveals little about the quality of the works involved, it does demonstrate the effect of material conditions on the publication and reception of foreign literature in the English-speaking world, including how often, and, it must be said, understandably, publishers' concerns about the bottom line influence their ultimate decisions. The archives thus shed light on the history of unpublished translations as well.

4. Perhaps most importantly for students and practitioners of literary translation, the manuscripts offer a unique insight into the nature and process of literary translation itself, from inception to publication, including early drafts, the submitted manuscript, editor's revisions and copy editing, further revisions for galley proofs, and the final text. The complexity of this process is often greater than that which generated the original text, and the result almost always reaches a wider and more numerous audience.

William Weaver, whose archives are at the Lilly, offers a revealing example of this intricate process. In a diary entry in 1956 Weaver laments: "Here I am 33 yrs. old, unknown, unsuccessful, broke, and homeless." Yet within a decade he had established himself as one of the finest translators of contemporary Italian prose in America. By the time Umberto Eco's first novel was creating a sensation in 1980, Weaver was the obvious translator of choice for the American publishers: "We have acquired Eco, *Il nome della rosa* in devout hope you would lend your marvelous skills & prestige to the translation." Weaver accepted at once, and although he found the work "horribly difficult," he was justly proud of the result. He sent the corrected

galley proofs his to editor at Harcourt, noting: "I feel like Wotan
gazing on Valhalla (*"vollendet das ewige Werk"*—or words to that
effect). I hope our edifice lasts a bit longer than four nights."

But William Weaver's manuscript of *The Name of the Rose* is
the most heavily edited I have ever seen, with Drenka Willen at
Harcourt revising practically every line. The translation in its final
incarnation was widely praised and the book itself was a best-seller,
catapulting Eco into worldwide notice for the first time. But by the
time Eco's next novel came along, Weaver was begging for a lighter
editorial hand.

When Weaver forwarded the manuscript of Eco's *The Island of the
Day Before* to the publishers, he included a special note for the copy
editor: "Over the past ten months, I have given hours, days, weeks
of thought to the problems of this translation. There is not a word,
indeed not a comma, that I haven't pondered, sometimes changing
it, then changing back, until I was—almost—satisfied. So spare the
red pencil as much as you can. Be careful, it's my heart."

And in the final analysis, these archives do lead into the heart
of the matter, toward what translators and readers alike care most
about, how great literature can change our lives.

•

And now in closing I would like to add a few final words about
Mike Heim.

Mike's environmental activism and his aversion to spending
money on himself were well known to his friends, although he was
generosity itself toward others. On a visit to Indiana University I had
arranged for him to be picked up at the airport. My email about the
car elicited this typical response: "I know you meant well by ordering
the limousine, but I believe in the most public kind of transportation
and in the least use of gas. If I remember correctly, there is a shuttle

every hour or two from the airport, and I'm perfectly willing to take it. I'd probably have needed the limousine if I'd come in on Thursday, but now that there's no rush why not cancel the reservation. (I realize that money is not a big issue, but another of my vagaries is that I am penny-wise and pound-foolish, and it did cost $40 to make the necessary change in the ticket. Since the shuttle must cost less than the limousine, here's a way to recoup some of that.)"

And here is his reply to an email I sent from the Banff Center for the Arts in Canada, where he had served as a senior translator-in-residence:

> Dear Breon: I'm jealous. I love the snow, and we've been having record-breaking highs. It's been in the eighties or nineties and lip-cracking dry. It really gets me down. But I'm writing during a wonderful downpour—not enough to alleviate our multi-year drought but wonderfully refreshing. I'm so glad to hear that things are going well with *The Tin Drum*. I look forward to hearing the rest of the saga when you're here in the spring. I'll then tell you my saga, but here is the twenty-five words-or-less outline, since you're implicated. Since it was obvious I would not be doing the new Grass novel (though the Grass people kindly sent me all the materials as if I were), I decided to drown my sorrows in my first (and last, I'm sure) Chinese project. You are "implicated," as I put it, because you introduced me to Sumie Jones, who invited me to Tokyo [and things went on from there]. Although it's a short novel it will take me forever because I still have to decipher (rather than read) each sentence. At times I despair, at times I exult. But I think I've found the tone for the narrator, who's an interesting and simpático kind of guy with a rich lexical range. So it's not only the challenge of the language (Chinese) but the challenge of

language (the English) that attracts me to it. More when we meet. P.S. By the way, people are now telling me I look like Obama—at least in his incarnation on the 26 January *New Yorker* cover. I take all the compliments I can get.

And here is the last email I was ever to receive from him—typically recommending something good to read:

> Dear Breon: Priscilla and I think you'd both enjoy the novels of Marina Warner (a friend), especially *In a Dark Wood*, *The Lost Father*, and *Indigo*. The funniest book I've read in years is Alan Bennett's *The Uncommon Reader*. Guaranteed to put anyone in a good mood.

Among the lives of the translators I wished to honor today, Michael Henry Heim's life shines forth in every way: his profound generosity, his amazing talent for languages, his sensitive and subtle translations of the most difficult texts, his dedication to his students, his courage in the face of every obstacle. Each time Lynda and I visited Mike and Priscilla in their home, it was like entering a verdant garden of thought. We talked and talked and never felt we were finished. Mike was a great teacher, and I learned greatly from him. But he was, perhaps above all else, a model of moral and intellectual integrity. He made me want to be a better person. Lynda and I are deeply grateful to Mike and Priscilla for all they have given us, and I am grateful to his colleagues, his students, and to his university for allowing me to express that gratitude.

Heim at a dinner with Günther Grass.

MICHAEL HENRY HEIM: A THEORY

ESTHER ALLEN

"It's what you do that counts, ladies and gentlemen,
what you do that counts."
—Serebryakov, in Anton Chekhov's Uncle Vanya
(translated by Michael Henry Heim)[1]

I. The Gift

I met Michael Henry Heim for the first time at 9 A.M. on February 28, 2003. He'd arranged the meeting in an email a week earlier. Apart from having read his translations (including Aleksandar Tišma's *Book of Blam,* which I'd just finished), I'd had no previous contact with him and was startled and delighted to receive a message out of the blue from a person I admired. At the time, I was Chair of the Translation Committee of PEN American Center, the New York chapter of the international writers' organization, and the brief note addressed me in that capacity. He'd noticed a letter to the editor of mine that *Harper's* had published a few months earlier and agreed with it. There was something he wished to discuss in person. Could I set up a meeting at the PEN offices?

---

1 In *Anton Chekhov: The Essential Plays* (Modern Library, 2003), p. 110.

270

He flew in from Los Angeles on a red-eye and came straight from the airport to our meeting, scheduled early in the day so he could move on to whatever work it was that had officially brought him to town. Though he'd been a member of PEN American Center for many years, only one of the three PEN staffers who joined us around the table that morning had met him before. I wasn't the first to be struck by his resemblance to Abraham Lincoln. In his early 60s, he was lanky, gentle, soft-spoken, attentive, and a bit awkward, the shape of his beard deliberately underscoring the likeness to the guy on the "heads" side of the penny. The all-night flight hadn't affected him; he was composed and energetic and had ridden the subway in from the airport; he used public transportation whenever possible. I can't quite remember whether, that first time, he brought his habitual gift of Meyer lemons from his backyard tree in the briefcase that was his only luggage. I think he did.

He got straight to the point. He was concerned about the paucity of literary translation into English and admired the various initiatives PEN's Translation Committee had taken to address that situation. Accordingly, he and his wife Priscilla had decided to donate $500,000 to establish a fund at PEN to support literary translation into English. He said this in a quiet, matter-of-fact tone, with a hint of embarrassment. My mind went blank. The PEN staffers weren't entirely sure they'd understood. He had to repeat himself.

There was, he quickly added, one stipulation: the donation was to be absolutely anonymous. He didn't want to have to talk to anyone, ever, about having given away this money. No one was to know he and Priscilla were the donors.

We all must be wondering, he continued evenly, taking in the expressions on our faces with some sympathy, how a professor in the UCLA Department of Slavic Languages and Literatures and his wife were able to make such a donation. He explained: the money came from a death benefit the U.S. government had paid his mother when his father—a Hungarian-born composer who enlisted in the U.S. military during World War II—died following an accident at a military base. Heim was a toddler at the time and had little memory of his father. The family had invested the money when it came in and left it to grow in the decades since. Mike had recently turned sixty, and he and Priscilla had decided this was what they wanted to do with it.

That was how I came to see Michael Henry Heim as an activist.

Before going further into the origins, aims, nature, and arc of Mike's activism, let me add a few details to this part of the story.

1) Some months later, when all the paperwork was complete and the donation was deposited in PEN's coffers, the amount of money given by Mike and Priscilla Heim was not the $500,000 he'd pledged at that first meeting, but $734,000. It was at the time and I believe still remains the largest single donation PEN American Center has ever received.

2) Why was the gift so much larger than the pledge? It had always been Mike and Priscilla's intention to donate the entire contents of the account inherited from his mother some years earlier. But Mike was indifferent to money and had only a vague idea of how much was in that account. He'd pledged half a million as a lowball guess. It was a nice, round number.

3) Donating the money was, in Mike's eyes, the least of his contribution to what has been known, since his passing, as the PEN/Heim Translation Fund. In the early days, he worked diligently to establish effective methodology and criteria for the Fund's grant-giving program, drawing on his long experience with grant-making organizations such as the National Endowment for the Arts. Once the Fund began accepting applications, Mike was the hardest-working member of the Advisory Committee that evaluated each year's crop of 150 or so submissions. Polyglot that he was, he assessed three

or four times as many projects as most of the other judges, devoting unstinting attention and sensitivity to each one.

Those in the non-profit world accustomed to dealing with donors and their demands will have trouble lending credence to this last detail. When the inevitable disagreements among Advisory Board members arose over which projects would receive funding, Mike never won the day for his favorites by revealing himself as the Fund's donor. All Advisory Board members held equal sway in the debates that preceded the final awarding of the grants.[2]

II. The Invisible Rightness of Being [Mike]

A panel on "The Politics of Translation," co-sponsored by New York University's Department of Comparative Literature, was convened on September 16, 2003 to launch the PEN Translation Fund. The panelists were Susan Sontag, Ammiel Alcalay, Michael Hofmann, Steve Wasserman, and Michael Henry Heim; I moderated. The proceedings, subsequently published in PEN's magazine,[3] attest that Sontag, Alcalay, Hofmann, and Wasserman offered insightful diagnoses of what Hofmann described as "the delusive self-sufficiency" that the immense global reach of the English language had induced in Anglophone readers: "English is running a colossal and intolerable surplus with the rest of the world," Hofmann, a poet who translates from the German, declared, predicting that the future of translation into English would be "a deluge of nothing." Alcalay, a poet and scholar who translates from Serbo-Croatian and Hebrew, pointed out that the publishing marketplace engages in "a form of

---

2   For more information on the PEN/Heim Translation Fund and its history of grant-giving go to http://www.pen.org/content/penheim-translation-fund-grants-2000-4000.
3   "The Politics of Translation," *PEN America* 3:6 (2005) 133-141.

censorship" when translations from other languages are excluded; he praised the "freer space of independent publishing" but added that it presents its own set of problems, most notably a privileging of formally innovative texts. Regarding the foreign-language books that *are* published in English, Alcalay mourned the U.S. tendency "to talk about translations as if they were removed from either personal or collective politics." Wasserman (then editor of the *Los Angeles Times Book Review*) and Sontag both deplored U.S. anti-intellectualism and attributed the paucity of translation to "American resistance to the idea of achievement and of quality, the idea of standards in literature" (Sontag) and "a totalizing metropolis country whose economy is most entangled with the economies and the fates of people the world over, but whose own people are becoming more and more parochial" (Wasserman). All of which, taken together, formed a realistically gloomy diagnosis of the state of literary translation in the U.S. in 2003.

Mike's brief remarks were of a different order. He wasn't concerned with *why* "America Yawns at Foreign Fiction," as a *New York Times* headline had put it that summer.[4] Instead, he proposed a solution: a prestigious new print magazine that would enhance the literary sophistication of readers in the United States by presenting them with the finest works of contemporary world literature in translation. Such magazines had existed in many countries behind the Iron Curtain prior to 1989 and were read by most literate people; as a result, he'd been hugely impressed by how knowledgeable, for example, the Hungarians he met during those years were about international literature. He wanted something similar for the United States. He stated this and took his seat.

The evening had begun with the usual interminable sequence of

---

4   Stephen Kinzer, "America Yawns at Foreign Fiction." *New York Times*, July 26, 2003.

introductions. Responding to a highly detailed version of his biography read out by the NYU professor who presented him, PEN president Joel Conarroe had quipped "She googled me," which brought the house down. It was the first time I'd heard anyone use "Google" as a verb.[5] At a moment when the power of the Internet was surging and the imminent demise of print media had for years been one of the U.S. print media's fondest clichés, Mike's earnest proposal for a new high-end print magazine must have struck the editors of *PEN America* (who had no idea he was the donor of the Fund the panel was launching) as about as relevant, timely and feasible as a call for a new horse-drawn trolley in lower Manhattan. Mike's contribution to the panel did not appear in the magazine's published transcript.

A lifetime as a translator had accustomed Mike to more painful slights than that one. If he noticed the omission he never mentioned it to me. What has now become apparent is that he was right. Though he slightly misidentified the medium (even if the *New Yorker* did publish an "International Fiction" issue at the end of 2005), he was strikingly prescient regarding a phenomenon that has steadily grown more significant in the ensuing decade: the emergence of a distinct sphere of U.S. publishing, both print and digital, devoted to literary writing in translation. 2003 saw the launch of the website *Words without Borders*, a pioneer among what is now a host of sites and, yes, print magazines in English (based within and outside of the English-speaking world) devoted to publishing and commenting upon literature in translation.[6] An ever-increasing number of houses that—like Open Letter, publisher of the book you're reading right

5 The OED gives September 14, 2003, as the first recorded use of "Google" as a verb in a print publication—an article published in the Glasgow *Sunday Herald*.

6 In addition to WWB, other translation-centered websites, magazines, blogs and programming initiatives to have gained prominence during this period (to list only those not focused on a single language or country) include Absinthe, Asymptote, the Center for the Art of Translation and Two Lines, Circumference, the Complete Review, Ezra, Reading in Translation, Three Percent, Translationista, etc.

now—primarily or exclusively bring out literature in English translation have also been founded and new ones are continually emerging.[7] After a decade's successive vogues for Steig Larsson at one end of the literary spectrum and Roberto Bolaño at the other, in 2014, "much of the literary establishment [is] enthralled"[8] by the Norwegian Karl Ove Knausgaard, translated by Don Bartlett, whose work was introduced by Archipelago Books, another of the new translation-centered houses. BookExpo America, the nation's largest annual book fair, devoted its 2014 Global Market Forum to translation. It all sounds quite a bit like the more globally sophisticated literary community within the United States that Mike was envisioning.

While the bleak analyses, caveats, and forebodings of his fellow panelists remain relevant, both Mike's optimistic vision of what Anglophone literary culture *should* look like (more oriented toward world literature) and his practical program for *how* that could be attained (by a newly expanded publishing niche) were not some blindly retrograde fantasy but were spot on target about a shift that would indeed occur over the decade that followed—thanks, in no small measure, to his own interventions.

Only much later did Mike mention that as a freshman at Columbia University he was briefly enrolled in a course taught by Susan Sontag, then a young adjunct. He didn't care for her style of pedagogy and dropped the class, though he later followed her rise to international literary celebrity with interest and was grateful for the support she gave to authors he championed and translated, such as Bohumil Hrabal, Danilo Kiš, and Milan Kundera. Another of his

---

7 Other houses besides Open Letter and Archipelago, founded or re-launched in the last decade and devoted exclusively or primarily to translation include: AmazonCrossing, Autumn Hill Books, Deep Vellum, Frisch and Co., Europa Editions, Gallic Books, Hispabooks, Le French Book, New Vessel Press, Other Press, Ox and Pigeon, Restless Books, Wakefield Press, etc.

8 Liesl Schillinger, "His Peers' Views Are in the Details: Karl Ove Knausgaard's *My Struggle* is a Movement." *New York Times,* May 21, 2014.

undergraduate courses at Columbia—one he stuck with and recalled with gratitude—was taught by Gregory Rabassa. "What has left the deepest impression on me," Heim wrote in a review of his former professor's 2005 memoir, *If This Be Treason*, "is Rabassa's unconditional and uncompromising commitment to a cause—the cause of cultural mediation as represented by translation—and the vitality that radiates from the prose of an octogenarian who has lived a professional life devoted to a cause."[9]

III. A Theory of Mike

The figure of Anton Chekhov frames Mike's career. His first book was *Anton Chekhov's Life and Thought: Selected Letters and Commentary*, in collaboration with Simon Karlinsky. The last of his translations to be published in his lifetime was of "Easter Week," a story by Chekhov. In the years between, he did all the major plays. "Like his beloved Chekhov, whom he translated and taught, Mike was a profoundly human and egalitarian man," Boris Dralyuk, one of Mike's students, wrote in memoriam.[10] To read Mike's Chekhov is to recognize certain central perceptions, preoccupations and stances that author and translator shared: the warm personal and professional generosity, the loving community of family and friends both men devoted themselves to sustaining, the intensity of commitment to cause, the concern with nature and ecological sustainability, and a largely tacit distaste for a certain sort of intellectual posturing.

Chekhov gives fullest voice to this latter tendency in the character of Uncle Vanya, who denounces his brother-in-law, the retired

9   "A word man from the word go." *Los Angeles Times*, August 14, 2005.
10 "Michael Heim, An Appreciation." UCLA Slavic Languages & Literatures, In Memoriam: Michael Heim. http://www.slavic.ucla.edu/in-memoriam.html (Accessed June 9, 2014).

professor Alexander Vladimirovich Serebryakov, in the most vehement terms:

> [The professor] does nothing but complain about his misfortunes, though in fact he's been extraordinarily fortunate . . . For twenty-five years he's been chewing over other people's ideas about Realism, Naturalism, and who knows what other nonsense. In other words, for twenty-five years he's been pouring one empty glass into another. But oh, how sure of himself he is, how pretentious![11]

Like the elderly Casaubon, whom George Eliot had skewered in *Middlemarch* a quarter-century earlier, Serebryakov has spent his life constructing theoretical overviews of cultural phenomena, overviews that enjoy a certain intellectual glamour for a time and then pass out of vogue and into irrelevance. Meanwhile, Vanya, the "devoted bailiff," has spent his life creating the material conditions that make these flights into abstraction possible.

Mike was no Vanya, and didn't feel cheated of anything. He neither deplored nor resented the dominance of theoretical discourse within the humanities during his lifetime and spoke with considerable admiration of a number of colleagues whose theoretical studies mattered a great deal to him, among them Mikhail Bakhtin, Roman Jakobson, Pascale Casanova, David Bellos, Barbara Cassin, Lawrence Venuti, and his dear friend Efrain Kristal. Their work bolstered the cause and, as he says of Bakhtin in *A Happy Babel*, "helped me to see things in books . . . that I would have missed otherwise" (47). He was grateful for that but had little interest in engaging directly in theory himself. He understood translation itself as an enactment of the issues the theorists debated in the abstract: the inherent ambiguity

---

11 *Chekhov: The Essential Plays*, 67.

of language, the relationship of signifier and signified, form and content, the politics of the world republic of letters, the ownership of a translation, the question of untranslatability. He opted to address those issues primarily within and via his translations.

Chekhov famously explained that he lacked "a political, religious, and philosophical world view—I change it every month—and so I'll have to limit myself to the description of how my heroes love, marry, give birth, die, and how they speak."[12] Likewise, the knowledge Mike sought was grounded in local sites of human thought, behavior, language, and culture. He might best be described as a philologist, interested in the precise characteristics that connected languages and set them apart from each other, valuing literary works for the specific qualities that could make them relevant in contexts other than those that produced them. Mike preferred situational particulars to generalities: his mind focused on individual words, grammatical structures, narratives, literary works, writers, languages, situations of cultural interanimation. These intrigued him for what they were, and for the inevitably unpredictable ways in which each act of translation transformed them—and not as evidence to bolster a theoretical position or demonstrate the existence of a pattern. The Procrustean imperative of literary theory and criticism irked him a bit. "A translator must deal with every single word," he said during his 2011 talk on "The Three Eras of Modern Translation" (92), whereas a study can dispense with those parts of the original that simply don't fit in with its argument.

If the academic arena of his time sometimes seemed to have forgotten how to value a contribution like his, that neglect mattered to him only insofar as it affected a younger generation of scholars who shared his concerns. He felt fortunate to have been allowed to pursue

---

12 *Anton Chekhov's Life and Thought: Selected Letters and Commentaries,* ed. Simon Karlinsky, trans. Michael Henry Heim (Harper and Row, 1973), 115.

his career as he wanted to pursue it. The lesson of "the difficult, unheroically heroic stand of hard work, of plowing through"[13] that Mike derives from *Uncle Vanya* in his introduction to the play can serve as a definition of his own approach. And indeed, translation is one of the unheroically heroic tasks that Vanya undertakes to support his intellectual brother-in-law. ("Father! . . ." Serebryakov's daughter Sonya exclaims in Act Three, "Remember when you were younger and Uncle Vanya and Grandmother sat up night after night translating books for you . . .")[14]

Mike's primary concern was always the practice of translation and the political, commercial, cultural, and academic structures that defined and controlled that practice. His vision encompassed and transcended the individual works he translated, but he did not care to express it in "theory" as "distinguished from or opposed to *practice*" (to cite one of its definitions in the OED). Rather than writing monographs about the structures within which translation occurred, he voiced his understanding and critique—which was inevitably *theoretical*, under another definition of "theory": "A scheme or system of ideas or statements held as an explanation or account of a group of facts or phenomena"—in what he did.

Mike intervened directly to make the Anglophone world more hospitable to translation. He was a literary theorist whose theories took the form of actions. And when those actions could be carried out behind the scenes, collectively or anonymously, so much the better. He had little ambition for renown or the overt exercise of political power and was almost chagrined by his own scant tolerance for celebrity and wealth. Though he spent his career in the hierarchical realm of academia, his goals had little to do with a personal ascent up the echelons of conventional power structures. The UCLA sociologist Gail Kligman recalls chatting with a colleague at the edge

13 "Introduction," *Chekhov: The Essential Plays*, xiv.
14 *Chekhov: The Essential Plays*, p. 101.

of the campus swimming pool when they saw a lean figure in the distance going through the contents of a trash barrel. When she waved, her colleague asked, "You know that homeless man who likes to hang around here?"—and was startled to learn that this was one of the university's most distinguished faculty members. Mike's students reminisce that his office, piled high with the cans, bottles and newspapers he energetically recycled, seemed more like a transfer station than a professor's enclave. Or, perhaps, like the Prague cellar where Haňt'a, narrator of one of the novels Mike translated, operates his hydraulic compacting press, full of

> bags, crates and boxes raining down their old paper, withered flower-shop stalks, wholesalers' wrappings, out-of-date theater programs, ice cream wrappers, sheets of paint-spattered wallpaper, piles of moist, bloody paper from the butchers', razor-sharp rejects from photographers' studios, insides of office wastepaper baskets, typewriter ribbons included . . . a cobblestone buried in a bundle of newspaper to make it weigh more or a penknife and a pair of scissors disposed of by mistake, or claw hammers or cleavers or cups with dried black coffee still in them, or faded wedding nosegays wound round with fresh artificial funeral wreaths.[15]

There was much that Mike opposed, as his vigorous rummaging through UCLA's trash bins to repurpose the detritus of a throwaway society attests. In the nation of rugged individualists, Mike espoused a self-construal that was resolutely interdependent and community-oriented, even as he remained a robustly independent thinker. His indifference to material gain or status and the depth of his commitment to others were, in their way, expressions of dissent from a

---

15 Bohumil Hrabal, *Too Loud a Solitude*, trans. Michael Henry Heim. (Harcourt, 1992), 4.

society that assumed all its members were propelled by an engine of universal self-interest. Yet though he greatly admired many oppositional activists (Tomáš Masaryk, Václav Havel, György Konrád) and translated some of them, his own activism was rarely oppositional. His characteristic approach was to identify positive structural solutions to the issues that concerned him and work, little by little, for years or decades, to implement them. Just as Mike and Priscilla's concern for the environment was lived out in the ordinary details of their daily habits—Priscilla once showed me the small, lone plastic grocery bag that contained all the garbage their household generated in a week—Mike's theory of "cultural mediation as represented by translation" was part and parcel of everything he did.

During his talk on the eras of modern translation (86), Mike said, "We're moving in a vector toward something that I think does exist, and we want to keep it existing." It's what a biologist might say about a species whose numbers are dropping, or an ethnolinguist about a language with fewer and fewer speakers. Mike's work was about keeping something—call it cultural mediation, literary translation, a certain idea of world literature, literary humanism, or whatever you like—alive.

The first era of modern translation he identifies is *reactive*. The example he gives is Max Hayward and Manya Harari's 1958 translation of Boris Pasternak's *Dr. Zhivago*, published in the West after the Soviet authorities refused to publish it in the USSR. A recently declassified 1957 CIA memo describes *Zhivago* as "more important than any other literature which has yet come out of the Soviet Bloc." The memo goes on to express the Agency's deep concern that the book "should be published in a maximum number of foreign editions, for maximum free world discussion and acclaim . . ."[16] In these

---

16 CIA memo dated December 12, 1957, published by the *Washington Post*, April 5, 2014, to illustrate Peter Finn and Petra Couvée, "During Cold War CIA used 'Dr. Zhivago' as a tool to undermine Soviet Union."

days of NSA global data mining, it's difficult indeed to imagine a time when U.S. security forces could express such urgency about the translation of a literary novel! Nevertheless, it wasn't a golden age; literary translation was understood as little more than a passive tool for advancing the nation's geopolitical goals.

Mike dates the beginning of the second era, the *active* period, to 1974 with Philip Roth's Writers from the Other Europe series for Penguin Books. This is also the period when his own career was being consolidated; his first translation of Kundera—*The Book of Laughter and Forgetting*—appeared in Roth's series in 1981. The commercial success of various translated works during the 1970s and 80s translated into greater cultural stature for translations, and for the translator. "We begin to have 'superstar translators,'" Mike said, adding, "though I hate to use the word" (89). Uncomfortable with any star system, he knew, nevertheless, that success in the marketplace benefited the cause.

Defining the third, post-1989 era as *proactive,* Mike cited the Center for the Art of Translation itself—founded in 1994 to "broaden cultural understanding through international literature and translation"—as an early example of new empowerment. He noted that the development of the academic field of Translation Studies had also been a boon: "Now you could say this is a legitimate field. It isn't just something that a few people are doing in a back room somewhere" (91). Mike's celebratory account of the sixty-year ascent, legitimization, and revitalization of the translator's work both within and outside the university, then reaches what might seem an odd conclusion. "How," he asked at the end of his talk, "do we keep the translator, and more importantly, of course, the *translations* visible? The translator, I think, is less important" (96).

Is this a return to a purely instrumental notion of the translator's role, a restoration of the translator's invisibility? I'd argue that it's better understood as a claim that the work of art is more important than its creator, the work of cultural mediation more important than the individual figures who carry it out: a protest against the self-branding imperative of late capitalism that was anathema to Mike's moral code. In keeping with that code, Mike praised his hosts and their contribution to the cultural evolution he'd been describing in his talk, but left aside all mention of his own role.

IV. Mike's Theory, in Practice

The editors of a 2008 Festschrift published in Mike's honor begged its readers to keep in mind "the impossibility of acknowledging adequately his contributions in all areas."[17] Indeed, there is no way to fully describe all that Mike did to bring about, support, consolidate, and prolong what he called the *proactive* phase of modern transla-tion. Susan Harris, a founding editor of *Words without Borders* who first met Mike when she was an editor at Northwestern University Press in the 1990s, offers a well-informed glimpse into the unknow-able dimensions of Mike's influence:

> . . . as I combed backlists and sorted through suggestions, he seemed to be everywhere. A classic Russian novel of addic-tion? Mike. Short stories from the Serbian Borges? Mike too. Chekhov's letters? Take a guess. Mike translated the first books I acquired, a co-publication of Croatian writer Dubravka Ugrešić's *Fording the Stream of Consciousness* and *In the Jaws of Life;* I was thrilled—starstruck, actually—to

---

17 *Between Texts, Languages and Cultures: A Festschrift for Michael Henry Heim,* eds. Craig Cravens, Masako U. Fidler and Susan C. Kresin. UCLA Slavic Stud-ies, New Series, VI (Bloomington, IN: Slavica, 2008), 3.

meet him, and to work with him later on his sly translation from Czech of Josef Hiršal's *Bohemian Youth*. Beyond translating, he was always happy to provide reader's reports on novels from virtually any East or Central European language. In the academic community, where egos tend to run in inverse proportion to accomplishments and accessibility declines with seniority, Mike stood out not only for his productivity, but for his modesty and generosity of spirit. At conferences and events he was mobbed by translators at all stages of their careers, but he wasn't swanning about: he was huddling with them, working on their texts, no matter their language or affiliation. I began to understand the number of people he'd worked with, trained, and simply helped, and the effect he'd had on the field in both official and less formal ways. His sensibility imbued the discipline. He was everywhere off the page as well.[18]

An outline of Mike's structural interventions in the field and the underlying theoretical positions that led him to undertake them has to begin where Harris does, in Mike's work as a translator. Though that work starts with Chekhov, a figure of absolute canonical status, and though it went on to encompass other writers widely acknowledged as classic, Mike was always aware of the perils of canonicity, the risk of fossilization, the perpetual need for new discoveries and new transmissions to keep the interconnectedness of cultures in motion. The first of what might be described as Mike's principles—to use a favorite word of his—derived from the publications of a lifetime, is: *All literary canons are fluid and must be continually renewed*

18 "Michael Heim, Everywhere, Always." *In Other Words: The Journal for Literary Translators* 40 (Winter, 2012), 56.

with new material. "Don't only assign Chekhov's plays," he warned teachers of literature during his 2011 talk. "Make sure you assign at least one contemporary work of translation that students wouldn't have heard of otherwise." (96) Mike had met Hrabal during a 1965 visit to Czechoslovakia and his second published translation, in 1975, was a collection of Hrabal's stories titled *The Death of Mr. Baltis-berger*—the very first translation of Hrabal's work into English. His commitment to further expanding the literary horizons of Anglophone readers remained unwavering.

Characteristically, Mike listed only twenty of his books on his UCLA web page. Even some of us who thought we knew him well imagined he'd produced perhaps thirty or forty and were startled when the bibliography assembled for this volume (pp. 97–104) from UCLA records and a search of library and publisher's catalogues turned up sixty works translated, edited, or written by Mike over the course of his career.[19] The fact that more than half the books listed there remain in print at this writing attests to the enduring quality of Mike's skill as a translator and the acuteness of his judgment; if he was going to stake his name on a work, he wanted it to be one that would be of lasting interest.

This acumen also enabled him to identify a number of fictions that resonate almost uncannily with events that happened well after they were written or translated. Mike's translation of Tišma's 1972 *The Book of Blam*, which takes place in the Yugoslav city of Novi Sad in the immediate aftermath of World War II, was first published in 1998. In the novel's concluding paragraph, its eponymous central

---

19 In fact, the bibliography is undoubtedly incomplete; in *Happy Babel* Mike mentions translations of Sylvie Richterová and Pavel Kohout, whose publication or stage production could not be verified. Meanwhile, as Cathy Popkin notes in the bio of Mike included in her 2014 Norton Critical Edition of *Chekhov's Selected Stroies*, "There is more than one brilliant translation by Heim out there that fails to credit his work."

character, Blam, looks out over his city's spires and rooftops and imagines the next cataclysm:

> "It is . . . as though the terrible heat of a weapon had melted them and, upon cooling, they had taken on a new asymmetrical, ungainly shape, the shape of ruins. It is a scene from the coming war, the site of his future summons."[20]

In 1999, NATO bombers rained destruction upon Novi Sad for two months. Literary translation was no longer a propaganda instrument for the Cold War; it had become a prophetic contextualization of current upheavals.

Heim in Novi Sad, Yugoslavia, September 1984.

---

20 *The Book of Blam* (Harcourt, Brace, 1998), 225-226.

Here's a second position inherent in Mike's immense bibli-ography: *Literary fiction can afford us a crucial understanding of history.* "The Novel That Predicts Russia's Invasion of Crimea" reads the headline of an article by Michael Idov posted March 3, 2014 on the *New Yorker* blog. Vasily Aksyonov was a visiting professor at UCLA in the late 1970s and there he met Mike, who ended up translating two of his books. *The Island of Crimea*, written in 1979 and published in Mike's English in 1983, describes a fictional Russian invasion of Crimea and "eerily anticipates this week's news." What makes the novel more than good satire, Idov adds, "is its miraculous restora-tion to relevance every time Russia takes a hard turn." The novel's "spooky prescience" is particularly intense this time around: "it's hard to see the newly minted Crimean prime minister's last name as anything other than life completely curdling into metafiction. It's Aksyonov."[21]

The prophetic power of the narratives Mike translated is enig-matic and manifold. On a flight to California in the fall of 2013, I was reading his 1982 translation from the Hungarian of István Örkény's 1977 *The Flower Show*, a satirical novella about a Hun-garian TV producer named Aron Korom who aspires to make a documentary called *How We Die* that will track real people through the final weeks of their lives and on their deathbeds. ("Ularik, who

---

21 Idov was writing the article in Russia and must not have been able to get his hands on a copy of Mike's translation, though he mentions it. A comparison of Idov's rendition of the novel's first line with Mike's speaks volumes about the other skills Mike brought to bear on his work, in addition to his eye for texts of lasting relevance:

Idov: "Who wouldn't recognize, amid the crazed architectural flourishes of Downtown Simferopol, the assertive skyscraping simplicity of the pencil-like home of the Russian Courier."

Heim: "Everyone knows the *Russian Courier* skyscraper, insolent in its pencil-point simplicity amid the wild monuments to architectural self-expression in downtown Simferopol."

was head of Documentaries, won the argument. Instead of *How We Die*, which sounded too serious, the film was televised as *The Flower Show*."[22]) It's a short book, and when I'd finished, I took a magazine from the seat pocket in front of me and began leafing through it, only to confront an ad for a Showtime series that premiered November 1, 2013, titled *Time of Death: Real People, Face to Face with their own Mortality*. Cold War media satire to U.S. reality TV in 26 short years. That isn't quite what Mike had in mind when he tried to find someone to make a version of Örkény's novella for television. This tale of life (or death) imitating art comes full circle in Mike's reminiscence of his one encounter with Örkény—just two week's before Örkény's death: "he told me that the idea for the novella came to him in New York, while he was watching a show on a similar theme, and he re-set the story in Hungary." [42]

One of the strongly-held convictions Mike worked longest and hardest to scaffold is that *literary translation is a primary, necessary form of literary scholarship*. This position was at odds with the standard idea of translation in the U.S. university during much of Mike's career. Michael Flier sums up the view that prevailed in 1979, when Mike went up for tenure: "Translation was considered a secondary activity, something scholars engaged in to earn extra money or to make particular foreign publications available to monolingual American students" [124–125]. Translations were for rank beginners or those outside the discipline, and hence of little or no interest to those within. It's an attitude that seems rather strange in our era of TED talks and Massive Online Open Courses (MOOCS), when it is widely understood that all academic disciplines, even the most arcane regions of the hard sciences, must justify themselves beyond

---

22 *The Flower Show, The Toth Family*, translated by Michael Henry Heim and Clara Györgyey (Budapest: Corvina Books Ltd, 2001), 11.

their disciplinary boundaries, and even beyond the university. After the tanks rolled into Prague in 1968, Mike stood between Russian soldiers, Czech citizens, and German journalists and helped them all communicate. In the same way, Mike's translations stand between his discipline and the general reader, between the literatures of the European continent and those of the Anglophone world—to the benefit of all.

That Mike's tenure decision was "no open-and-shut case," as Michael Flier notes, is quite astonishing. By 1979, Mike had collaborated on the aforementioned edition of Chekhov's letters, which, writes Cathy Popkin in 2014, "has been the standard for decades." He was sole author of a textbook for contemporary Czech that was twice reissued in the 1980s and was later described in the Festschrift put together by his colleagues in Czech studies as "methodologically groundbreaking."[23] He had collaborated on an anthology of readings in Czech that would also be reprinted during the 1980s. He had published the first English translation of one of the most significant Czech writers of the twentieth century (still in print), and had translated three of Chekhov's four major plays, with a translation of the fourth well underway, for critically-acclaimed stage productions in Los Angeles, Houston, Pittsburgh, Cincinnati, and the Stratford festival in Canada. (Decades later Mike's Chekhov plays would be published as a Random House Modern Library Classic, still in print.) He had translated a contemporary Russian play for the stage, collaborated on an anthology of Hungarian folk literature, written and published the obligatory scholarly monograph on nineteenth-century Czech poet, politician, and journalist Karel Havlíček Borovský, and completed most of his translation of Kundera's *The Book of Laughter and Forgetting*. I will not even mention the articles. By

---

23 *Between Texts Languages and Cultures*, 3.

1979, his work had made a lasting impact on the field of Czech studies, the discipline of Slavic Languages and Literatures, and the broader literary culture of the day. What were the achievements of his contemporaries whose tenure decisions *were* "open-and-shut cases"?

The granting of tenure meant that Mike could work more effectively within the system to bring about recognition of the legitimacy of translation within the U.S. university. He understood that *literary translators need formal training in the practice of translation itself.* In the mid-1980s, he established what quickly became a legendary course at UCLA called Comparative Literature 285 (Workshop in Literary Translation), which he taught in alternate years. A group of students in a 1994 iteration of the course were so engaged that when the quarter ended they asked to keep meeting on an informal basis: thus was the Babel Group for Translation Studies born. Ten years later, graduate students in the Babel Group, under Mike's guidance, would organize the first in a series of International Conferences for Graduate Literary Translators.[24]

Having helped train a generation of translators, Mike worried for their future, and continually sought ways to make translation a viable activity for every phase of an academic career. When the Salzburg Global Seminars convened Session 461 at Schloss Leopoldskron in February of 2009 on the subject of "Recognizing and Promoting the Critical Role of Translation in a Global Culture," Mike chaired the working group on "The Role of the Academy in Promoting Translation." One of the key recommendations the group made was that

---

24 See "The UCLA International Conference for Graduate Literary Translators." *UCLA Graduate Quarterly* Spring 2004, 15. Following its 2004 inauguration at UCLA, the Graduate Student Translation Conference would subsequently convene biannually at the University of Iowa, Columbia University, and the University of Michigan.

"Universities should recognise the translation of literary and academic works as scholarship and evaluate it as such."[25] Catherine Porter, then president of the Modern Language Association, took part in that working group, even as she was organizing the 2009 Convention of the MLA on "The Tasks of Translation in the Global Context." Following the MLA convention, Mike, Porter, and several others including former MLA presidents Michael Holquist and Marjorie Perloff, worked for many months to draw up a set of guidelines for evaluating translations as scholarship, finally adopted by the MLA's Executive Council as an MLA Statement in February of 2011.[26] Another girder in place in the edifice of translation Mike spent his life constructing.

The MLA Guidelines were a long-term project, envisioned as early the 1999 interview in Timişoara, when Mike formulated a goal that would increasingly become the focus of his work in the years that followed:

> I think it is important that all over the world there be a sustained interest in translation, since with this kind of training you create a team of active people, that is, people who will not wait for the publisher to sign a title that has to appear. If every university with a strong comparative literature department began to produce qualified translators,

25 "Part II: Working Group Recommendations. What is the Role of Literary Translation in the Educational Process?" *Tradutore, Traditore? Recognizing and Promoting the Critical Role of Translation in a Global Culture.* Salzburg Global Seminar Session 461 Report, 25. Downloadable at http://www.salzburgglobal.org/fileadmin/user_upload/Documents/2000-2009/2009/461/SessionReport461.pdf (accessed June 9, 2014).

26 See Modern Language Association, "Evaluating Translations as Scholarship: Guidelines for Peer Review." http://www.mla.org/ec_guidelines_translation (accessed June 9, 2014).

they could start to work immediately, and then there would be more opportunities for foreign authors to reach their audience. This is true everywhere, not just in our country. [33–34]

Naturally, one of the concepts Mike instilled in the students who passed through his workshop—the *active team* he was forming—is that *literary translators must be proactive agents of cultural mediation.* Noting the obstacles and barriers his graduate student translators encountered in the publishing marketplace, Mike devised other structural interventions to make their work more feasible. In 2003, when we were establishing the parameters of the PEN Translation Fund, he insisted that the Fund not follow the lead of other grant-givers in the field such as the National Endowment for the Arts and the National Endowment for the Humanities, which require letters of recommendation and a substantial record of publication as a condition of eligibility. Applicants to the Fund are judged solely on the quality of their work, which opens up the competition to the sort of proactive young translator Mike believed in.

The impact of the Fund, which to date has supported 108 translation projects from dozens of languages, is by no means limited to the viable way forward it has offered fledgling translators. Jason Grunebaum received a Translation Fund grant in 2005 for the translation from the Hindi of Uday Prakash's *Girl with the Golden Parasol.* While the grant was a great boon to Grunebaum—who knew his work was going very much against the tide, given that no U.S. publishing house had brought out a work by a living Hindi novelist in more than a generation—the effect on Prakash was even greater. "Uday credits the PEN award with turning things around for him at a point when things looked so bleak and he was so disillusioned that he was ready to quit writing," Grunebaum told an

interviewer in 2010.[27] Prakash is among many writers to have been
greatly heartened by learning of a PEN Translation Fund award for
his or her work in that unlikeliest of quarters, the English-speaking
world. After living in Detroit for most of a decade, Iraqi poet Dunya
Mikhail finally saw her work translated into English after Elizabeth
Winslow, her translator, received a grant from the Translation Fund.
Chinese dissident poet Liao Yiwu was published in English for the
first time after his translator, Wen Huang, applied for a grant from
the Fund. And the list goes on.

The establishment of the Fund at PEN American Center was
a catalyst for the renewal of commitment to translation in PEN
centers across the globe. In 2005, with support from Bloomberg,
English PEN established a biannual Writers in Translation award to
assist in the marketing and promotion of selected works of literary
translation. In 2007, International PEN's Translation and Linguistic
Rights Committee and the Institut Ramon Lull published *To Be
Translated or Not To Be,* a comparative overview of forms of support
for literary translation in a number of countries. Mike's contribution
was a central factor leading to the creation of PEN American Center's World Voices Festival, which, since 2004, has brought writers
working in many languages around the world to New York City for
an intensive week of programs and panel discussions each spring.
As he understood: *Translation is a central component of literature itself,
which is revitalized by support for translation.*

In addition to bolstering Mike's "active team" of translators, the
Translation Fund was explicitly aimed at correcting a flaw in the

---

27 Annie Janusch, "The Jason Grunebaum Interview" (March 1, 2010). Quar-
terlyconversation.com, http://quarterlyconversation.com/the-jason-grunebaum-
interview, accessed June 9, 2010. In the wake of support from the Translation
Fund, *The Girl with the Golden Parasol* was published by Penguin in India and by
Yale University Press in the U.S.

marketplace, a flaw that, as Ammiel Alcalay had pointed out in the panel that launched the Fund, functioned as a form of censorship. Mike shared with the French sociologist Pierre Bourdieu the view that *the publishing marketplace is not only a necessary object of study but an arena for action.* This meant, for starters, that the Fund sought to ensure that the projects it supported were brought to completion and ultimately published. Translators receive only half the money upon awarding of a grant; the rest is delivered when the project is complete. The Fund's Advisory Board, which selects the grantees, includes editors whose reputations ensure that the publishing industry takes note of the projects that receive their imprimatur. To date, 60 of the Fund's translation projects have been published, and more are coming out all the time.

Mike had worked with commercial publishers from the beginning of his career and had no fear or revulsion of the marketplace, though he expected so little from it in the way of personal gain that the first time he received substantial royalties for a book—his 1999 translation of Hans Magnus Enzensberger's *The Number Devil*—he assumed a mistake had been made and mailed the check straight back to the publisher. His interest in studying and affecting the marketplace long predated the establishment of the Translation Fund. In the years after the great turning point of 1989, Mike was increasingly dismayed by what was happening in the publishing industry, as the systems for cultural transmission that had previously existed, including Roth's Writers from the Other Europe series, came to an end or were transformed. He had seen the effect a translated bestseller like *One Hundred Years of Solitude* or *The Unbearable Lightness of Being* could have on U.S. culture. He wanted to see more of that kind of thing, and only the marketplace could make that happen.

In 1991, Northwestern University Press launched a new series called Writing from an Unbound Europe, with Mike on the editorial board. As an editor, Mike sought out models and best practices that could enhance the series' impact on U.S. literary culture. In an article from the mid-90s he expressed dismay that the readership for contemporary world literature "is now in danger of falling prey to economic pressures."[28] He noted that publishers in the German-speaking world had maintained and expanded a readership for work in translation, and therefore interviewed three German editors to "determine the extent to which their practices are applicable here." Mike wanted to know everything, including details about which marketing techniques had proven most effective. Among the practical lessons he recorded was the importance of catalogue descriptions "that stress connections with common human experience and with equally or better-known writers of German culture." Translation studies theorists might dismiss this as rank "domestication," but Mike had no such qualms: what mattered was to sustain and increase readership. If the familiar was a useful doorway into the foreign, so be it.

Mike's concerns were not limited to the U.S. marketplace but encompassed much of the global ecosphere of interlinguistic cultural mediation. *A Happy Babel* was an unintended side effect of his long work with the "Third Europe" cultural/society research group which organized the 1999 Timișoara Conference in order to rethink the cultural connections that constituted "Central-Europeanness." This was necessary because the fall of the Iron Curtain had released a flood of new cultural traffic between the countries of Eastern Europe and the West that threatened to displace the network of cultural connections that had formerly conjoined the region. Ten years later, Mike coordinated a special study of "East-Central European Literatures Twenty Years After," "to provide an overview of the course of Central European literature in the twenty years following the fall of the Berlin Wall." Rather than composing the overview himself, as he

---

28 Michael Henry Heim, "Revitalizing the Market for Literary Translation." *Translation Review* 48-49:1 (1995), 16.

certainly could have, he recruited a dozen young specialists who each contributed a recap on the country of their expertise.[29]

The increasing dominance of English as a vehicle for scholarship across the globe was another growing concern. Social scientists, historians, and specialists in many academic disciplines, whatever their first language might be, were tending more and more to write scholarly work in English. As new global ranking systems—starting with the Shanghai Rankings in 2003—began evaluating all universities worldwide into a single list, using the number of faculty publications in prestigious English-language journals as a central criterion, faculty everywhere were coming under increasing pressure from their institutions to publish in English. Many scholars concluded that writing directly in English was their best means of reaching a global audience, having an international impact in their fields, and bolstering their institution's reputation. Andrzej Tymowski's contribution to this book gives a detailed account of the formation of the American Council of Learned Societies Social Science Translation Project in 2004, with Mike and Tymowski as principle investigators. From the set of "Guidelines," which that project, too, resulted in, I derive another of Mike's principles: *Translation into English enhances the literary and scholarly capital of all languages by allowing writers and scholars to continue to work in their first language, while still reaching a global audience.* One clear outcome of the "Guidelines" is "Considerations in the translation of Chinese medicine," published by the UCLA Center for East-West Medicine in 2014, and dedicated to Mike.

In an era when "interdisciplinarity" is an academic buzzword—however many obstacles to cross-disciplinarity remain in place—Mike's career clearly evinces the belief that *the boundaries between disciplines and fields of knowledge are artificial constraints that must not be allowed to define or limit one's own interests and areas of endeavor.*

---

29 *East European Politics & Societies* 23:4 (Fall, 2009), 552-581.

The aforementioned work on translation in the social sciences is only one example among many. Here's another: while a wide gulf exists in many language departments between the literary scholars and applied linguists or pedagogy specialists, Mike remained devoted to applied linguistics and second language acquisition throughout his life, both as a teacher and as a second-language learner.[30] He once told me he was annoyed that UCLA required a minimum of 13 students in order to allow a foreign language course to proceed, since it limited the number of languages he could teach: "Where am I going to find thirteen kids who want to learn Slovenian?" Meanwhile, the fact that he was officially a Slavicist did not stop him from learning and working in German, Dutch, French, Italian or, at the end of his life, Chinese.

According to Priscilla, his interest in the language began when he was in high school. He had a job at a French bank, where he formed a friendship with the janitor, a Chinese thinker with whom Mike had long discussions about the nature of good and evil. Mike then studied Chinese as an undergraduate. He returned to it at age 60, for the sheer intellectual challenge, no doubt, but for other reasons, as well. Much in contemporary China was recognizable from the Soviet Union of Mike's early career, but while the translation of Soviet dissidents was an instrument of U.S. foreign policy during the Cold War, Chinese dissidents, and contemporary Chinese culture in general, had found no similar reception in the West. The introduction to the ACLS Guidelines cites Chaohua Wang on the disparity between Chinese intellectuals' deep engagement in translating Western thought in China and the scant translation of Chinese thought in the West.[31]

---

30 UCLA's Center for World Languages did a good deal to document Mike's work in applied linguistics. In a video made by the Center, "Michael Heim Speaks on Learning Languages" (https://www.youtube.com/watch?v=RfCiTD4ShLA), he speaks in four languages about what motivated him to learn each one.

31 *One China, Many Paths* (Verso, 2003), 9-10.

Mike's work with Chinese in the last decade of his life took him to China several times. He helped bring a Confucius Institute to UCLA to promote Chinese culture, and served on its Advisory Board. He contributed to the UCLA-Fudan University workshop in Scholarly Translation, held each summer from 2009-2012. He began developing an innovative elementary Chinese textbook/dictionary. "The reason why I feel I can write such a textbook," he told an interviewer, "is that I'm really learning the language almost from scratch, but I'm observing myself learning the language after studying and teaching languages for almost fifty years, so I think I have something to offer that other people don't have."[32] And of course he tried his hand at translating a Chinese novel (Breon Mitchell cites Mike's description of the experience on 267). "Had he been given a couple more years, I'm confident that his contributions to Chinese language pedagogy would have been substantial," says Howard Goldblatt, one of the foremost translators of Chinese in the U.S. who, with his wife Sylvia, became close friends of Mike and Priscilla. Lin Lin, a former translation student of Mike's, has taken over the textbook/dictionary project, Priscilla tells me. For, of course, Mike had been working with Chinese students at UCLA on his cause. He wrote me about a translation into Chinese that a Fulbright student was doing, under his guidance, of his friend Rosanna Warren's *Ghost in a Red Hat*: "the poems," he said, "only get better. I see more and more each time."

The novelist Caleb Crain, author of an important 1999 article on Kundera and his translators (cited by Michelle Wood, 199), recently told me that he was surprised and delighted when Mike wrote him many years later to ask for permission for a Chinese exchange student he was working with to translate Crain's article into Chinese—another language whose exiled writers live among readers who

---

32 "10 Languages and Counting." A podcast posted on the UCLA Center for World Languages website: http://international.ucla.edu/cwl/article/103979.

know their work primarily in translation. Which brings us to a final theoretical premise that underlay everything Mike did: *Translation enriches texts by transforming them.*

There was one project Mike did not bring to fruition, though he pursued it down many avenues over the years. Of all the interventions in the publishing and academic marketplace that he dreamed up, this was the most ambitious, and he never gave up on it. He mentioned it to me even during our last conversation. Mike envisaged an industry-wide system in Anglophone publishing to address and remedy the disparity between the vast worldwide flow of translation from English and the small trickle of translation into English. This system would allow Anglophone publishing houses or widely-translated Anglophone writers to voluntarily, automatically donate a small percentage of the moneys received from the sale of translations into other languages to a fund supporting translation into English. It doesn't exist yet, but that doesn't mean it won't. I'm not sure what principle of Mike's we might derive from this project, except, perhaps, that *almost anything is doable: you just have to be patient, keep looking for a way to do it, and take it step by step.*

CODA: CHEKHOV, WORD FOR WORD

Raymond Carver's final story appeared in the *New Yorker* in June, 1987. Shortly thereafter, Carver learned he had lung cancer; he died of the disease a year later. The story, titled "Errand," was included in the collection *Where I'm Calling From*, published after his death. It also appeared in *Best American Stories, 1988*, and was awarded first prize in *Prize Stories, 1988: The O. Henry Awards.*

"Errand" describes the final days and deathbed scene of Anton Chekhov in a hotel room in the German spa town of Badenweiler.

Carver says he began writing the story after reading Henri Troyat's *Chekhov*; an editor at E. P. Dutton had sent him a copy of the newly published biography early in 1987.[33] The bulk of Carver's story relies on historical figures, incidents and citations taken from the biography, while the final pages describe a fictional bellboy whom Olga Knipper, Chekhov's widow, sends out on an errand to find an undertaker.

Carver's friend, the novelist Douglas Unger, was at Yaddo, the writers' retreat, when "Errand" first came out:

> . . . it so happened that there was a copy of Henri Troyat's biography of Chekhov around. James Salter noticed that the death scene in the biography and a large part of the death scene in "Errand" were almost exactly alike, almost word for word. That caused quite a stir and discussion among the writers there.[34]

Carver is one of the most celebrated and written-about U.S. writers of the latter half of the twentieth-century, and the relationship between "Errand" and Troyat's *Chekhov* has come in for much analysis. Charles E. May, Lionel Kelly, and Claudine Verley have all published studies of "Errand" which state, variously, that Carver "may have consulted . . . Troyat,"[35] that he "was prompted to write the story while reading Troyat . . ."[36] or that the story "is a work of

---

33 "On 'Errand'" in *No Heroics, Please: Uncollected Writings*, ed. William L. Stull (Vintage Contemporaries, 1992), 123.

34 "Douglas Unger," in Sam Halpert, *Raymond Carver: An Oral History* (University of Iowa Press, 1995), 123.

35 Claudine Verley, "'Errand,' or Raymond Carver's Realism in a Champagne Cork." *Journal of the Short Story in English* 46 (Spring 2006, Special Issue on Raymond Carver), 148.

36 Charles E. May, "Reality in the Modern Short Story." *Style* 27:3 (Fall 1993). See also Charles E. May, "'Do You See What I'm Saying?': The Inadequacy of Explanation and the Uses of Story in the Short Fiction of Raymond Carver." *The Yearbook of English Studies* 31 (2001), 39-49.

homage . . . inspired by Henri Troyat . . . [that] adheres closely to Troyat's account."[37] Of these three, only Kelly even names Michael Henry Heim, and then only to credit him as the biography's translator in a source reference.

More recently, the novelist John Dufresne commented on his blog that as he and a creative writing class were reading "Errand," they began looking at the degree to which the story was "borrowed" from "the Michael Henry Heim translation of Henri Troyat's biography." Their conclusion:

> Carver lifted passages whole cloth from Troyat. Large chunks of nine paragraphs, comma for comma, word for word, in some cases.[38]

When using descriptive text by "Troyat/Heim" (as the critic Martin Scofield, who has also compared Carver's story to Troyat's biography puts it),[39] Carver generally made certain alterations, as in this line, one of a dozen equally similar passages identified by Dufresne:

> Troyat/Heim: "Dr. Ewald spread his arms in a gesture of helplessness and left without a word."

> Carver: ". . . he threw up his hands and left the room without a word."

The passages in Carver's story that exceed this degree of similarity to follow Heim's translation with word for word precision are

---

37 Lionel Kelly, "Anton Chekhov and Raymond Carver: A Writer's Strategies of Reading." *The Yearbook of English Studies* 26 (1996), 220.

38 Johndufresne.com: "The Errand," posted September 12, 2011. http://johndu-fresne.com/blog/2011/9/12/the-errand.html (accessed June 9, 2014).

39 "Story and History in Raymond Carver." *Critique* 40 (Spring, 1999), 276.

quickly identifiable: they all appear in quotation marks. When, for example, Chekhov describes his famous metaphysical argument with Tolstoy, the only difference between the words in "Errand" and those in the biography is Carver's contraction of "don't."

Tolstoy, writes Carver/Heim/Chekhov,

> assumes that all of us (humans and animals alike) will live on in a principle (such as reason or love) the essence and goals of which are a mystery to us . . . I have no use for that kind of immortality. I don't understand it, and Lev Niko-layevich was astonished I didn't.

All in all, 28 sentences in "Errand" are identical to Heim's rendering of passages from the correspondence of Chekhov, his widow, Olga Knipper, Tolstoy, Alexei Suvorin, Maria Chekhov, and other Russian sources for Troyat's biography.

Douglas Unger spoke to Carver on the phone from Yaddo shortly after "Errand" was published and told him about the consternation the side-by-side comparison to Troyat's *Chekhov* had caused.

> [Carver] told me that he had read the biography, was fascinated by it, and decided to use it when he got the idea for his story. To his mind it was no different from using parts of a story one of his friends had told him around the table.[40]

Carver "wasn't worried about his debt to Troyat and Heim," his biographer Carol Sklenicka confirms. "[I]nstead he believed, 'I couldn't stray from what happened, nor did I want to.'"[41] The *New Yorker's* fact-checking team, which duly went over the piece, apparently

---

40 *Raymond Carver: An Oral History*, 123.
41 *Raymond Carver: A Writer's Life* (Scribner, 2010), 451.

agreed with Carver that Heim's translations of the many citations that appeared in the story were a kind of objective fact, like an accurate date, the correct spelling of a name, or the correct transcription of speech into writing: no more and no less than "what happened."

Troyat's biography was an uncharacteristic departure for Mike. It was the only biography he translated, and though French was the first foreign language he acquired, he translated only one other work from it, Kundera's play *Jacques and His Master*, which premiered in the U.S. in 1985 at the American Repertory Theater in a production directed by Susan Sontag.

Just as his prior work translating Kundera from the Czech had led him to Kundera's French play, it was his expertise on Chekhov that brought him to Troyat's biography. Like all biographers who write in a language other than that spoken by their subjects, Troyat had devoted much effort to translating citations from correspondence, diaries, news articles and other sources. Translation of Troyat's translations into an English twice-removed from the original was rightly deemed a bad idea and the volume was wisely entrusted to someone who knew the language of the biography's subject and all the original source material extremely well. Mike's "Translator's Note" to *Chekhov* explains that all citations appearing in it were rendered directly by him from the Russian; where the texts cited had previously appeared in *Anton Chekhov's Life and Work* (1973), on which he collaborated with Simon Karlinsky, he reproduced those translations and gratefully acknowledged the permission of Karlinsky and the publishers to do so.[42]

Translation is a complex process: "Two people never translate the same sentence the same way," Mike declared to his Romanian

---

[42] Henri Troyat, *Chekhov*, trans. by Michael Henry Heim (E. P. Dutton, 1986), vii.

interviewers (48). Nor does one person: it's almost impossible for a translator to go back over his or her work without doing some tinkering. At the launch of the PEN Translation Fund, Michael Hofmann decried the common notion that "anyone else would do the identical job if your dictionaries were the same."

> In fact, you wouldn't do the same job two days running; I certainly wouldn't. Translation is a human activity and you bring human fallibility and human distinction to it.

Going over the citations in Troyat's *Chekhov* that had appeared in the earlier volume, Mike made changes. The 1973 version of the afore-cited lines from the letter to Mikhail Menshikov of April 16, 1897, in which Chekhov bemoans Tolstoy's oppressive metaphysics, was different. In the earlier version, Chekhov bemoans Tolstoy's assumption

> that all of us (men and animals) will live on in some principle (such as reason or love), the essence of which is a mystery . . . I feel no need for this kind of immortality, I do not understand it, and Lev Nikolayevich was astonished that I don't.

In 1986, the parenthetical "men and animals" has become "humans and animals alike," perhaps due to the growing feminist consciousness of the era, or perhaps to Mike's relationship with Priscilla, whom he met shortly after the first version was published and married in 1975. Further along, the "essence" has now been joined by practical "goals," and the goals are no longer a general mystery but a localized one, a mystery "to us." The 1986 substitution of "I have no use" (a utilitarian statement) for 1973's "I feel no need" (an emotional declaration) injects another note of characteristic practicality. The new version, the other words, reflects the evolution of Mike's life and thought in the dozen or so years that elapsed between the two projects.

1987 was a busy year for Mike. Two stage productions of his translations of plays by Yuri Lyubimov were mounted, one at the American Repertory Theater in Cambridge, Massachusetts and the other at the Arena Stage in Washington, D.C. His second translation of a book by his former colleague Vasily Aksyonov, this one titled *In Search of Melancholy Baby*, was published, and he was back at UCLA, newly promoted to full professor, after having spent 1985-1986 as a visiting associate professor at Harvard. "I don't think Mike had any idea of Carver's lifting of material," Priscilla writes me.

Chekhov's death belongs to no one, least of all to Chekhov himself. It has been retold innumerably, by Olga Knipper and Schwöhrer, the doctor, who were there, and by countless journalists, biographers, commentators, critics, fiction writers, and translators, in countless languages, who were not. Each brings his or her own subtle emphases, preconceptions, personal obsessions and preoccupations to bear; each translates the story, and Carver, too, among all the others. Part of the impact of reading his tale of the death of an author lies in the harbinger of Carver's own imminent death it contains, though he was unaware of that as he wrote it.

Carver did not intend for his story to be a tribute to Michael Henry Heim, either. But one of translation's many lessons is that an author's intentions are only one element in what a text means, and not necessarily the most important one. The abashed bellhop at the end of the story, slow to become aware of what has happened and uncertain of what to do or how to react in the presence of an event as momentous as the death of Anton Chekhov, is a stand-in for Carver and for the story's readers. But Mike's role, in Carver's story, is that of Chekhov himself. Chekhov speaks in Mike's words. For a privilege that great, invisibility is a small price to pay.

Mike and Priscilla in the 1970s.

Heim practicing viola in the woods, 1976.

CONTRIBUTORS

Henning Andersen is a professor of Slavic Languages and Literatures at the University of California, Los Angeles. A Guggenheim Fellow, he is a member of the Royal Danish Academy of Sciences and Letters.

Bente Christensen has translated numerous works from French into Norwegian, including novels by Balzac and Jules Verne and Simone de Beauvoir's *The Second Sex*. She is a former vice president of Norwegian PEN and the International Federation of Translators.

Andrei Codrescu is a Romanian-born American poet, novelist, essayist, screenwriter, and commentator for National Public Radio. He was Mac Curdy Distinguished Professor of English at Louisiana State University from 1984 until his retirement in 2009.

Michael Flier is the Oleksandr Potebnja Professor of Ukrainian Philology at Harvard University. His research interests include Slavic linguistics and the semiotics of medieval East Slavic culture.

Maureen Freely was born in the U.S. but grew up in Turkey, where her family still lives. She was educated at Radcliffe College and has spent most of her adult life in England. A professor at the University of Warwick, she is currently the President of English PEN. She is perhaps best known for her translations of five books by the Turkish novelist and Nobel Laureate,

Orhan Pamuk, and for her campaigning journalism after he and many other writers, scholars, and activists were prosecuted for insulting Turkishness or the memory of Ataturk. Her sixth novel, *Enlightenment* (2007), covers some of the same ground. Her seventh, *Sailing through Byzantium*, takes place in Istanbul during the Cuban Missile Crisis and was named one of the best novels of 2013 in the *Sunday Times*.

Celia Hawkesworth was for many years Senior Lecturer in Serbian and Croatian at the School of Slavonic and East European Studies, University College, London. Among her many translations are two works by Dubravka Ugrešić.

Michael Henry Heim was a professor of Slavic Languages and Literatures at the University of California, Los Angeles. His complete bibliography includes 63 books and staged plays.

Breon Mitchell is Director Emeritus of the Lilly Library and Professor Emeritus of Germanic Studies and Comparative Literature at Indiana University. He has translated works by Franz Kafka (*The Trial*), Günter Grass (*The Tin Drum*), Heinrich Böll (*The Silent Angel*), and Siegfried Lenz (*Selected Stories*) among others.

Andrzej W. Tymowski is Director of International Programs at the American Council of Learned Societies, serves on the editorial board of *East European Politics & Societies and Cultures,* and teaches academic writing at the University of Warsaw.

Dubravka Ugrešić is a European writer. Born in Croatia (Yugoslavia), she now lives in the Netherlands. Among her numerous literary prizes and awards, the most recent is the Jean-Améry-Preis für europaische Essayistik (2012). Twelve of her books have appeared in English, four of them in translations by Michael Henry Heim.

Rosanna Warren teaches in the Committee on Social Thought at the University of Chicago. She is the author of five volumes of poetry, as well as *Fables of the Self: Studies in Lyric Poetry* (2008). A Guggenheim Fellow, she has served as Chancellor of the Academy of American Poets and her work has been awarded the Pushcart Prize and the Academy of Arts and Letters Award of Merit in Poetry, among other prizes.

David Williams received his PhD from the University of Auckland, New Zealand in 2012. Michael Henry Heim was one of the examiners of his thesis. Among his translations are two books by Dubravka Ugrešić. He is the author of *Writing Postcommunism: Towards a Literature of the East European Ruins* (Palgrave, 2013).

Michelle Woods is an assistant professor of English at State University of New York, New Paltz. She is the author of *Translating Milan Kundera* (2006) and *Kafka Translated: How Translators have Shaped our Reading of Kafka* (2013).

Alex Zucker has translated novels by Czech authors Miloslava Holubová, Jáchym Topol, Petra Hůlová, and Patrik Ouředník. His forthcoming translations include Heda Margolius Kovály's *Innocence, or, Murder on Steep Street* (Soho Press), and Tomáš Zmeškal's *Love Letter in Cuneiform* (Yale Press). He lives in the Greenpoint section of Brooklyn, NY.

Russell Scott Valentino, Sean Cotter, and Esther Allen.
Photograph by Anne Magnan-Park.

Esther Allen is an associate professor at Baruch College, City University of New York. She is co-editor of *In Translation: Translators on Their Work and What It Means* (Columbia University Press, 2013). Her most recent translation is *Zama,* by Antonio Di Benedetto (New York Review Books Classics). In 2006, the French government made her a Chevalier de l'ordre des arts et des lettres.

Sean Cotter is an associate professor of Literature and Translation Studies at the University of Texas at Dallas. Awards for his translations from the Romanian include the Three Percent Best Translated Book Award and a National Endowment for the Arts Translation Fellowship. He is the author of *Literary Translation and the Idea of a Minor Romania* (University of Rochester Press, 2014) and the translator of Mircea Cărtărescu's *Blinding* (Archipelago Books, 2013).

Russell Scott Valentino is the author of two scholarly monographs and the translator of seven book-length literary works from Italian, Croatian, and Russian. He served as editor-in-chief at *The Iowa Review* from 2009 to 2013 and is currently president of the American Literary Translators Association, Senior Editor at Autumn Hill Books, and Professor and Chair of Slavic and East European Languages and Cultures at Indiana University. His latest book, *The Woman in the Window*, will be published by the Ohio State University Press in 2014.